About the Editors

Pracha Hutanawatr is a social activist and intellectual in Thailand. A former Buddhist monk and student radical, he has been involved since the mid 1970s in exploring the application of Buddhism to contemporary society. He has worked under the guidance of of Buddhadasa Bhikku, a renowned innovative Buddhist monk and philosopher and Sulak Sivaraksa, an influential independent thinker and activist in Thailand. In 1988 Sulak and Pracha co-founded the International Network of Engaged Buddhists.

Pracha Hutanawatr's areas of interest include the application of Buddhist principles to social reconstruction, holistic approaches to rural development, Asian spirituality, deep ecology, social justice and green politics. The programmes and organizations he currently directs are all searching for new, practical Asian alternatives to the present mainstream approach to development and globalization.

His present positions include: Director of the Wongsanit Ashram near Bangkok; Deputy Director of Santi Pracha Dhamma Institute; Programme Director for Grassroots Leadership Training; and a board member of the Spirit in Education Movement.

He has published several major books in Thai and is the translator of works by Thich Nhat Hanh, Fritjof Capra and E. F. Schumacher.

Ramu Manivannan is a teacher, scholar and peace activist from India with an inter-faith religious and spiritual background. He has been deeply influenced by socialist values and the Gandhian tradition and is committed to non-violent, decentralized models of community self-sufficiency. He believes in freedom and democracy as important values, but considers that they must be based on social justice if they are to be of relevance to ordinary people. He is also a critic of the modern state system because of the violence associated with it.

He has been closely associated with the Alternatives Movement in India and other parts of Asia, and is the founder of the Spirit in Life Movement, which is a grassroots initiative committed to exploring non-violent alternatives and community participation. He is an Executive Member of the Nonviolent Peaceforce, USA/Belgium, an associate member of JUST, Malaysia, and was co-convenor of the Nonviolence Commission of the International Peace Research Association (IPRA). His many voluntary roles in India include serving as co-ordinator of Friends of Tibet-India in Delhi, and of the Burmese pro-democracy movement.

A Reader in Political Science at the University of Delhi, he is the author of several books, including *Shadows of a Long War: Indian Intervention in Sri Lanka* (1988), and (editor) *Social Justice, Democracy and Alternative Politics: An Asian-European Dialogue* (2001).

Participants in Volume 1

Ashis Nandy
Sulak Sivaraksa
Helena Norberg-Hodge
Tu Weiming
Mahmoud Ayoub
Bishop Julio Xavier Labayen
Abdurraman Wahid

Participants in Volume 2

Walden Bello
Vandana Shiva
Chandra Muzaffar
Arief Budiman
Satish Kumar
Nakamura Hisashi
Venerable Samdhong Rinpoche

PRACHA HUTANUWATR AND RAMU MANIVANNAN | editors

with Jane Rasbash

The Asian future

Dialogues for change
Volume 1

Zed Books
LONDON | NEW YORK

The Asian future: Dialogues for change, Volume 1 was first published by Zed Books Ltd, 7 Cynthia Street, London N1 9JF, UK and Room 400, 175 Fifth Avenue, New York, NY 10010, USA in 2005.

www.zedbooks.co.uk

Cover designed by Andrew Corbett
Set in Arnhem and Futura Bold by Ewan Smith, London
Printed and bound in Malta by Gutenberg Press Ltd

Distributed in the USA exclusively by Palgrave Macmillan, a division of St Martin's Press, LLC, 175 Fifth Avenue, New York, NY 10010.

A catalogue record for this book is available from the British Library.
US CIP data are available from the Library of Congress.

ISBN 1 84277 342 9 cased
ISBN 1 84277 343 7 limp

Contents

To Sulak Sivaraksa, our beloved teacher

Foreword

Suffering in the present world is overwhelming. Seeing suffering clearly is the first step towards the cessation of suffering. Great compassion and wisdom come from this clear seeing, without which there will be no liberation – spiritual, political or otherwise.

It is my great joy to see this collection of dialogues by socially engaged Asian intellectuals of great calibre who articulate so rigorously their search for a better alternative to the present scenario. Deeply rooted in the diverse spiritual and political traditions of Asia, these voices present unique Asian contributions to our present debate about the future of humanity from a non-Western perspective. This is an important first step towards a necessary intellectual balance that we badly need at this moment at the global level.

I am positive that this book will be a contribution to the shifting of perspectives on how we analyse the causes of our suffering, re-visualise alternative futures, and pave the path toward those visions. Without this shift, the world's suffering will not be improved at any substantial level.

Civilisations do not need to clash. The human nature of compassion and understanding teaches us that all civilisations can co-exist. Some civilisations may have more aggressive elements; others are more tolerant. However, if we mindfully draw lessons from the past history of human suffering, there is no other way to live together in this shrinking globe but by listening deeply to each other, to those who think and see things differently from us, and also to nature.

A particular message to the strong and the dominant is that one can benefit greatly by listening deeply to the weak and the marginalised. The kind of wisdom coming out of their hearts is something one lacks when one is strong and dominant. Humanity needs to draw on that wisdom to live together in mutual respect and harmony.

His Holiness The Dalai Lama

Introduction

The Asian Future records a search. The aim of the search is to define who we Asians are – politically, intellectually, culturally, morally and spiritually. To search implies dissatisfaction. Even after the end of colonialism and at the beginning of a new era of political independence, Asia is still under pressure. Young intelligentsia and concerned intellectuals are dissatisfied with the ethos of our societies. At both conscious and sub-conscious levels we find, if we look carefully, that we still experience the domination of the West. This is true at both the intellectual and psychological levels and also within our economic and political systems.

Undoubtedly certain sectors of Asian society are 'catching up' with the West in terms of material well-being and economic and technological development. Some sectors have even been able to achieve a level of social justice in terms of distribution of wealth and with a parliamentary political system. These include Japan (very affluent) and Kerala in South India (less affluent). Many other Asian countries and sectors of Asian societies are more affluent than they once were.

However, at best these economic achievements are a mixed blessing, for they are based upon the stimulation of greed, competition, violence and individualism. Traditionally, in Asia, these characteristics are regarded as the root causes of unhappiness. They are responsible for all kinds of other problems in contemporary society.

People are compelled to search for more money, wealth, power, recognition and sensual gratification. The cycle never ends. Hence the high rates of suicide, mental illness, stress, alcoholism, over-consumption and drug addiction in those 'successful' sectors of Asian society. We believe this is also true in other, non-Asian, societies around the world.

We should be aware that the well-off sectors have achieved their prosperity through the exploitation of and structural violence against the poor majority and the natural environment. Unfortunately the less affluent people are subjected to heavy pressure – from educational institutions and the mass media – to regard those success stories as the model, and to look down upon their own way of life accordingly.

By the time Asia gained independence from Western colonisation, most of the Asian elite had lost confidence in their own cultural values. The elite are educated in the West or receive Western-style education in their own countries. They come to feel that they belong to a type of society that is intrinsically inferior to the West. So they have to 'catch up' with all the latest fashions of the West. This even includes the progressive elite 'catching up' with progressive Western political thought.

Once elite circles accept that a society is backward and underdeveloped, they feel that the people urgently need to be modernised and 'developed'. Through educational institutions and the mass media, this inferiority complex of the elite spreads to the people at large. This is a process of cultural uprooting. People in every stratum of society feel that they are not good enough.

When we walk around Tokyo, Bangkok, Delhi, Seoul, Manila and the other Asian capitals, we see many youngsters dyeing their hair blonde or red. They eat out at Pizza Hut, Kentucky Fried Chicken and McDonald's. Their hairstyles and eating habits are not just a temporary fashion of young people: they reflect a vivid and deep cultural and spiritual sickness in Asia. Their society has become one where they cannot be proud of who they are and have to try to be someone else.

Actually, we can see this phenomenon of deep colonisation in all societies in the contemporary world. Everywhere people are made to feel that they are not good enough by consumer monoculture. This process of alienation is required to sustain the continuing process of globalisation.

In fact, any society with a structure that undermines the self-respect of its members is an unhealthy society. You cannot be a mature and happy person and part of a healthy community by rejecting what you are and who you are. This does not mean that we have to confine ourselves to all the structures of traditional roles and responsibilities. It means that we have to reject the notion that we belong to a lesser race, class, gender, religion, culture or civilisation, whoever we are, whatever we are.

Once we are firmly rooted in self-respect and in our own cultural values, we can make healthy and critically aware choices for the future from various sources. It is in order to combat this 'catch-up' mentality that dominates the whole of Asian society and this basic alienation that dehumanises our people that we have put our energies into producing these two volumes of dialogues challenging Western political thought. There is still much to be done to heal the deep spiritual and political crisis that came with colonialism. We must fight to regain our spiritual and intellectual integrity in defining and redefining who we are and to recover our long-lost self-confidence rooted in our ancient cultures, traditions and indigenous wisdom.

Somewhat to our surprise, we find the intellectual articulation from these various ancient Asian traditions, as expressed here by the best minds in Asia, to be rigorous, relevant and full of vitality. They spoke gently but strongly, deeply rooted in tradition but very appropriate to contemporary society, with a sense of humour but straight to the point.

Each interview is complete in itself yet, reading them together, they have a clear affinity. Each is unique yet part of the whole. When we look at them together we can say to ourselves – 'Yes! this is Asia: diverse and unique – yet the unity is there.'

To take part in these dialogues we chose activist-thinkers: deeply rooted in their traditions and also strongly committed to working for social change. This is about looking backwards in order to go forwards; using indigenous wisdom as a base to encounter the challenges and opportunities of modernity with dignity. While specific questions vary according to each individual, the general outline of enquiry is the same, covering the following areas.

- Overview and critique of the present system: analysis of the present society in Asia; pros and cons of capitalism, globalisation, consumerism, the 'tigers' economic model, the Japanese model; Mahathir and Lee Kuan Yew's approach to Asian cultural values and modernisation; successes and failures of communism/socialism in the Asian context; assessment of environmental degradation; the grassroots movements and the role of NGOs; the importance of alternative power structures in society.
- Alternative worldview and philosophy: the effects of the Eurocentric worldview; the concepts of modernisation and the dominant paradigm of development; the supremacy of scientific knowledge, the right to conquer nature, never-ending technological progress, unlimited-economic growth, the virtue of competition, private property, equality, liberty, freedom, democracy, individualism and human rights; modernisation in Asia; human beings and nature; the Asian meaning of sustainability; industrialised markets; Asian cultural roots and inferiority complex; concepts and attitude to power.
- Vision for a new Asian society: the basic characteristics of a good and sustainable society, the type of political culture; the concept of government and leadership in an alternative political order; the concept of service as opposed to the concept of power; the role of institutions in the new politics, parties, international groups, community organisation, religious bodies; the idea of decentralisation, the political manifestation of spirituality; the causes of growing religious fundamentalism; spiritual resurgence and alternative politics.

3

- From here to there: how to build a just and sustainable society with a spiritual basis; revolution or reform; violent and nonviolent methods; the agents of change; a particular class building alternative communities; changing life styles; starting a new education; the concept of civil society and how to strengthen it; the role of NGOs, citizen groups, religious organisations; the building of alternative institutes, such as business, banking, and so on.

We were amazed by the richness of these dialogues. Altogether we spoke to 14 people. Abdurraman Wahid (Indonesia), Chandra Muzaffar (Malaysia) and Mahmoud Ayoub (Lebanon/US) are Muslims. Samdhong Rinpoche (Tibet/India), Sulak Sivaraksa (Siam) and Helena Norberg-Hodge (Sweden/Ladakh) are Buddhists. Satish Kumar (India/UK), Ashis Nandy (India) and Vandana Shiva (India) are Gandhian/alternative thinkers with the unique spiritual background of that subcontinent. Tu Weiming (China/US) is a Confucian scholar. Bishop Labayen (The Philippines) is a Christian strongly influenced by Marxism. Arief Budiman (Indonesia/Australia), Walden Bello (The Philippines) and Nakamura Hisashi (Japan) are Asian left intellectuals strongly identified with Asian culture in general. These people are all deeply rooted in their particular cultural traditions, which to a great extent inform their political views. But none of them is dogmatic and all are very open-minded thinkers – and activists too, to varying degrees. We regard Helena Norberg-Hodge as an 'honorary Asian' because of her deep understanding of Buddhist Asian values derived from her study of Ladakh's people and culture.

It is vital to recognise that the geopolitical and cultural specifications of what is Asian are very diverse. There is huge complexity of human migrations, and socio-cultural and religious interaction among the peoples and societies of Asia. Consequently the inherent limitations of this project in representing the collective voice of Asia should be duly recognised by the reader. We earnestly believe that this is only a beginning, and hope to continue this dialogue with thinkers, scholars, social activists, and political and community leaders from other parts of Asia. We deeply respect and recognise the fact that this dialogue judiciously represents the principles of diversity that are so intrinsic to the culture and traditions of the East. We also hope that this book provides an opportunity for wider dialogue among Asians and between Asians and peoples from other parts of the world.

These two volumes have taken shape within the Alternative Politics for Asia project, which is part of the Alternatives to Consumerism venture at the Santi Pracha Dhamma Institute, Bangkok. Many people have helped us greatly, and we would like to thank them. First and foremost, the interviewees, who generously managed to fit in many hours for the interviews despite their very busy schedules. We regard them as our teachers. We would also like to thank Jane Rasbash, who was then the co-ordinator of Alternatives to Consumerism. Her support has been of great help in making this project run smoothly. Many thanks go to those who assisted with the transcription of the tapes, especially political science students at Delhi University and volunteers at Wongsanit Ashram. We would particularly like to thank the native English-speakers whose hard work helped with the editing, especially Christine Dann, Jane Rasbash, Jill & Graeme Jameson and Ronald Suleski. We would also like to thank Burint Saray and friends at CCFD, who saw the importance of this work and co-ordinated basic funds for the project. Thanks to Barbara Clarke and Robert Molteno at Zed Books for their support and encouragement. Special gratitude to our beloved wives Jane and Sheela, for without their understanding, assistance and endless support these volumes would not have been possible.

Pracha Hutanuwatr and Ramu Manivannan

1 | Ashis Nandy

Ashis Nandy was born in the 1930s in India. He is one of the most prominent and outspoken Asian intellectuals. In India, he is a leading thinker, public intellectual and social commentator. His work covers a vast terrain. He provides an approach that is at once theoretical and empirical, literary and ethnographic, civilisational and local. Nandy is active at all levels. His key areas of interest are the political psychology of violence, cultures of knowledge, utopias and visions, popular culture, futures and genocides. In South Asia and beyond he has played a critical role in establishing crucial links between North and South. His outstanding contribution has been to provide a critique of dominant knowledge systems. His voice has helped to conscientise both the North and the ruling elites in the South about their own suppressed traditions of knowledge and dissent.

Nandy works as a sociologist and clinical psychologist, and has for thirty-five years been a Fellow at the Centre for Study of Developing Societies, Delhi, and is chairperson of the Committee for Cultural Choices and Global Futures. He is associated with the Commonwealth Human Rights Initiative, the Transnational Foundation for Peace and Future Research and the Institute of Postcolonial Studies. Past positions include Director of the Centre for Study of Developing Societies, a Woodrow Wilson Fellow, a Fellow at the Institute for Advanced Studies in Humanities, Edinburgh, a UNESCO Professor at the Centre for European Studies at the University of Trier, and a Regent's Fellow at the University of California, Los Angeles. He has monitored democratic elections in India, Bangladesh and Pakistan on behalf of democratic and civil rights movements. He served on the jury of the Asia–Pacific Public Hearing on Crimes Against Women Related to the Violence of Development and the World Court of Women Against Racism, as part of the World Conference on Racism, Racial Discrimination, Xenophobia and Related Intolerance. Both were organised by the Asian Women's Human Rights Council. He also served on a jury of public hearing on the Sardar Sarovar (Narmada) dam project.

He is a prolific writer, his major books and publications being: *Alternative Science*, *At the Edge of Psychology*, *The Intimate Enemy*, *The Tao of Cricket*, *The Illegitimacy of Nationalism*, *The Savage Freud and Other Essays in Possible and Retrievable Selves*, *An Ambiguous Journey to the City*, *Traditions, Tyranny and Utopias* and *The Blinded Eye: 500 Years of Christopher Columbus*. He is the co-author of *Science, Hegemony and Violence*, editor of *The Secret Politics of our Desires*, and co-editor of *The Multiverse of Democracy*.

Oxford University Press is bringing out an omnibus edition of his works, of which the first two volumes, *Exiled at Home* and *Return from Exile*, have been published. The third volume, *A Very Popular Exile*, will be published shortly. Nandy's works have been translated into a number of languages. He has also contributed to major human rights reports, including, in Delhi (2000), the People's Tribunal on Environment and Human Rights.

RAMU MANIVANNAN: How do you see the nature of the present system of governance, especially in the third world?

ASHIS NANDY: It is mostly comical. More seriously, the nature differs so much from country to country that it is difficult to generalise. At best, one can say that many 'controlled' democratic forms of governance and most of the alternatives supplied by Leninist Marxism have collapsed. They have been eased out of power in many places and are holding on to power in a few cases, usually through naked autocracy or military might. But they are now mostly marginal players on the world stage. The dominant ideal now is liberal democracy as defined by the Western liberal democracies. I suspect that this is also not much of a solution, because liberal democracy presumes a homogenised population and advocates a form of citizenship in which individuals technically have an equal right to vote and participate in governance. Usually, however, the citizens have the right to participate only through elections. Between elections, they have little political say.

The citizens' opinions count because they change regimes every four or five years. In the actual process of governance, however, the citizens are mostly spectators. There is also a tacit assumption in liberal democracies that ordinary people know nothing about governance. They do not know the technicalities of governance and they do not have expert knowledge of diplomacy, national security, developmental planning or economic management. In addition, they are not interested, except in some of the ritualised, telegenic aspects of governance. The citizens are presumed to be more deeply interested in such important things as shopping, entertainment, spectator sports, and making money. Therefore, the system sets up and depends on experts, professionals or specialists who are never fully or directly answerable to the people. These experts occupy an ever larger space in modern democracies as decision-makers in crucial areas of life. This mode of governance is winning new victories every day all over the world and has reduced the power of the citizen in every liberal democracy.

Simultaneously, the growth and reach of the media have produced another kind of problem. Nowadays, leaders in democratic polities are chosen the way South Asians choose their sons-in-law. Political parties choose leaders taking into account their physical looks, public presence and communication skills. A political leader is expected to be mediagenic and attractive in the way a film star is. As a result, the quality of leadership is declining in every democracy. Leaders are not chosen on the grounds of their political qualities. Ronald Reagan, during his eight-year rule, saw nearly 2,500 films. Reportedly, he was functional as President for not more than two hours on an average day. He gave his press conferences entirely under the guidance of his advisers and fought elections under the supervision of his media experts and political handlers. He served as a front and one wonders if he had any political substance inside. He was set up as an attractive and impressive communicator who articulated the opinions, beliefs and preferences of a whole range of experts and specialists who constituted a network of special interests.

This is only an example, but it hints at the kind of problem we are facing in this part of the world. Because of various historical and cultural phenomena, including the experience of colonialism, the fear of the people is deeper in our part of the world. We feel we do not understand the people, nor do they understand us. We are also convinced that people do not know, that we must give them solutions and they must accept them. If they do not, we consider them irrational, superstitious and stubborn. There is built-in legitimacy in our countries for such rule by specialists and professionals. There is built-in legitimacy for a style of governance that distances the rulers from the people.

We also often lack the scepticism that many in the Western world, over-exposed to all forms of media, have begun to display towards audiovisual media. Consequently, as democracies in Asia and Africa become more media-intensive, they also become more manipulative.

MANIVANNAN: Why do we need to be governed by this kind of system at all?

NANDY: Well, that is an open question. I do not believe people need to be governed. I believe that people can govern themselves reasonably well. If they were left alone, they would govern themselves even better. There is a drought going on in parts of India at this moment, quite a bad one. There is severe water scarcity. In many places, the government seems to be at its wits' end. Yet every report shows that communities and villages that have taken care of their water needs by themselves, through their own traditional systems of water storage, harvesting and management, have done better. Whereas people depending on the government and experts for water management through dams, canals and other forms of water supply have been thrown into deep crisis.

PRACHA HUTANUWATR: In Asia, we are still largely following the colonial system of governance, including the colonial model of administration and political representation. This is also true of Thailand, which was never formally colonised, but the nature and style of governance is Western. What are your responses to the situation?

NANDY: If we look at it closely, we see that it is a sign of our intellectual defeat. We were defeated not only by the force of arms but also by the belief that those who have power possess right ideas, and those who do not have power cannot but have wrong or useless ideas. What you say is true of many countries in Asia, not only of Thailand. This is equally true of much of Africa, where I have noticed little or no deviation from the Western model or system of governance. Africa is no longer colonised. In fact, in many countries there, the Western model is in total disarray. Yet they are trying hard to integrate themselves into the globally dominant system of governance. I am not surprised that Thailand is doing the same. This is the thrust of our times. At some point we shall have to reverse the process.

PRACHA: Do you believe in people governing themselves? If not, what kind of governance do you believe in?

NANDY: I believe in minimum governance. I believe that the government should get off the backs of the people. This is the slogan of conservatives in many liberal democracies in the West. But in our context it has a different meaning, and has tremendous potential for liberation and emancipation of the people because the state systems are invariably distant from them. The state systems here are dismissive of the ideas, life-support systems and occupations of the people. They are dismissive even of their democratic rights.

MANIVANNAN: Is this close to Henry David Thoreau's idea that the best government is the one that governs least?

NANDY: Certainly. I shall put it this way. Because we have set up more or less alien structures of governance, even a democratic regime cannot easily intervene in or effectively alter our style of governance. We would perhaps do better to have a decentralised system of self-governance in which the central authorities perform the role of distant, benign monitor and interfere minimally in local government.

MANIVANNAN: What we are discussing is related to the nature of state that has emerged in recent times. The twentieth century has been looked upon as a period of consolidation of the nation-state system, though the consolidation has been going on for centuries. How would you rate the nation-state system and its relevance today?

NANDY: I think the nation-state system has little cultural relevance to this part of the world, except probably as a force of destruction. Its only positive value is that it allows us to negotiate the present global system. We are neither monolithic national entities nor homogenised masses. There is no melting pot in any of the countries in Asia. We have tried to create such melting pots and have produced artificial melting pots in every society. We expect every individual citizen to melt in these pots in the long run. Even in the West, this melting-pot system has not been as perfect as the modern theories of state presume. In Asia, the system has been a calamity. True, the idea of a state system is not a product of the twentieth century. It has grown over at least 350 years. But the immense power of modern economic, military and media institutions consolidated the idea in the last century. Yet it has remained a fragile arrangement in much of Asia, where the survival of the state is often more dependent on the security apparatus and the power of the state. The most important point is that these societies, particularly in South and South-east Asia, have been tolerant societies, perhaps not by design but by default. They did not operate with ideas of nationality, but with that of communities. India, for instance, has eighteen hundred languages and dialects and twenty thousand castes. When we talk of the Brahmins of India, we often do not know that they can be of two thousand kinds, most of whom do not know each other, do not speak each others' languages, and do not intermarry. But people always talk about how the Brahmins keep themselves at a distance from other castes. As it happens, they have also been distant from each other. These communities have links but they are also autonomous.

We have not thought about how to build on this odd principle of diversity. The traditional systems of governance in each of these societies held in respect and in fact built upon this principle of diversity. We, on the other hand, have learnt to feel inferior when our societies are not as homogenous and unified as Western societies are. Not that Western societies are entirely homogenous, but in some of them the idea of the nation-state has gone very deep. France is a good example. In the popular French concept of nation-state, there is less scope for diversity. We have tried to follow that model and think it ideal. When we do not exactly follow that model, we think we are making compromises. Actually, these are not compromises but a way of paying homage to the traditions of diversity in our societies. People think that if we do not pay minimum respect to the traditions of diversity, even the imperfect nation-states that many societies of Asia have put in place would be jeopardised. Otherwise, Asian states have shown no intrinsic commitment to diversity.

PRACHA: Why do you consider diversity so important?

NANDY: Diversity is important because we live in a world where the cultural gene pool is shrinking every day in a way similar to the way biodiversity is shrinking globally. In North America, hundreds of varieties of apple have already come down to less than ten, I am told. I do not frankly appreciate the question, 'what is the use of diversity?' Diversity is a value in itself. If we do not have diversity, we shall be left with only homogenised, uniform cultures. If for some reason future generations want to or are forced to come out of that state, they would have no option left in the real world and they would have to invent diversity.

Diversity gives you different vantage points and different baselines, which allow you to have different points of departure. Diversity can be seen as a series of human experiments about how to organise life, particularly public life, how to organise governments or self-governance. We have choice as long as we are diverse. If we find that liberal democracy is exhausted or has run its course, we can look for a different kind of democracy that is more decentralised and people-oriented and does not have the institutionalised fear of the people that is built into our present system of governance. But if we destroy diversity now, we might find that we do not have enough alternatives to choose from, experiment with or build upon.

PRACHA: How do you view the formation of nation-states in Europe and the way this concept of the nation-state has been used in practice in other parts of the world?

NANDY: That is a very wide-ranging question and I am not a world historian. But an important point to remember is that the idea of the nation-state spread to the countries outside Europe, in Africa, Asia and Latin America, not through cultural diffusion but through colonialism and the rise of imperial states. The nation-states that the Asians saw in operation during the nineteenth century and the first half of the twentieth were mostly the imperial states. After de-colonisation, they usually saw the new nation-states being built on structures bequeathed by the imperial states. Only the rulers or incumbents were new. Therefore, despite the introduction of the system of electoral democracy, the basic idea of the state has to some extent remained imperial. The idea of the imperial state mediates between the classical concept of the state and the nation-state as it operates in large parts of the Southern world, particularly in Asia. This compromise has created problems for us. This particular form of nationalised, post-colonial, imperial state has a deep fear of the people. They are seen as subjects and not as participants in governance. This idea of the subject insists on a certain basic distance between the pursuits of the state and the lifestyles of the people.

PRACHA: What are the sources of the modern nation-state? Where did it originate?

NANDY: The crude, simplified answer is that the nation-states came into being in the West with the decline of the monarchies. The republican regimes began to take shape as the monarchies began to collapse. The cementing bond, the relationship between the people and the state, became weaker or, at least, seemed weaker to the elite. Traditionally, the monarchs mediated between the sacred and the profane, heaven and earth. They had a natural legitimacy and within their kingdoms at least could be certain of the loyalty of the people. After the demise of monarchies, the European elite became apprehensive about the sustainability of people's loyalty to the state. They felt that nationalism could be a good way of ensuring this loyalty. The idea of nation, nationality and nationalism became salient in that context.

That is one way of describing how the nation-states emerged from the ruins of the *ancien régime* in Europe. In large parts of Asia and Africa, people did not see themselves as part of any nation-state because they did not see themselves as nations. They saw themselves as communities and you cannot start calling them nations and expect them to behave accordingly overnight.

The more people refuse to give unthinking legitimacy to the state, the more the state insists on its priority and coerces the population into becoming loyal citizens. Part of the coercive nature of the state in Asia and Africa arises from the fear that the citizens are not automatically loyal to it. Indeed, in some countries of Europe and in North America this loyalty is easier because the masses are relatively more homogenised and have little to fall back upon except the nation-state. Therefore, the idea of nationalism sustains the idea of state, whether in football matches or in wars. If you are French, then you automatically owe allegiance to the French nation-state, the French football team and French cuisine.

In our societies, life is organised differently. It is not organised around atomised individuals. Societies are 'salad bowls', not soups. Despite what politicians and statist intellectuals say, there is no cosmic melting point called the 'mainstream' in which people melt, as reportedly they do in the United States. The United States is a country of the uprooted. People came to it from all over the world and it was easier to homogenise them. Perhaps the idea of nation-state can partly resolve the crisis of identity for the uprooted and offer them a primordial sense of belonging.

Though displacement and uprooting are increasing dramatically in our societies, we have lived in communities for centuries, probably for millennia. We cannot quickly become a set of isolated individuals, owing allegiance only to the state, whether it is an Indian, Chinese, Indonesian or Thai state. The more we demand of citizens that they talk and behave not as members of communities but as individuals – isolated, atomised citizens – the more they learn to hide the fact that they have other allegiances, too. As the state becomes more nervous, it shrilly asks the people to be citizens first, and hence be submissive to the state's authority, and members of religious and ethnic communities second. People sense the nervousness and quickly learn the language of the state and begin to show, sometimes flamboyantly, their allegiance to the ideology of the state. But they also learn to camouflage and protect their other, less respectable loyalties. It is well illustrated by Wail Khan's 'notorious' claim, which went something like: 'I am a Pakistani for the last fifty years, a Muslim for the past 1,400 years, and a Pathan for 5,000 years.' It is a self-defeating project.

PRACHA: Is there any relationship between the emergence of the nation-state in the West, the formation of capital, and the rise of capitalism?

NANDY: There is, and others have written about it at length. I can add little. However, a psychological relationship between the two may not be that obvious. I think only atomised, psychologically uprooted individuals, owing allegiance to only an abstract, reified idea of the nation-state can give such centrality to a kind of commerce that is entirely impersonal and contractual, thoroughly rational, and not touched by any concept of vocation. There is a difference between a job and a vocation. When Thai peasants till the land, they are not professionals pursuing an occupation. They are not only producing something for the global market. What they produce has symbolic value and cultural meaning. It exhibits certain continuity between their ancestors and their children and grandchildren, a connection between their past and their future. Work is seen simultaneously as a source of well-being, survival, worship, leisure and as the affirmation of their culture, which is radically different from capitalist forms of production. In the last analysis, capital has no respect for culture. It can have respect only for itself.

In Japan, rice cultivation is not only a production system but also an essential part of a cultural system. It binds Japan to its past. It provides meaning to Japanese life, although the Japanese may not dare to say so any more. They have to give, apologetically, economic reasons for persisting with rice farming in Japan. They are often asked why they have such high tariffs on rice produced elsewhere in the world and why the rice Japan produces cannot be produced in another country at half the cost? They are asked if such enormous subsidies to farmers are economically justified? The answer should be that it is culturally justifiable. But the Japanese would not say so openly. The second most powerful economy in the world does not or cannot say that rice cultivation is essential for cultural continuity in Japan. It is like saying that the Red Fort at Delhi should make an excellent tourist hotel, and Indians giving elaborate economic reasons against it.

Yes, I do think that the atomisation, alienation, isolation and loneliness of the individual citizen under the nation-state system, the disregard for community life, and the fear of cultures has something to do with the capitalist political economy. My suspicion is that this partly explains the success of capitalism and the reasons for the failure of socialism and Marxism. Millions of people seem willing to get uprooted, alienated and atomised to make money; capitalism leaves you ample scope to do so while having some symbolic access to culture and community.

PRACHA: Can you elaborate on the last point?

NANDY: Socialism and Marxism tried to fight the capitalist system without fighting the nation-state system. They lacked basic respect for people and their cultures. They respected people as a proletariat, but did not respect them as functioning cultural entities. Socialism and communism wanted to learn nothing from the people; they always wanted to educate people. Nor had they any respect for traditional systems of knowledge, which their ideologies saw as dispensable or disposable. Communism glorified a concept of revolution in which only the proletariat had a role to play, not the oppressed in general. It believed that people needed to be taught, trained and readied for radical transformation. Above all, communism had no sense of priorities. Like many comic rationalists who infest public life in the South, the communists were more hostile to astrologers who told your fortune and cheated you of a few Bahts than to necrophiliac scientists who promised perfect security through nuclear weaponry or the billion-dollar cosmetic industry selling permanent youth, or the global medical establishment selling perfect painlessness and immortality.

PRACHA: Is Marxism the child of modernisation?

NANDY: Certainly. It is the child of the European Enlightenment and modernisation. It is a dissenting child, but a child none the less. The main concern of Marxism is to establish the structural basis for a just modernisation, which many might say is an oxymoron, an impossibility. Any social movement must, to succeed, understand the idiom of the people. This idiom includes their cultural values, their cultural knowledge pool, craft and other artistic traditions. That is a tall order, but the time has come for us to move beyond the ruins of nineteenth-century European ideologies, which promised to show us a direct path to secular salvation.

PRACHA: This largely explains the causes of the communists' failure in Thailand.

NANDY: Does it? I am not surprised.

MANIVANNAN: You are talking about the imperfect fit between the Western concept of the nation-state and the worldview that goes with it on the one hand, and our traditional ideas of state, society and the development of the post-colonial situation on the other. Do you see any possibility for the emergence of alternatives to the present system of governance and the nation-state model?

NANDY: Alternatives are always there. I do not think such large entities as cultures and civilisations can be defeated so easily. It is not possible to turn the world into a replica of the United States of America. The United States draws people from different parts of the world into a single man–machine system, with the hope of providing them with a new identity over a generation or two. The European experience with the alternatives, on the other hand, has always been coloured by a form of social evolutionism that often verges on racism. Socialist and Marxist theories are no exceptions to this rule. They have a built-in bias against the non-West, particularly its diverse cultural repertoire, categories and systems of knowledge. They are seen as depositories of superstition or irrationality. As I have already said, I have no objection to fighting superstitions, but I believe that we must fight the larger and more powerful ones first. There are many elements of irrationality in the consumption patterns of the West, which people there do not want to see as irrational.

MANIVANNAN: I want us to return to alternatives. How do you see the future of alternative visions? Can people revive them?

NANDY: First, as a mark of respect for and celebration of alternative visions, we should not expect only one to emerge, but hundreds and thousands of them. Who are we to specify what should be the alternative? Our role is to empower diverse alternatives. Out of the dialogue between various alternatives will emerge certain major tendencies or trends that will help to organise the world of the future. We do not know what the more relevant alternatives will be? It is not possible to predict their configuration now. It will certainly emerge from the dialogue between the existing and emerging alternatives. The creation of an alternative world order is the work of millions. We should be humble enough to accept that we cannot produce an Asian Buddha or even Gandhi in our times to give us a solution acceptable to all. There cannot be and there should not be a single alternative. I like to visualise a world in which alternatives will be as diverse as the lifestyles of the people. It requires a world where there is no large, dominant, phagocytic system hostile to and trying to destroy all alternatives. Large systems are acceptable only if they are accommodating and respectful towards the least powerful alternatives, where the larger systems are in essence the creation of smaller ones.

PRACHA: Are some basic values essential for bringing together these alternatives?

NANDY: Yes, but I do not think it is necessary to strive for a consensus on them. These basic values usually cross barriers of cultures and civilisations. For instance, childhood has especial privileges in all societies. There is an element of sacredness or a touch of transcendence even in secular world-views. There are limits to violence, and life is valued, in all cultures.

PRACHA: What about democracy?

NANDY: Democracy is one apparently modern value for which there is wide support worldwide for two reasons. First, contrary to the belief of the moderns in this part of the world, in parts of Africa and among the native American communities long traditions of living with diversity have already created an important base for democracy. In South and South-east Asia, even dissent has often enjoyed an especial status. These parts of the world have always been open to the idea of plurality and democracy. They may not be democratic in your way or mine, but the idea of democracy does not appear alien to them. Indeed, their concepts of democracy should serve, within the modern world-view, as windows through which we can glimpse possible non-modern and post-modern concepts of democracy. The term post-modern here does not have the same meaning that it has for the 'postmodernist'. I am alluding to the chronological significance of certain ideas that at one time looked retro-gressive and tired. Modernism has come to its fag end.

No era in this world has lasted more than a few hundred years, though every era has behaved as if it was going to last forever. Even the dark age of Europe lasted only three to four hundred years. Modernity has already lasted four hundred years. In several areas of our life, knowledge and social organisation, we have already started moving beyond the modern age. One of the values of the modern age that may survive the age's demise is democracy. It may not be liberal democracy, as we know it today, which is being reconceptualised and celebrated as a gift of Europe and globalised capitalism. I am talking of ideas of democracy that are intrinsic to this part of the world. I think the Buddhist vision has always been democratic. Several socio-religious movements in this part of the world, such as the Bhakti movement in India during the medieval and post-medieval times, have been profoundly democratic. Politically, it can be read as a democratic revolution. Islam has a built-in concept of democratic justice. Sufism in some of its incarnations has pushed that principle to its logical, transcendent conclusion. I think these different concepts of plural de-mocracy will begin to interact with each other. There will be mutual learning and cross-cultural dialogue on plurality. I do not see much future for regimes that attempt to banish democracy in the name of Asian values or family values or even socialism. Their efforts are doomed.

MANIVANNAN: You appreciate the principle of diversity, the revival of com-munity values and the grass-roots orientation to politics. You also think that the communities should be allowed to grow and develop into fuller entities.

NANDY: Yes, that is one way of putting what I want to say. I should, how-ever, add a footnote. I am impressed by the fact that the new modes of global governance through economic institutions (such as the World Bank or the IMF or the GATT) and through the global nation-state system seem so insecure when facing small communities, movements or even individuals resisting integration into the dominant system of governance. This insecurity persists despite their total dominance of the global political economy. This does not indicate the self-confidence of a victorious system. It reveals a deep sense of being fragile and vulnerable and a fear that if you leave even a small commu-nity alone or a social movement untouched, it will ultimately overwhelm the dominant system. This is an important lesson; we must notice it and learn from it. The response to the Seattle demonstration is itself a classic example of this insecurity. The spokespersons of both the IMF and the World Bank claimed that they shared the values of the demonstrators, who were otherwise misinformed and misguided.

PRACHA: When you talked of alternative governance, you mentioned the role of state as a monitor. Can you say little more about that?

NANDY: I mean to say that we cannot go back to our past. There are things we cannot dismantle. We are in communication with each other across the globe. There should be some scope for modes of governance having a global reach. We cannot have global media without some global regulatory authority to check civil or criminal misuse of media. Similarly in other areas of life: there should be some monitoring authority to ensure that global institutions conform to minimum norms. I do not know what shape these institutions will take in the future. I am merely pointing out possible areas where the state might have an important role to play, as an intermediary between the global and the local.

MANIVANNAN: Are you talking about the need for building a global mech-anism to ensure accountability of global institutions?

NANDY: Yes. We need regulatory norms to check excesses and the misuse of power. Obviously, in areas like media, communications, arms control, geno-cides, we need global bodies. Arms are becoming a serious problem all over the world. We cannot control them only through local initiatives. It is difficult to check ambitious, desperate despots at the local level alone, without any simultaneous, large-scale global intervention.

PRACHA: On the one hand, you talk of the need for the revival of commu-nities and grass-roots politics. On the other, you advocate the need to build a global mechanism of control. What is the link between the two?

NANDY: Actually, I am pleading for some minimum role for the state that only the state can perform. I am suggesting that the state, instead of dabbling

Ashis Nandy

in things that it knows little about, could profitably concentrate on things that it can possibly handle. In India, the state does not have good regulatory bodies to handle corporations' transgressions or to control corruption, but it runs hotel chains, tourist agencies and sports bodies.

The state was not a stranger in our part of the world. We have lived with the idea of the state for millennia. They were not democracies, but they were sometimes 'consociational'. I borrow the term from Arend Lijphart to mean a state that takes into account communities, not only individual citizens. Some of these states allowed different communities and regions to have different levels of allegiance to the state, a principle from which contemporary states also might have something to learn. As a result, probably, they also survived longer. The Mughal Empire, which preceded British rule in India, lasted for nearly four hundred years. That is, its tenure was double the length of British rule in India. Such was the resilience of the convention of the Mughals and the political culture they built that during its first eighty years, the British Indian state tried to follow them in religious and educational policies, revenue system, customary laws and even official language, which was Persian. For a hundred years, the East India Company ruled India under the mandate of the Mughal Empire. The Mughal state lasted so long not because it saw itself as a nation-state but because it learnt to take into account the diverse cultures and power systems of the society. The Rajputs, for instance, were major co-sharers of power in the Mughal Empire. It was on the Mughal system that the British were partly to build the colonial princely order.

Likewise, the traditional Thai state was a good example of how different peoples and communities could be accommodated within an unconventional state system. The king simultaneously meant different things to different people and was never a homogenising principle. The Thai monarchy symbolised not only the unity of Thailand but also the diversity of Thai society. He was not only a Buddhist king but simultaneously made sense to his Hindu and Confucian subjects. There were Brahmins who participated in the rituals of the state and presided over life-cycle rituals such as dynastic births, marriages, coronations and deaths.

I must hasten to add here that I am not preaching a return to a mythical golden age of India or Thailand. I am suggesting that we could have learnt more from the indigenous state systems and avoided mechanical adoption of textbook versions of the nation-state.

PRACHA: In Thailand, all these have changed, largely after the adoption of a new constitution. A lot of diversity has been destroyed. The plural bases and values within the society have been eroded. The new colonisers come from within. Bangkok, for instance, enjoys a special status in comparison with other parts of the country in every respect – social, economic and political.

NANDY: This has been happening in virtually every country. The Thai king has been reduced to the status of president of the country. But some of the older ideas of plurality might have survived. In Thailand, you notice individuals and communities that are more than they seem. One can see how the ideas of the state and political identity could have been given another kind of meaning in our part of the world in the Thai model itself. There are Thais who are simultaneously Thai and Chinese, Thai and Indian, Buddhist and Confucian, Buddhist and Muslim, and Buddhist and Hindu. Cultural plurality exists not merely at the community level. Many individuals belong to more than one religion, culture and nation.

Let us not forget, however, that democracy is one modern value that is not yet as destructive as other ideas and values of modernity. When people have an unfettered right to elect their rulers, creative possibilities open up in a society. This is because people in a democracy do not bring to the public sphere their votes alone. They bring their ideas, values, loves, hates, preferences and anti-preferences. These 'contaminate' the democratic process. Politics becomes the vehicle of the power of the people and, through them, of their culture.

On the other hand, there is also an element of openness in the democratic process. It allows open mobilisation of people on grounds of caste, class, ethnicity, socio-religious difference and nationality. That is, democratic mobilisation takes place not exclusively on the basis of cultural identity. It also takes place on the basis of prejudices, stereotypes and collective memories. This has led not only to enormous ethno-religious strife, but also to the hardening of the boundaries between the different ethnic and religious groups. In India, for instance, nearly 15 per cent of communities have multiple identities in terms of religious faith, but religious divides have become stronger over the last fifty years. This negative contribution of democracy we can no longer overlook. Similarly with ethnic divisions in Sri Lanka. We blame the politicians, but do not see the problems inherent in a system that demands mobilisation based on criteria that are traditional. Particularly in societies where other forms of organisation and criteria of mobilisation are weak or unavailable.

MANIVANNAN: India had an experience of this kind of mobilisational strategy when the Jan Sangh in Punjab in the 1950s asked Hindu Punjabis to declare their mother tongue as Hindi instead of Punjabi. The Sikhs not only questioned the validity of the claim but also held the rejection of Punjabi by the Jan Sangh to be one of the seeds of communal polarisation in post-independence India.

PRACHA: You are talking about the need to move beyond modernity. I am quite certain that what you are saying is different from 'postmodernism'. Could you clarify the distinction more clearly?

NANDY: I see 'postmodernism' as a variety of modernism that is less informed by the limitations of orthodox modernism. But I also see it as a way of controlling and containing dissent. Conformity is often less of a problem to the winners of the world than is the nature of dissent. The most powerful systems are never built only on formations that support them but also on predictable and manageable dissent. Such systems always try to monitor dissent. They concede the legitimacy of dissent but ensure that the dissent is of a given type. Particularly, all large modern systems of dominance have tried to spell out the criteria of legitimate dissent. They have insisted that dissent, to qualify as sane dissent, should also be modern. One of the problems of postmodernism is that it is centred on Western universities. This has reified dissent and shifted its locus to academe, away from the chaos, violence, unpredictability and dirtiness of the grass roots, the slums and, most important of all, the informal sector of knowledge, close to the victims. As the capitals of dissent move to the West, dissent, to be audible or convincing, has to be whetted by dissenters in the Western intellectual mainstream and knowledge industry. In the last century, we learnt our dissent from socialists such as Robert Owen, then from the likes of Marx and Lenin, and now our children are learning it from the postmodernists.

PRACHA: In other words, postmodernism is Eurocentric.

MANIVANNAN: I would like to return to the issue of alternatives. In view of our discussion about the need for building alternatives and the role of civil societies, what do you think is the relevance of grass-roots movements? From this point of view, what do you think are the strengths and weaknesses of the grass-roots movements in our part of the world?

NANDY: The first part of your question is not entirely legitimate. We never ask what is the relevance of the modern nation-state. We do not ask what is the relevance of the modern communications system. But when it comes to the question of NGOs, we always love to ask about their relevance? That is not the right way to look at it. Whenever someone asks me this question of relevance, I mention the comment of my friend Fred Chiu, an activist associated with a number of NGOs and trade unions in Hong Kong and Taiwan. He says, 'wherever modern civilisation has gone, it has taken with it syphilis'. For modern capitalism, NGOs are like syphilis. Wherever global capitalism has gone, it has produced NGOs'. NGOs are a natural response to global capitalism. They are the natural response of ordinary people, communities and victims. It is much like the birth of trade unionism as an almost automatic response to industrial capitalism. With industrial capitalism dying, trade unionism is also dying. The question of relevance does not arise in such a context.

It is difficult to answer the second question. Many ask about the strengths and limitations of grass-roots movements in our part of the world because they are not comfortable with NGOs or, for that matter, even with the idea of NGOs. They see hundreds of NGOs come into existence and hundreds of them die, often after a short, inglorious life. They see NGOs constantly fighting with each other and suspecting each other's motives. Every NGO functionary thinks that his or her organisation is the best and others are simply inefficient, compromised, or driven by a fundamentally faulty analysis of the world. Many find this situation difficult to cope with. Actually, to some extent it is in the nature of NGO activism to be bogged down in interpersonal conflicts of all kinds because, to survive in their world, they have to be a bit self-righteous. The situation is aggravated by another feature: most of them are single-issue NGOs. Take the case of opposition to the building of large dams. Suppose an NGO is formed to fight a planned large dam on grounds of environment, displacement of people, protection of forest wealth, and the rights of the forest people. Once the dam is scrapped owing to protests, or the protests fail and the dam is built, the *raison d'être* of the NGO vanishes. In this sense, there is nothing wrong with an NGO closing down, because it has achieved its purpose. Even if it fails, it often succeeds in spreading certain forms of awareness among the people. In the end, it becomes more difficult to build another dam.

In India, at least two major anti-dam movements (Tehri and Narmada) are going on at this moment. Both may fail. But if they do, the leaders of the movement, Sunderlal Bahuguna and Medha Patkar, will fail only apparently. They have both already succeeded beyond all measure. In the last eight to ten years, no serious proposal for a large dam has come up in India. The reason is simple. Politicians build dams not because their hearts bleed for people or because they are concerned about efficient water management in the country. They build dams because it gives them prestige, an enlarged vote bank and financial kickbacks. It also provides them with political slush funds and the power of patronage. Once the issue of the dam itself comes under heavy public scrutiny, politicians lose much of their interest. They do not want to build a dam when there is no hope of earning even a cent. They also do not want to be involved in a controversy. Instead of being a political asset, the dam then becomes a liability. Up to a point, the anti-dam movement in India has succeeded in creating such a situation. It is not correct to judge NGOs by their apparent successes and failures. We must judge them from a larger perspective.

Finally, most NGOs are narrow and rigid in their concerns because none can fight for an important cause against all odds without being single-minded. Even more important, single-issue NGOs do not consist of persons with single-issue concerns. It is usually only a matter of a single-issue programme. If you are fighting against nuclear weapons, it does not mean that you do not know that other countries are also producing nuclear weapons or that there are finer aspects of military balance and political bargaining involved. Nonetheless, you have to close your mind to that if you want to be politically effective. I am more or less convinced that this mode of coping through ideological and operational closure is typical of the NGO world. It is one of the characteristic features of NGO activism. But they must be judged in terms of their long-term implications.

MANIVANNAN: How do you assess the interplay of the power centres such as the state, civil society and transnational corporations in the politics of nations?

NANDY: That is again a very broad question and I can answer it only partly. First, it is obvious to all of us that the power of the state in the contemporary world is diminishing finally. It may be expanding when you look at the coercive apparatus of the state, but the coercive apparatus alone cannot ensure the legitimacy and reach of a state. The significance of the state is already beginning to diminish in the minds of people. Few activists talk today about the state as an engine of social change or as an instrument of radical intervention. I think this is a healthy development. Generations of social activists have tried to use the state for social change, leading to much devastation, cruelty and bloodshed. In most cases, the state used the activists for its own purposes. In Cambodia, using the instrument of the state, they virtually killed or exiled forty per cent of their own people for the sake of the remaining sixty per cent. When the killers were through, some Cambodian scholars claim, the country was left with some 250-odd people who could take care of the affairs of the state. One can make the case that some leaders of the group that did the killings were trying to actualise the model that they picked up during their student days in the famous French universities. People talk about how bad Pol Pot was, but nobody talks about the complicity of the Sorbonne.

The point I am trying to make is that somehow the early romantic view of the nation-state as a major instrument of social and political change has now faded. But the state is receding in the global scene in other ways, too. There are two kinds of the depreciation in its value. It is declining in the West because many countries are willing to 'sell off' aspects of the sovereignty of the state for the sake of economic prosperity. The European Union is a good example of the diminution of state power and the scope of the state with the active support of the electorate. Many Europeans have begun to believe that the European Union will give them a better life than the individual European states have given until now. That is their expectation, whether right or wrong. Simultaneously, there are efforts to control states that are outside the global nation-state system to some extent by imposing limits on sovereignty. Take, for instance, the attempts to control states that have poor human rights records or states called rogue states. People are aware that for them you need supra-state institutions. Even when you support that kind of supra-national institution to serve your national interests, you cannot help strengthening institutions that may some day judge your own human rights records according to criteria not entirely compatible with your own purposes. Read the recent Amnesty International report on the United States of America for an illustration of the point I am making. The European Union now has a human rights commission with supervisory powers that supersede the sovereignty of individual European states. Individual states often find it difficult to control.

All this has abridged the place of the state in human affairs over the last few decades. It is in this context that the new economic globalisation is taking place. The multinational companies have begun to exercise power in a world where most states have diminished in stature and lost their capacity to exercise full sovereignty and power. I would have applauded this decline of the state but for the fact that we have not been able to put in place any mechanism that can seriously monitor the activities of multinational corporations, the major non-state players today. The largest multinational corporation today is larger than several member states of the United Nations put together. Then there are multinational bodies that are not recognised as multinational corporations but act like them. The entire development aid sector is one of the ten largest corporations in the world, though it does not call itself one. Nobody seriously monitors it. In India, for instance, only 20 per cent of the money meant for poverty alleviation actually goes to the poor. The poverty experts and the poverty bureaucracy consume the rest. This is not my data but what an Indian prime minister said some years ago, and none has yet refuted him. Then there are multinational corporations of another kind, which cater to the global market in arms, drugs, money and laundering. An elaborate set of conventions binds them together.

In these respects, the present forces of globalisation are qualitatively different from earlier ones. It is not that we did not have any multinational companies earlier. The British and Dutch East India Companies were also technically multinational entities. They ruled some countries in our part of the world for long stretches of time. So, even that is not new. We have seen how multinationals function for more than two hundred years. What is prob-

Ashis Nandy

ably new is the kind of cultural exchange they are promoting by unbridling consumption. Traditionally, when cultural exchanges took place, the imports usually went through an elaborate process of cultural adaptation. The results were often creative. The idea of the novel, as a literary form, came to this part of the world as part of colonial expansion and colonial education. Countries in South and South-east Asia and China made excellent creative use of the novel and marked out a space for this kind of creativity within the local cultures. South and South-east Asia, for instance, had epics. Yet the idea of the novel must have filled a void somewhere, for many writers took to the form so easily. Of course, the novel did not remain the same in the region; it was reshaped and its contours changed. Likewise, Africa and South America have made a wonderfully creative use of the idea of the novel. Asia has in the same way redefined and adapted the cinema in this century; the Japanese, the Chinese, the Indians and more recently the Iranians have made excellent use of the medium. It has acquired cultural depth and offers scope for new modes of cultural creativity. Then there are the more obvious examples. India until medieval times did not have chilli; we only had black pepper. Chilli came from Latin America. But now people associate chilli more with Indian cuisine than with Latin American. The chilli has been Indianised. I am sure that the history of chilli in Thailand is not very different, and look what the Thais have made of it.

However, the emphasis has shifted to another kind of cultural commerce. In it, the scope for cultural creativity is much less, because the imports do not undergo much cultural adaptation. A hamburger is the same in Tokyo, Cape Town or Mexico City. Blue jeans do not differ whether you buy them in Bangkok, Berlin or Buenos Aires. These cultural forms do not change drastically when crossing cultural borders. If you change them too much, the consumers will not accept them. Coca-Cola is the same all over the world. The cultural message it carries may differ a bit, but not the artefact itself. This leaves less scope for individual or collective imagination or creativity. When you drink Coca-Cola, you drink not merely the contents of the bottle; you also drink a brand name. A Calvin Klein T-shirt is not merely a garment.

MANIVANNAN: You have earlier talked about the crisis of leadership in the world. I look at this problem as a consequence of two processes. First, there is a marked decline in values and commitment in the leadership, though a few leaders remain inspirational role models for the entire world. Second, leaders are not emerging from the grass-roots for various reasons, including the idea of state and power held by people in the grass-roots movements. How do you look at the present crisis of leadership in Asia and the world at large?

NANDY: Well, if you are talking about leadership at the level of the nation-state, one can think of institutional changes that will throw up new kinds of leaders. If you are talking about leadership as an organic part of communities, we have little control over it. We can celebrate the good and shed tears over the bad. We can do nothing more about it. We have little control over communities and we should be prepared to accept this fact. It is up to communities to deliberate on this question. We can only invite them to do so.

About the other kind of leadership, we certainly have a bigger say, because we participate in choosing it at the regional and nation-state levels. That leadership is a creation of the democratic process and we do speak our mind about it through the electoral system. How we do so is an open question. My suspicion is that we have not utilised the democratic process adequately. We have simply lamented the fact that the quality of leadership is going down. I have not heard many NGOs, movements or activists seriously discuss mainstream political leadership. They are somehow reluctant to address issues of this kind, because even when they are opposed to the state, they take the state and its leadership for granted. As if a hostile state and a venal, manipulative leadership were stable formations and eternal concepts.

I have already said that a movement or an activist group has every right to be a single-issue organisation, but I shall be happy if it does not entirely neglect the open democratic process. For that process is not only linked to the nation-state system, it itself links the nation-state with the larger society. This linkage provides an opening within the democratic system that has not been adequately utilised. We may be critical of the state or choose to remain indifferent to the existence of the state, but we cannot neglect the opportunity provided by the democratic system about the choice and the quality of leadership. We have voluntarily shrunk our options in this respect. First, we are so suspicious of the nation-state that we do not like to touch it, and we try to keep it outside our domain of activities. Secondly, a large proportion of social movements and activists are apolitical, even when talking all the while about politics. They judge politics in purely moral terms and find it wanting. Politics requires a different kind of moral sensitivity; 'moralism' is anti-political. That said, the civic engagement of an NGO is itself a form of politics, linked to the revival of civil society. For that politics to succeed, the NGOs must remain aware of and respond to other forms of politics. More so, since both forms operate within the same public arena.

MANIVANNAN: We have been talking about leadership and political changes. What kind of changes do you foresee in the near future? What would you consider a real political change and what means you would advocate to facilitate it?

NANDY: Let me use here one of my favourite quotes. After Mohandas Karamchand Gandhi died, there were many obituaries, but the one I like most was by Arnold Toynbee, the historian. I heard of it second-hand, years afterwards. Toynbee said something like, 'henceforth, humanity will ask its prophets: are you willing to live in the slum of politics?' He did not have initiatives of civil society in mind, but state politics. Toynbee's message is clear: prophets and saints are a dime a dozen in South and South-east Asia; among them, only a few are prepared to enter the dirtiness of politics. Yet, politics remains the major means of changing human destiny. Gandhi called politics *yugadharma*, something that yielded codes of conduct for our times.

The time has come for us to recognise this and explore the full possibilities of politics. I said earlier that democratic politics is one open sector in the modern world that allows large-scale mobilisation and intervention. We cannot, for instance, get into the business of starting an alternative multinational corporation to fight the existing multinational corporations. It would be self-defeating. Again, it may not be impossible but it will certainly be a back-breaking job to set up an alternative media empire that will capture public imagination.

However, it is still possible to influence or even shape the democratic process. We can always help society, when facing a choice between two scoundrels, to choose the lesser evil. Politics is the art of the possible. Thailand holds a good record in this regard. People involved in civil society initiatives have never ignored the other politics, perhaps because a long list of authoritarian rulers deliberately maimed the democratic process. And the connection between civil society initiatives and mainstream politics has always been obvious to Thai activists.

PRACHA: Is there any possibility of evolving an international body that will help to monitor the multinational corporations?

NANDY: We have to look at this task issue by issue and sector by sector. It cannot be too broad or general in approach. It has to be much more specific to become politically feasible and operationally meaningful.

PRACHA: Do you see the possibility of building a system of global governance based on direct elections, to create a world government resembling the United Nations?

NANDY: I do not consider it possible. The Western governments would not like to push the idea of global democracy that far, even if they are democratic at home. They stand to lose their power and it may even prove to be a disaster for them. We would have to wait. The waiting may not be worthwhile or necessary, because global governments can only be global and may not possess the sensitivity required to attend to local needs and aspirations. It will have cultural implications, too, due to its very nature. It may turn out to be like another multinational corporation.

We need global institutions, not a global government. I am personally hostile to all proposals for a world government. In Asia, we sometimes dream of a world government because we have lost confidence in our cultures. It is not that multinational corporations have defeated us fully. But we feel defeated because of our earlier encounters with the West. Let me give an example. According to one set of data, roughly two-third of all Indians use traditional healing systems. Most of them also go to modern doctors. In fact, they accept both. I do not think that the picture is any different in China or in Thailand. Even in the United States in 1998, for the first time, Americans spent more money on non-modern medicines than on conventional ones. But the people do not have confidence in their own instinctive choices; they choose rightly but apologetically.

The American Medical Association has recently published what amounts to a white paper on acupuncture. It lists the beneficial effects of acupuncture in some situations and in some kinds of illness. Things have changed in recent years, but I have met many Chinese doctors in my life who think that acupuncture is nonsense, a remnant of past superstitions and a slur on China. I have also met many Indian doctors who not only feel the same way but also advocate stringent punishment for modern doctors soft on non-modern medicines. A famous middle-aged Indian film and stage actor started life as a modern doctor. Two years ago, he appeared in a television advertisement for an ayurvedic general tonic, and the Indian Medical Association promptly revoked his membership. We suffer more from the fear of traditional healing systems than do the major multinational pharmaceutical companies. Virtually all of them have, in fact, established research institutions to tap indigenous knowledge and identify herbs and plants used in traditional systems of health care.

We are insecure about our traditions and we are insecure about modernity. We see ourselves as more modern than the moderns themselves. People seem confident, but the professionals, the intellectuals, the bureaucrats and our rulers do not seem to be confident. This is our problem.

Dialogue of Civilisations

MANIVANNAN: How relevant is the Eurocentric world-view to our lives in this part of the world? For that matter, what has been its impact on the world during the last few centuries?

NANDY: You are giving me too wide a mandate; I shall be tempted to go on and on. Well, as far as Eurocentric values are concerned, naturally they are useful and relevant to Europe. If we say that Asian values are relevant to Asian societies, we cannot but admit that European values should be relevant to European societies. However, there is now a disjunction of sorts in the global scene as far as world-views are concerned. When we say 'European world-view', we usually mean by it the world-view of modern Europe.

This world-view began to crystallise in the sixteenth and seventeenth centuries (though some, such as Ivan Illich, trace it to earlier centuries) and acquired its full-blown form in the nineteenth century. In Asia, we know this Europe, for this Europe ruled us and continues to dominate the world, culturally at least. The United States of America is a child of this Europe. After saying all this, however, let us not forget that there was a Europe before the seventeenth century. That Europe has survived the hegemony of modern Europe during the last two hundred years. It may have survived in the interstices of cultures, but it has survived. Parts of Asia know and remember this other Europe too, the Europe of pre-colonial days, agricultural societies, early Christianity and the Gnostic cults. Later, the Europe of dissenting visions, reflected in the works of such people as Goethe, John Ruskin, Leo Tolstoy, William Morris, William Blake and William Wordsworth. It is no accident that one of the great proponents of Asian values, Gandhi, considered three people his spiritual gurus and two of them were Europeans, one American. They were Tolstoy, Ruskin and Thoreau. He claimed that his theory of non-violence came not from *Bhagavadgita*, but from the Sermon on the Mount. Technically that might be an Asian sermon from an Asian prophet, but it came to Gandhi from Europe.

That other Europe, let us not forget, has been marginalised within contemporary Europe itself. Indeed, that defeated Europe lives with more dignity in some other parts of the world. We have to hold that Europe in trust somewhat in the manner in which the banks keep the property of a dead person for heirs who cannot be found easily. We have to preserve aspects of Europe for a future Europe. I am sure that some day true heirs of that other Europe will emerge and lay claim to their patrimony from us. Others can also hold parts of our cultures in trust. This once happened in the case of Greek philosophers like Plato and Aristotle. Hellenic studies were dead in medieval Europe. The Arabs held them in trust and Arab civilisation treasured Greek culture and civilisation. For centuries Europeans who wanted to study the Greek philosophers had to go to Arab universities. And the Hellenic medical system, in the form of Unani, is much more vibrant in South Asia than in Greece. Something like that can happen again.

If we remember this half-forgotten Europe, European and Asian values may not seem so incompatible. It is a pity that the term 'Asian values' has itself become controversial and pejorative. It is also a pity that many human rights activists and NGO stalwarts use the expression 'Asian values' as a term of abuse. It is associated with people who are not known for their strong commitment to democracy and human rights. Lee Kuan Yew, Mahathir Mohamad of Malaysia and the present Chinese communist regime are examples. By default, we have in one sense granted them a monopoly on Asian values. The Dalai Lama and Aung San Suu Kyi also represent Asian values. So did Gandhi. They represent Asian values in a much more authentic and creative way than those who talk about it loudly. The Nazis did not exhaust European values, though the likes of Heinrich Himmler constantly talked about protecting European values. I do not think that the self-proclaimed defenders of civilisational values represent either Asia or Europe.

MANIVANNAN: You have mentioned the positive aspects of the Western world-view as well as the Asian. What exactly has gone wrong with the Euro-centric world-view during the last two to three centuries as far as our lives are concerned? This question is based on the realistic perception that we have to co-exist with the West, by choice or by historical circumstance, though I would not concede that it is our destiny.

PRACHA: I also would like to retain a balance of perspectives in our understanding of the Western world-view. I think it has both positive and negative aspects.

NANDY: I have not gone into details in this matter here, though I have done so elsewhere. The reason is simple: even Europe has more than one ancestor. Europe is vastly diverse culturally. At least one major contemporary philosopher, Hans-Georg Gadamer, considers that diversity to be Europe's greatest cultural asset.

PRACHA: Can we then restrict ourselves to the role of the modern West and its impact on our lives? From the beginning of the modern West in the seventeenth century to its full unfolding in the nineteenth century, its values have exercised enormous cultural influence on other societies and civilisations.

NANDY: In some respects, these modern values can also be used creatively. They have been a challenge to us. I do not think that great civilisations crash or crumble under the impact of thirty new television channels or the flooding of the market with hamburgers and Coca-Cola. If civilisations are so fragile and cannot withstand such flimsy threats, they do not deserve to survive.

Far more critical is the fact that contemporary Europe has posed several challenges to us, to which we have not yet adequately responded. Well, in some respects we have, in other respects we have not. Japan, when all is said and done, has responded to the Western challenge with tremendous energy, hard work and innovativeness. Yet I am afraid that Japan's economic and technological success has made the Japanese imbibe many of the values of the West. They have tried to defeat the West at its own game. This is all right up to a point. But culture is not a game in which you can say that your day is made because you have defeated someone from who you learnt the game. This is like a strong Australian team getting a thrill after beating a weak English team in cricket, because cricket is quintessentially an English game. This particular approach has its own limitations and consequences. Japan has begun to face these limitations after its grand success. Japanese identity or self-definition is under stress. Its own slogan, 'Western technology and Japanese spirit', is no longer adequate, because the Japanese spirit has been shrinking over the decades. On the other hand, the culture of Western technology has expanded in Japan over the years. This is a lesson that many of us have to learn. What Japan may learn in the area of economics, others may learn in the area of warfare and military technology. India will also learn its lesson when copying the West in the area of nuclear technology. It will not bring the country any success or glory, only self-defeat.

Malaysia, Thailand, South Korea and Taiwan will all learn the same lesson in different ways. After all their success, some questions remain unanswered. For instance, the question whether we have to be so much like the West in the long run, just to do well economically? Is this the concept of doing well? Is this the ultimate goal of our societies? Are there options we have not explored because we did not have confidence in our values and world-views? We thought that we must succeed first, in the Western sense of the term, and then we can try to protect our culture. This is not as theoretical a question as it looks; our pursuit of modernisation and development has already extracted a massive toll. Our countries are not large, uninhabited expanses where only small communities existed, as is the case for North America. We cannot have a free run over vast expanses of land and resources through a bit of healthy genocide. Here people have lived in cities, towns, villages and wilderness for centuries. Our societies are thickly populated, with a delicate balance between nature and the livelihood of the people.

We are now trying to introduce a model of development that is contemptuous of the needs for survival of a large section of the people. We have, all of a sudden, tacitly declared that a large part of our population is obsolete and redundant. As if many of the neighbours living around us have lost their right to exist. We have begun to think that this is the only way to overcome the problem of excess population, to get rid of those whose economic relevance and productive capacities are dispensable, according to us. They include millions of artisans and thousands of agricultural communities that cannot compete to produce and profit from globally marketable goods. They include communities of artists and musicians that have pursued their vocation based on centuries of traditions that have no place in today's world. We have declared a section of our fellow human beings as burdens on our societies. We have deliberately transported them into the past and begun to refer to them as though they were historical entities that have become obligingly extinct. Whenever we see them or think about them, our official intellectuals and media call us romantic lotus-eaters. This is a major tragedy of our times.

MANIVANNAN: I would like to draw your attention to a specific debate within Africa, Asia and Latin America. Some scholars, thinkers and activists have been demanding compensation from the West. They say that their people and societies have suffered enormously from the West's exploitation of their material and human resources. Now, when we are discussing the world-views and other civilisations, how would you respond to such claims for compensation?

NANDY: In principle, I support the claim. But we know that this compensation will not be paid in reality. The West also knows it. For we all know that if we really measure the suffering inflicted on the Southern world in monetary terms, the West will be reduced to a much lower level of prosperity. The compensation would be truly enormous. We have seen the extent of compensation paid by the Germans for the genocide of Jews and for the use of slave labour during the Second World War. If you use similar criteria for the compensation that will have to be paid to Africa for the Atlantic slave trade or to Asia for its colonisation, it will be so huge that no country responsible would ever consider paying even a fraction of it.

But after saying all this, if we look at the world as an integral whole, as an integrated, living organism, with all its peoples as interconnected parts of a common humanity, there is another kind of price that the West has already begun to pay. Let me give an example. As you surely know, much of the African slave trade was used to supply cheap labour to produce two major crops in the New World – sugar and tobacco. Now, over the last two centuries these two products have also taken an enormous toll in the West. Look at the data on the number of people suffering from sugar- and tobacco-related diseases in North America and Western Europe. If you make a rough estimate of the lives lost in the African slave trade and offset the figures against the loss of lives from sugar- and tobacco-related diseases, they will not be very different. There is a cycle of natural justice – you can call it a moral universe – which has its own logic. Sometimes I wish that the Israeli state had the vision to return

Ashis Nandy

the money given to them as reparations to support anti-racist work in Europe and within Israel itself. That is probably what Simone Weil and perhaps even Martin Buber would have recommended.

MANIVANNAN: It is a great irony indeed. In Vedic philosophy, there is a beautiful metaphor on cause and effect. It says, what you consume today would consume you tomorrow. We eat flesh (of animals), fruits and vegetables (of plants and trees). After our death, our bodies decay to supply energy to the plants, trees and animals. It is a wonderful imagery. In one of your articles published in *Resurgence*, when America was celebrating the arrival of Columbus in the continent five hundred years before, you talked about the way the slaves were transported from Africa like sacks of potatoes, to create a new, prosperous, just democracy. Nearly a third died on the way. I am happy that our discussion touches upon that historical tragedy.

Can we now shift our focus to some other major concerns of our time? The concepts of modernisation and development are integral to the Western worldview. How relevant to us are concepts such as progress, economic growth, private property, collective ownership, equality, liberty, freedom, democracy, individualism and human rights?

NANDY: There are too many concepts in your list and they are too diverse. But the most crucial one is the idea of progress. It is related to several, if not all, of the other concepts you mention. Popular 'progressivism' and the theory of progress have been, on the whole, disasters for us. They might have done some good here and there and might have powered some social reforms, but usually it has legitimised change for the sake of change and sanctioned every form of violence on ordinary human beings in the name of social change. The contemporary world has gradually lost all ability to appreciate beingness. We have no capacity to appreciate ordinary people and everyday life. We want to improve them. The same with things. We always want them to become bigger and better. Both are seen as normal human yearnings. We have no time to celebrate or even savour our lives and successes; we are constantly thinking about our next step in becoming or getting.

These ideas of becoming and getting found some of their most vulgar expressions in the nineteenth century. Cultural differences lost their intrinsic legitimacy and were fitted into a model of social evolution. The cultural identity of Asia or Europe was no longer relevant. The idea of such identity can naturally have not much meaning if everyone is seen as perpetually climbing a historical ladder. In that unending process, everyone is so busy with the job of climbing that no one has any time to look at the surroundings.

It reminds me of a story I read in my childhood. It was by a famous Bengali writer, Shibram Chakrabarty, who wrote for children. It is the story of a man in Calcutta who lost his wallet to a pickpocket. As he had seen the thief who picked his pocket, he ran after him. But the thief ran faster and soon vanished into the alleys of the city. The victim felt humiliated; he did not want this to happen to him again. He began to practise running. As it happened, a few years later, his pocket was picked again. This time he confidently chased the pickpocket and soon caught up with him. But he could not stop; he had practised running too long. He passed the thief and kept running. When he did not return, the family members informed the police, who declared him missing. The story ends with the police getting the information that he had crossed the borders of India and had been last spotted in Burma. He was still running.

That is actually our story. The West has humiliated us, and so we have decided to defeat the West at its own game. But we cannot stop now. Even societies which have been enormously successful and prosperous, like Japan, cannot stop. They are still running; they themselves do not know what they are running towards.

PRACHA: What is the basis of this myth of progress? Where has it originated? You have also talked about social Darwinism. Does the idea of progress have anything to do with Darwinism?

NANDY: Yes, partly. People like Herbert Spencer directly translated Darwinian evolutionism into social evolutionism. The great social critics of nineteenth-century Europe – the Utilitarians, the socialists in general and the left Hegelians in particular – also contributed to the myth. Industrialisation and modern science, too, strengthened it by seemingly opening up the possibility of unending progress. Within a century, evolutionism was applied to virtually every field of enquiry, even in areas like child development. Now, the modern world cannot even think of the child as a child; it sees childhood as a stage on the way to adulthood. In many societies in this part of the world, particularly in India, people worship Lord Krishna as a child-god. The child's innocence and creativity symbolise spirituality and divinity. This is true of Christianity, too. Childlikeness has a special meaning in religion. By the end of the nineteenth century, Europe had lost these traditions. Everything – every culture, every society – has become a preparatory stage for something else, thanks to social evolutionism. The results were even more tragic when evolutionism was introduced in areas like race. Virtually all the major bloodbaths and genocides in the twentieth century were conducted in the name of social evolutionism. Do not be taken in by claims that Nazism was an irrational movement and a throwback to the past. The Nazis built on past racism, but sought sanction consistently from biological evolutionism and eugenics. To them, politics was a matter of health that required ruthless cleansing of the unhealthy, the diseased and the genetically handicapped. The approach made a lot of sense to many people, and not only in Germany.

Discrimination against the blacks in the United States of America was justified within the same mould. The terror mounted against Russian farmers during the Soviet drive for collectivisation was also an exercise undertaken in the name of progress, guided by scientific history. That progress demanded blood sacrifice. The theory of progress has served as an excellent modern, rational, efficient way of eliminating your fellow human beings for the sake of climbing that mythical ladder or to move to the higher planes of history. In Cambodia, when the Marxists killed more than one-third of the population for the sake of progress, I am sure they were prepared to kill 49.9 per cent of their own people for the welfare of remaining 50.1 per cent. This kind of cost calculation is now usual in human affairs. The social evolutionism of the nineteenth century still rules our consciousness.

PRACHA: I would like you to relate this idea of progress to the Asian situation. Is there any specific way that the Asians look at progress?

NANDY: Asia is a vast and diverse continent. I cannot claim to know many societies in Asia. I can only talk about a few of the Asian cultures and civilisations to which I have some exposure. The idea of progress has always been associated with development-in-stages. It is also a package; it is never simply an improvement in material conditions. The idea of improvement is open-ended, but not unending. It does not usually offer much scope for absolutisation. It is a bit like Nagarjuna's idea of unmasking reality, it is like an onion; you peel off a layer to find a reality that can be further peeled to reveal another layer of reality. The process is unending.

That story has a subplot too. In the case of modern sciences and social sciences modelled on the Enlightenment concept of science, once you have pierced the manifest reality and revealed the underlying reality, you are closer to truth. The underlying reality, of course, varies with disciplines. In modern medicine, for instance, once you reach the language of the body in your diagnosis, you have already reached hard reality. You cannot demystify any further. In Marxism, once you have identified the material base and structure of class relationships, you are closer to truth. In psychoanalysis, once you have reached the level of psychosexuality, you have moved closer to reality. It cannot be further demystified.

This is debatable. For such a model of demystification protects the expert, the vanguard and the healer from radical criticisms of their theories and from self-criticism. If you try to show, using Marxist categories, that those who are fighting for a classless society have themselves become a class with its own interests, that these revolutionary heroes are not outside space and time, that would be considered a very unfriendly act. There is little Marxist analysis of Marxism, and psychoanalysis of psychoanalysis. *Medical Nemesis* by Illich was seen as anti-medicine, though it is a book some doctor somewhere should have first thought of writing. However, once you have learnt to speak the language of the body, it also can begin to serve as a defensive mask. You feel you are a purveyor of a fully rational, optimised system of knowledge, not subject to criticism by the laity. I think it would be good to apply Nagarjuna's imagery as an antidote to the idea of progress and the closed systems and one-way modes of demystification that the various theories of progress have underwritten.

PRACHA: Can you elaborate a bit more on Nagarjuna's philosophy?

NANDY: I was only using Nagarjuna's imagery. I was referring to his belief that no interpretation is an end in itself, nor does it allow you to know the ultimate truth. Truth is a matter of constant enquiry and continuous search. It is not a final destination that one can reach and rest afterwards, on the assumption that all one needs to do after arrival is to establish one's hegemony over the destination.

MANIVANNAN: What is the role of the era of industrialisation in the West, in the development of the idea of progress and the dominant theory of development?

NANDY: Industrialisation has certainly contributed to the consolidation of the idea of progress and the present model of development. But the question is about the extent of industrialisation that is necessary. Like several other elements of modernity, industry is not *ipso facto* evil. It can be a necessary balancing factor against the excesses and the established rhythm of rural life. However, many things introduced as balancing factors in a society later turn out to be forces that need to be balanced. Dissenting or marginal strains become dominant strains. Today, industrialism has become cancerous. Cancer cells are not always, by themselves, pathological; it is their undifferentiated growth that leads to suffering. Similarly in human affairs, some degree of individualism existed in pre-modern times. It existed as a counterpoint to the dominant collectivist ethos. It was not modern individualism, but it was individualism all right. A person who renounced the world could be read as highly individualistic. Artists, writers and musicians could be individualistic to a fault, even in pre-modern times. This individualism was acceptable as long as it operated within certain limits. In modern times, uncontrolled and unmediated individualism has turned human beings into social isolates.

MANIVANNAN: You are talking about industrialisation and individualism. I

Ashis Nandy

37

am concerned about mechanical industrialisation and its impact on the West and on our societies. It is only in this context that we speak of the negative aspects of individualism. It is beside the point that it does have positive aspects.

NANDY: You have a point there. Though, unless you acknowledge the existence of other forms of individualism, you cannot understand the pull of the idea of individualism. However, I have to agree with you that the industrialisation of the present kind and, particularly, the production process involved in it, demands a mechanistic individualism. One of the best depictions of this demand and its pathological form can be found in the films of Charles Chaplin, particularly *Modern Times*. The individual is reduced to a mere cog in the wheel. In one sense, there is a built-in paradox in this kind of individualism. It protects the individual from the collectivity, but it also isolates and alienates the individual from others in society. Consumerism is often a desperate response to that isolation.

MANIVANNAN: While talking about the concepts of progress, industrialisation and individualism. I want to bring into the discussion the ideas of community and collectivity, not necessarily as an antidote to individualism, but to understand the relationship between the two. Gandhi spent considerable time and energy developing his idea of community ownership and community action. In Asia and Africa, there have been societies that have held the idea of community ownership as both a value and a practice. The idea of collectivity diffuses the individual's greed and, to some extent, restrains the drive towards a mechanical attitude to progress.

NANDY: Greed is one of the great unresolved mysteries of human nature. I think all human beings have a tendency to be greedy. Several societies have tried to contain greed through collectivism, often forcibly. The results have not been happy. Sometimes they have controlled freedom more successfully than greed. There are societies that concede that they have not been successful in containing greed. They are still searching for solutions, with a sense of impending defeat.

On the other hand, capitalism has clearly been designed to serve the purposes of greed. The culture of capitalism assumes greed to be a human quality or psychological trait that cannot be erased. It therefore strives to take advantage of this fact and build on it. The capitalist culture in effect says, let everyone's greed come into play openly and we can build something out of that as a check against greed itself. Personally, I do not see any sign of greed diminishing because of this; it seems to feed on itself.

MANIVANNAN: Do you think it is possible to achieve at least equality in our societies under the present circumstances?

NANDY: However politically incorrect this might sound, I am not a great votary of equality. I am willing to accept equality as a value and an ideal, but I consider justice more important than equality. I do grant the need for relative equality, but I believe that equality cannot be measured in absolute terms. It is difficult to assess our incomes and needs on uniform scales.

Any talk of equality must be tempered by a concern with justice for another reason. Absolute equality is possible only in a police state. My suspicion is that even after establishing a police state, one can ensure only a façade of equality; everyone in such a state knows who is more equal than the others. The experience of the Soviet Empire and China shows that the rhetoric of economic equality can sanction enormous political and social inequalities.

MANIVANNAN: Actually, you are talking of a just society. Justice is equal and equality without justice is not equality. Therefore, when you speak of equality with justice you seem committed to building a just society.

NANDY: Yes. It is necessary for us to accept the reality that human beings are not the same. They are different in their aptitudes, skills, contentment and attitude to life. Not everything can be measured in purely material terms. Happiness and leisure are classic examples of things that cannot be measured by any uniform standard. I might prefer to live in poverty just to get more leisure to pursue my interest in art, and yet I might be a third-rate artist. Do I have a right to choose? Do I have a right to be unequal to my neighbours not by being rich but by voluntarily remaining poor?

Ideally, our idea of individualism should include within it the individual's right not to seek material equality. Many do not seem to know where to stop. Nor do they have the time to stop and reflect. As I have said earlier, being is sacrificed constantly at the altar of becoming. Our search for equality should take into account that part of the story, too.

PRACHA: May I go back to a slightly different theme in this context? The negative aspects of the idea of progress and the dominant model of economic development must be resisted. We cannot allow them free rein because they cannot be controlled once you have unqualified individualism or greed.

NANDY: There have to be limits. Industrialisation has been pursued without any limit or self-regulation. This is also true of urbanisation. Only a few decades ago, Brazil was 80 per cent rural and 20 per cent urban. Today, it is 80 per cent urban and 20 per cent rural. Nearly half the population of Mexico lives in Mexico City. The situation in Buenos Aires is not much different. Bangkok is walking the same road. More than one-sixth of the people of Thailand, around ten million people, live in the city. We seem to have forgotten the principle of limits, which is so central to Buddhism. There should be a limit to change also,

Ashis Nandy

for the sake of psychological well-being and cultural continuity. Each tradition has its own distinctiveness. In Islam, the concept of justice is highly developed. In Buddhism, the concept of limits is crucial. In our contemporary world, the fear of losing in the Olympiad of nation-states rules the minds of many people. They are afraid of defining their limits, because of the fear of being left behind by other countries in the race for greater and greater prosperity.

MANIVANNAN: Do concepts like liberty, freedom and human rights in the West have relevance outside the West?

NANDY: These concepts have some intrinsic relevance cross-culturally, though not exactly in the way the West would like to believe. Liberty as an idea and as a value is shared by many non-Western traditions also. Near home, Buddhism, Christianity, Hinduism and Jainism share the concept of emancipation. The question of human rights is more complicated, because it has become a political slogan. Human rights cannot be absolutised, Mahathir Mohamad or no Mahathir Mohamad. For instance, there is the need to respect the rights of living and non-living organisms in the universe. Rivers have a right to be and you must respect them. What about the species rights of blue seals or tigers? Our rights also have to have limits, to prevent the extinction of other organisms. Rights will be meaningful only if there are limits to them.

Apart from that, sloganising human rights as a universal has certain specific hazards in countries like ours. What about young children being trained in traditional crafts by their artisan parents? What about classical instrumentalists like Amjad Ali Khan of Delhi who began to train at the age of 5 and started giving public performances and earning money before he entered his teens? Should we have prosecuted his parents for using child labour?

MANIVANNAN: I think rights keep growing as our lives become more expansive. It is one thing to talk about limits on rights and totally another experience to have to establish rights that may look new but are not actually so. They belong to us. The trial of Augusto Pinochet in England has practically ended the traditional impunity enjoyed by dictators abroad for crimes committed against their own people at home. He may have returned to Chile, but he will now certainly think twice before stepping out of his country again. He is likely to face further isolation in his own country, despite the support of the military. I support this development as an endorsement of the rights of suffering people all over the world.

NANDY: I can only agree with you.

MANIVANNAN: We would like to return to an issue that has already come up more than once in our dialogue and I want to hear your assessment of Asian cultures and traditions as alternatives to the Western world-view.

NANDY: Perhaps your question has not been appropriately worded. Why should the Asian cultural traditions be thought of as alternatives to the Western world-view? Asian cultures are not meant to replace European cultures and values. People have lived with these cultures for centuries. Europe has its cultural rights, too.

The problem is that we have somewhere lost the capacity to be ourselves. It is like saying that, for human babies, mother's milk is superior to packaged milk or cow's milk. There is little need to justify the use of one's language and culture. People are born and reared in certain languages and cultural systems. They are part of them and have a right to them. At some point, some of us began to think that Asian cultural values and traditions were not good because they differed from or were counterpoints to modern Western values and traditions. Now some of us have begun to think that Asian cultural values are good because they are a corrective to modern Western traditions. Both are dangerous positions. We need Asian values if we have to talk with Asians and work with them, to appeal to them or to touch their hearts. Normally, a person is at home in his or her own cultural traditions. Despite glib assessments of the so-called strengths and weaknesses of cultures and traditions by Westernised Asians, no serious political and social activist can avoid using the cultural idiom of the people.

MANIVANNAN: I agree with you. But I did not word my question clearly. There has been a major invasion by the Western world-view of non-Western parts of the world. The West's cultural influence is changing the way we think, eat and dress. We are now constantly thinking of catching up with the West because of this cultural invasion. Western categories are gradually taking over our lives. Our governments are imitating the West by adapting our political and economic systems to Western norms. Our people are adopting Western lifestyles and attitudes to the market and consumerism. We have not been able to challenge the West. When we talk about Asian alternatives, we do not want to transform the West; they have a right to their culture and traditions. But we are certainly concerned about defending ours against a domineering West. It will be too defensive to try to preserve our culture and traditions and not to try to transform the West and help the West to find its true ancestors.

NANDY: I grant you that and we have already talked about it. But we must sound here a word of caution. Let us hope that all this is temporary. For in the end, we cannot overdo the culture business. Culture itself is a form of resistance. It allows you to resist certain forms of oppression, inequity and injustice. That is important, but living in our own culture is also like breathing. The moment we begin to think about our breathing, it goes wrong and its rhythm is disturbed. We cannot breathe normally by being conscious about it. We can do *pranayama*, which is mindful or conscious breathing, but I am talking about normal breathing. I think, defying social scientists, culture should 'come naturally to us'. I can put it in another way. Great creative minds usually do not think much about the sources and methods of their creativity, about what creativity is or should be, or about the factors conducive to or retarding creativity. That absence of self-consciousness is healthy. I hope that we shall be able to say that soon about our cultures also.

After all, culture partly belongs to the realm of understanding and intuition. It is a normal part of our self and ensures continuity of identity, gives us a language and a framework for understanding the world. It also provides a sense of belonging and rootedness. It is absurd to talk of assessing a culture and choosing elements from it on extraneous grounds. It is like trying to assess a language and telling its native speakers not to use some elements of it because some grammarians have found them cumbersome or other languages have better usages.

PRACHA: You have earlier talked about the loss of confidence in our cultural values and traditions among our elite. There is also, if I may use the term, a sense of cultural suffering in our societies due to the one-way cultural interaction with the West. This has given rise to a sense of inferiority among the people and leaders in our societies. How do we overcome that problem?

NANDY: There is no single answer or solution to the problem. It can be attacked at many levels. In any case, I do not think that we can solve this problem by subjecting every Asian to psychotherapy or psychoanalysis. We can solve it only through politics. One partial solution is to empower our people. Most Asians have confidence in themselves. It is the elite and the small middle class that have lost cultural confidence. We must allow the democratic process to work itself out fully. That means that we should ensure that the elite and the middle classes no longer remain the dominant voices in Asia. They are a small constituency in a large continent. The ordinary people do not see the problem of cultural invasion of the West as a problem of vast magnitude. They may enjoy a bottle of Coke and watch a Hollywood film casually. Their interest in the West ends there, and to many of them it is mostly a passing fad. Ordinary people have confidence in their cultures and, once their voices become more audible, the feelings of inferiority we see around us will become a marginal phenomenon.

MANIVANNAN: You earlier mentioned our intellectual defeat at the hands of the West. How does that compare with the casual attitude or normal response of the common people to the West?

NANDY: Our intelligentsia comes largely from the middle class, which suffers from a sense of inadequacy and fear of being left behind. But then, we do not live in middle-class societies either. All intellectuals do not belong to the middle class and there are intellectuals from outside that hallowed circle, too. Hence, I suspect that our sense of intellectual defeat is not going to be a permanent feature of our cultural life. Many changes are taking place in this part of the world. There are attempts to recover the cultural space that we have lost. Our culture and traditions have been artificially marginalised; we have not lost them. They are still the cultures and traditions of the majority.

PRACHA: I hope it will not seem too harsh if I say that the urge for progress and the economic drive in East Asia has its roots in their sense of inferiority *vis-à-vis* the West.

NANDY: It is probably true. Frankly, I am prepared to accept some amount of economic growth. I am concerned about the development establishment, which itself is often a hurdle to growth. Developmental expertise, economic policy-making and even poverty removal are parts of a major multinational venture. But there is a need to undertake and enforce certain qualitative and quantitative changes in the economy for the sake of the poor and the deprived. The quality of human lives must improve and it is necessary to create conditions for that.

PRACHA: Your reference to the development structure and especially the role of the development bureaucracy in creating more hurdles reminds me of the saying that a health worker is not required if there is no illness in a community.

NANDY: Yes, a good doctor, who knows both when to act and when not to, makes himself or herself redundant.

PRACHA: We have talked of the other Europe. And I also notice a cultural shift taking place in the West. The rise of the Greens and the return of the likes of William Morris in the West's cultural life indicate that shift.

NANDY: It is pity that we in this part of the world have paid little attention to the shift. We have no clue to this transition in Western Europe and North America because our systems of information, knowledge and education still reflect the mainstream West. William Morris and William Blake are less known outside Europe because the systems of knowledge and education in operation in our countries allow you to know mainly the conventional thinkers and writers of the West. The shift is no longer marginal. Significant new voices, too, are emerging. It is important to recognise the contribution of the writers, thinkers and unknown activists to the social and cultural changes in the West. There is a particular style of social thought behind this new development. We should familiarise ourselves with it; it is in our interests to do so.

PRACHA: Especially since, in this cultural shift in the West, there is a lot of influence of the East.

NANDY: Yes, it is a different kind of cultural dialogue, taking place quietly, without fanfare.

Spirituality, Religion and Politics

MANIVANNAN: I have been greatly influenced by the life and teachings of Jesus Christ. I always remember one of his discourses to his disciples. In it he said, 'the kingdom of God is within you'. An atheist too has this space for the divine, though he or she may not recognise it as the dwelling of God. And even some sceptics might accept this inner space as the dwelling of the divine spirit that is in every living being. This unlimited space in mortal (human) beings is the home of our individual self, the source of our knowledge about the universe, and cosmic awareness. A pursuit of spiritual life is not an isolated action of relationship with the divine. It involves the holistic experience of identifying with the living and non-living organisms in the universe. Great social reformers are in touch with this divine spirit; that is why they are sometimes recognised as messengers of God and even worshipped as such.

I want to venture two propositions here. First, there is a spiritual crisis in the world today. We cannot solve our social, political, economic, cultural and ecological problems without addressing the spiritual crisis faced by humanity. Second, the spiritual advancement of a few, in seclusion, is a matter of debate. Many feel that the Buddhist monks in Burma have not taken up the cause of democracy in a way that would enable the people to follow them at a time when the entire Burmese society has been silenced by military rule. Yet these monks come from a great spiritual tradition that has an active interest in the well-being of society. Now, may we ask you whether you think spirituality should have its own political manifestation?

NANDY: I must clarify at the outset that we are talking about spirituality, not religion. Spirituality cuts across every kind of barrier and difference. Everyone, including a non-believer, is spiritual in some way. I am not a believer. Nevertheless, I do believe that a certain touch of transcendence is crucial in human affairs. Karl Marx, when he wrote about the ideal of a good life under communism, was thinking about the spiritual dimension of life. When we listen to great music from sitarist Vilayat Hussain Khan or vocalist Kishori Amonkar or the compositions of Bach, we experience a feeling of transcendence. It is part of our normal life. In public life, that touch of transcendence comes in different guises.

I would again refer to Arnold Toynbee's obituary of Gandhi in which he claimed that, after Gandhi, humankind would ask its prophets whether they were willing to live in the slum of politics. Spirituality need not be antagonistic or incompatible with politics, but the moderns like to believe that it is so. Yet many major figures of our time have tried to give a spiritual dimension to public life. Gandhi was only one of them. From Martin Luther King to Desmond Tutu, a galaxy of people have walked that path. They have shunned the bland secularism that the standardised theories of progress vend. The proceedings of the Truth and Reconciliation Commission in South Africa are evidence of this. The Sandinista regime had half a dozen priests in its cabinet. In recent times, the environmental movements have made a major contribution to this way of looking at the world. E.F. Schumacher tried to give a spiritual dimension to public life. His concept of environment is spiritual, and the way in which he conceives of environmentalism in public life has a spiritual component. It is no accident that the two greatest living Gandhians are neither Indians nor Hindus. Nelson Mandela and Aung San Suu Kyi have brought a touch of transcendence and spirituality into public life. I am told that both of them came to Gandhi's writings late in life, after people began to call them Gandhians.

This is natural. Gandhiansm is greater than Gandhi. It is the rediscovery of a hidden dimension in human life. Islam too is not merely fundamentalism. It is moving towards a spiritual resurgence against the excesses of orthodoxy. Right there in Iran, a number of thinker-activists, from Ali Shariati to Abdolkarim Soroush, have defied fundamentalism to give new meaning to the old links between culture and dissent. This cannot be explained away as romanticism. I believe that this particular social force will become stronger over time. For it links the vision of a desirable society to public interventions. For too long, we have gulped uncritically the idea of a desirable society lovingly gifted to us by the West. The emphasis on spirituality in politics and the emphasis on plural visions of a desirable society in our part of the world are both linked to a defiance of the European mainstream and the search for culturally embedded alternative visions of desirable societies in Europe itself.

MANIVANNAN: There are certain developments taking place in our part of the world and in the West to which I should like to draw your attention and seek your responses. People are drawn away from their socio-religious and spiritual traditions in the name of secularism and modernisation of society and politics. How do you respond to this development?

NANDY: Modern societies are inherently secular. There is no escape from that process. This in fact contributes to the rise of religious chauvinism and fundamentalism in a society. Because people are uprooted from their spiritual and religious traditions, they take the easy way out. They seek a community and

Ashis Nandy

a degree of mutuality through the revival of their socio-cultural identities, that is, through revivalism or fundamentalism. Revivalism is a modern, packaged form of socio-religious and cultural identity, a direct by-product of our times, not of traditions or religion. Such revivalism promises that you can have both your religious identity and modernity. It is an attractive promise to people threatened by a crisis of identity or a fractured self in an increasingly secular world. This is why the expatriates usually are far more vocal and aggressively chauvinistic. We can even perhaps say that the secularisation of society has contributed handsomely to the rise in fundamentalism.

MANIVANNAN: What you have given is a broad conceptual overview. Could you be more specific in identifying the causes for the rise in cultural chauvinism and religious fundamentalism today, especially in Asia?

NANDY: The specific reasons differ from society to society. But there are certain common trends that can be found. First, there is a double bind in fundamentalism. It seems hostile to modernity and it is an attempt to defy modernity. At the same time, it is a homage to modernity because fundamentalism cannot disown its modern parentage. Hence some of the inner contradictions of fundamentalism. For instance, we never find fundamentalists disowning either the nation-state system or military technology. This is common to fundamentalists and revivalists all over the world. They have never offered nor sought an alternative to the modern nation-state. They have always wanted to capture the modern state and use it as an instrument for their agenda. Actually, they also operate the state exactly the way their enemies do. And they love everything indigenous, but not indigenous military technology. Fundamentalists always seek the latest and most sophisticated military technology to fight their opponents. They are as keen to enhance the power of the state, once they have captured it, as the modernists are.

Secondly, revivalists are invariably nervous and insecure about their worldview. They cannot tolerate any alternative viewpoints or social diversity at any corner of their realm. Of even greater concern is that they do not tolerate diverse interpretations of the religion they fight for. The idea is to throttle any dissenting vision of religion or individual access to transcendence. Fundamentalists are perpetually fearful of the seductive charms of modernity, which they sense within themselves. The cruelty and ruthlessness of fundamentalism comes from this.

One of the important issues that we have not discussed so far is the role of ideology. Ideology is typically a feature of the modern mind. I am not talking of ideology in a Mannheimian or Marxist sense, but ideology as a standard social-psychological category as a particular kind of configuration of beliefs, values and thought. Ideology is supposed to tell not only who you are, but give an idea of your world-view as it stands in relation to your politics and social choices. Traditionally, people mostly had faiths. Religion is not usually an ideology but a matter of faith. In modern times, the importance of religion as faith has declined with the secularisation and demystification of the world. As a result, religion has become an ideology for many. They feel for religion the same way others feel for liberalism or socialism and they bring to it the same psychological configuration that underlies political and social ideologies.

This has some specific implications. For instance, to continue with the example of religion, there is a latent dislike among ideologues for the people whom their ideology is meant to benefit. The ideologues always feel let down by those for whom they work. I have gone through the literature of Hindu nationalism in India. One of the most surprising things that you find in the RSS [Rashtriya Swayamsevak Sangh] literature is that, despite much venom against the Muslims and the Christians, the real target of hate is the Hindus. The Hindus are seen as superstitious, primitive, effeminate, faction-ridden and disorganised. There is a long list of grievances against the Hindus and an elaborate programme to engineer them, to make them more organised, aggressive, disciplined and masculine. In Islamic fundamentalism, too, there is tremendous hostility towards ordinary believers, particularly if they do not conform culturally to the standard, nineteenth-century European concept of the Muslim. For instance, Islamic fundamentalists believe that all Indonesian Muslims are imperfect because their beliefs and practices have been contaminated by the influence of Buddhism and Hinduism. Likewise, they think that the Indian, Bangladeshi, Pakistani and Malaysian Muslims are flawed. These are the five largest Muslim countries in the world. The Afghan and Iranian Muslims do not fare much better, despite the presence of the Taliban and Ayatollah Khomeini's brainchildren. One of the first things the Taliban did in Afghanistan after taking control of the country was to issue several draconian decrees in the name of Islamic laws and practices. In Taliban's view, these steps were necessary first to eliminate the impurities that contaminated the lives of the Afghans, and ultimately to hammer them into better Muslims. Look at the absurdity of the situation: you try to polish up 80 per cent of the world's Muslims into good Muslims and then you are left with only a few who need no cultural engineering. You love Islam, but you hate the ordinary run of Muslims. This is typical of fundamentalism.

I can give you similar examples from Christian fundamentalism in the United States of America and from Buddhist ethno-cultural chauvinism in Sri Lanka. In this respect they are probably all the same. This is because the fundamentalists' ideology of religion is a substitute for faith. In this respect, religious fundamentalists have much in common with other kinds of ideologues. Feminism and Marxism show the same kind of hostility towards their targeted beneficiaries, for not being organised and disciplined enough to constitute a proper sisterhood or proletariat. This is also true of many Gandhians.

The real challenge, therefore, is to establish communication with the people in a way that will give them confidence in their own faith and not push them to embrace fundamentalism as a substitute for faith. This is a challenge that requires a different approach towards religion and spirituality. Religion and spirituality are something that comes naturally to people. We have made religion untouchable and in the bargain snapped our links with the people. Religion is like a village home we have abandoned, to live in a comfortable modern apartment in the city. Once you leave a house unused, the homeless and squatters come and occupy it. Then there is no point in screaming about the misuse of the home and blaming the squatters. The point is that you have abandoned the village home in the first place.

We have abandoned spirituality and religion as irrelevant and old-fashioned. Today, the fundamentalists of all hues encroach upon this space, though the territory does not naturally belong to them. Several societies in Asia, Africa and Latin America are facing this problem as a direct result or by-product of our loss of touch with our spiritual and religious traditions. The best antidote to this fundamentalism is to give confidence to ordinary, humble believers. The best antidote against the Hindu fundamentalism is Hinduism. This is true of Buddhism, Christianity and Islam, too. There may be alternative antidotes to fundamentalism, but they are more limited. This is because religion always makes sense to people. Soroush in Iran has publicly said that Islamic fundamentalism is not a religion. The Islamic fundamentalists in Iran do not know what to do with him. The Hindu revivalists had to kill Gandhi, not the secularists like Jawaharlal Nehru. They had not even attempted to kill anyone except Gandhi among the first generation of Indian leaders. He was the only person they tried to kill three times and succeeded in the third attempt. They did not see others as a danger to their ideology.

MANIVANNAN: My next question has two parts. First, there is a significant role spirituality can play in public life. It can provide a basis for reconciliation between people, cultures and societies and in resolving the socio-economic, cultural and political conflicts in the world today. I think we can address these problems more effectively if we can understand the spiritual dimensions of conflict resolution both at the international and intra-societal levels. Second, as many say, time heals everything. I think they mean that life itself can be a healer because of the working or awakening of the spiritual dimension in each human being. Can we apply our spiritual values and traditions to heal our historical wounds *vis-à-vis* other cultures and civilisations? Would it help us to recover our identity and our confidence in being ourselves?

NANDY: One of the most important markers of a post-colonial society is self-hatred, often manifest in hatred towards one's own people. The people represent an aspect of ourselves that we despise. The common people of our societies embarrass us and we always of think them as responsible for humiliating us in the larger world. We consider them illiterate, primitive, superstitious and irrational. We treat them as such and in the process feel threatened by them.

On the other hand, the logic of the democratic process increasingly brings the people to the centre of the political arena. We are afraid that they will soon begin to speak for themselves and not allow us to act as their spokespersons. The question of religion and spirituality assumes significance here. We become more nervous about working with the spiritual and religious traditions of the people because these traditions are closer to the people than we are. Giving people the right to use their own language, particularly a language that we neither respect nor handle well, makes us doubly uncomfortable. We feel that this would further strengthen them politically because they would bypass us more effectively. They speak the language of religion and spirituality; we speak the secular language of statecraft, development, progress and the concept of a global civil society, none of which makes any sense to ordinary people. They only understand the language of spirit and faith.

Hence my proposal that the restoration of the language of faith and spirit and establishing communication with the language of religion is a way of communicating with the people. It is a way of connecting to the people and overcoming our fears of them.

MANIVANNAN: What is the role of spirituality in building a just and sustainable society? It has traditionally been the basis of every sustainable society in the world. Considering the decline of spiritual values and traditions, I am a little pessimistic about the future of the idea of sustainability.

NANDY: One caveat before I respond to you. I would like to use the term transcendence instead of spirituality because of its scope and width. I do not think any society or person can live without its moments of transcendence. I say this as a non-believer.

PRACHA: I would like to link this concern for strengthening the spiritual base to our visions of an alternative political culture and leadership in our societies.

NANDY: We have already spoken, directly or indirectly, of a few aspects of a possible alternative vision of politics during the course of our discussion. I have already mentioned the need for decentralised polities and open-ended cultures and societies. I would also like to see the growth of republicanism of, if not villages, at least of small communities. Many indigenous communities not only in Asia, but also in Africa and the Americas had something close to this. What could have been fascinating experiments at the margins of the modern world have been dealt a death-blow by modern states. But then, the modern state is also not doing very well. We are being forced to look at other ways of managing our polities now. Our system of governance has become too distant and impersonal. It has also become too specialised and expert-driven.

Take the case of India. We have a population of one billion, an electorate of roughly 650 million, and five-hundred-odd parliamentarians represent the people and link them to the government. Well, they represent the people all right, but they have no direct links with the people. The constituencies are too large for that. These leaders have to rely mostly on media-genic issues, image manipulation and sloganeering to be elected. No wonder they are now expected to possess the qualities and the charisma associated with film stars and sports heroes, qualities that would cut across social divisions and interests. There is less emphasis on sustained work at local or national levels. Even when they seem to be doing work, it is too narrowly local and involves solving problems of daily life for their supporters. These gaps in the representational process also contribute to problems like corruption and nepotism in public life. There has to be some degree of decentralisation. The distance between the electors and the elected has to be reduced in some way. I do not know how to achieve that politically. Perhaps the fluidity and chaos induced by globalisation will give us a chance.

As I said, politics is becoming increasingly expert-infested. We are building new barriers to participation through these experts, as we are becoming more conscious and fearful of the power of the people. The people and even parliament are not seen as competent to handle crucial issues any more. The problem of development has been contacted out to the development experts. That is also true of diplomacy, planning, nuclear policy in particular and defence in general, energy, environment, and so on. The entire arena of public life has been sliced into several compartments and the slices are being handed over to small groups of experts. As a result, large parts of public life have become domains or fiefdoms of experts. India's nuclear decisions are made by a group of scientists and bureaucrats whose number may not exceed even fifteen. They may not even involve many politicians or the army. Indeed, the politicians have very little control over the functioning of these bodies, which are not directly accountable to the people. This is happening in other parts of the world, too, if that is any consolation.

This process will have to be contained. There is a need to restore the sovereignty of the people. Professionalisation of dissent is an attempt to depoliticise them. Politics must be restored to the people. This is one part of the story.

As for an alternative culture of politics, I do not know whether we can consciously build one. It has to emerge on its own from encounters and dialogues of people. Political culture is changing everywhere. I do not think that the culture of Indian politics is what it was thirty years ago. People are more open to ideas and they are less fearful of openly expressing their political choices. This is the effect of democratisation. However, I am more willing to discuss what kind of politics will lead to an alternative political culture than to specify the kind of alternative culture that I want. It is against my democratic principle to advocate a concept of alternative political culture. For such a culture, despite its beautifully worked-out contents, may be as authoritarian as many existing systems of governance. Let there be a thousand alternatives. People are quite capable of finding the right alternatives and weeding out the rest if the democratic process works. They are prior to even their charismatic leaders.

There is another reason why I am not eager to define the kind of alternative culture of politics I want. I believe that human beings are always more capable of reaching consensus on what they do not want than on what they want. If you say that we do not want a state system like the one the fascists built in Italy, everyone will agree to it. The moment you say that you want a state system like what Fidel Castro has built in Cuba, there will be more dissenters than conformists. We have always been more divided on the question of our ideal society and much less divided when we discuss the kinds of society that we do not want. This is no accident and it is a sign of healthy politics. Even the novels that talk of dystopias survive better than the ones that talk of utopias. Aldous Huxley's dystopia, *Brave New World*, survived better than his positive utopia, *Island*. There is something curious about the human mind. It intuitively senses that it could be more confident when defining social good and well-being negatively than when defining them positively. This is the way the human mind shares and transmits experiences. We address our preferences about an ideal society but we do so not directly, by specifying the contents of an ideal society, but through a process of elimination of what we do not want. This keeps democratic options open for the future generations, too.

PRACHA: I would like to address a far more basic and simple concern related to spirituality or a feeling of transcendence, as you like to call it. Why do

Ashis Nandy

we need to experience this feeling of transcendence and how does it occur? How is it relevant to our lives?

NANDY: I have not systematically thought about it. Why do we need it? I think because human creativity and psychological health need it. Such transcendence must take place at the level of the self. I am not speaking about the transcendence of the world or of reality but of self. Occasionally you should have the chance and the ability to get out of your self and watch the world and your self from outside. This play, with one's own self and its boundaries, has always been a source of human creativity. When I talk of creativity, I do not mean the creativity of great minds alone. I am not talking of Johann Goethe or Albert Einstein. I am talking about everyday creativity, including the arts of working, loving and living. Many societies have tried to institutionalise means to ensure such transcendence. Pilgrimage is one such venture, when you leave behind a part of your self and try to acquire a new awareness. When you return, your self is not the same. The experience of being a pilgrim gives you a touch of transcendence in your everyday life ever afterwards. In the process, you also become more aware of what you are, because you have met other realities of your own self. Simultaneously, you have also made others see you from a different and new perspective. A person who has undertaken a pilgrimage in his life enjoys a special respect and honour in the society.

But you do not often have to go that far. Even great music or poetry or great philosophy can give you moments of transcendence.

PRACHA: You have made a passing reference to Iran. How would you respond to the proposition that Islamic revolution in Iran itself is a form of alternative political culture?

NANDY: It may be an alternative from one point of view, but that is not my concept of an ideal alternative politics. I do believe that the Islamic revolution had something to contribute to Iran. At least it brought down an oppressive regime. The Shah of Iran in many ways was a disaster. However, I also feel that the Islamic revolution has turned out to be a disaster, too, in several ways. For it has been routinely reacting to the Shah ever since. The Shah is dead for us, but he is alive for them. His memory-traces define the enemy still, and these enemies are fought through a state apparatus and a police that remain direct descendants of the Shah's state and the Savak, at least psychologically. In other words, the Iranian revolution would not have taken place if the Shah had not been there in the first place. No Shah, no Iranian revolution. But that also means that they are still fighting a dead enemy, an enemy who is partly within.

However, after saying all this, I would like to point out that there were creative possibilities in the Iranian revolution that were not pursued. The revolutionaries became engaged in settling minor and petty scores. Above all, they showed little compassion. In some sense, they defeated themselves by blowing up the opportunities for genuine change that were available after the revolution.

I must emphasise in this connection my belief that, in our times, no revolution can succeed unless it has built-in principles of compassion, rights to self-expression and theory of non-violence. This is a tall order, because most revolutions have a built-in theory of violence. It is that theory that ensures their self-destruction.

PRACHA: You have earlier talked about feminism as an ideology. What is the significance of feminism in our search for an alternative political culture? Is it a part of the overall search for change everywhere, especially if we think of the feminist challenge to patriarchy as a challenge to a form of social hierarchy and political power?

NANDY: The question of gender has become a crucial metaphor of our times. I think that our overarching systems of oppression have been hyper-masculine. The language of masculinity has been the crucial component of them. I therefore consider the reaffirmation of the feminine vital. It is central not only to the humanisation of politics and public life, but also to the redefinition of our human self in large parts of the world. However, I would like to add that the issue of gender has a different kind of meaning in the non-Western civilisations. I do not think the kind of masculine domination or patriarchy that most feminists in the West talk about has existed as a living reality in much of the non-Western world. It is, for instance, a travesty of truth to claim that we are all mired in the system of patriarchy in the same way as American or West European women are. I know of several indigenous communities in Asia and Africa who have a different concept of women and power. I know of certain communities in India in which women have more rights than men do on issues such as property rights and divorce.

It is not an accident that the world's first woman prime minister came from this part of the world. Actually, all the major countries of South Asia produced powerful women politicians before the West did. In addition, suffrage for women and gendered job definitions in the modern sector have never been serious problems in our part of the world. Unequal wages and direct violence have been. There is a greater proportion of women in professions like medicine and engineering in the part of this world that in the West. Our Westernised feminists may think this an accident, but it is not so. This is because, while there is patriarchy, there are other principles in our societies to

Ashis Nandy

organise human relationships. Ordinary people and those seriously into grass-roots women's movements in South and South-east Asia will not be surprised by what I am saying. The concept of an androgynous Christ might have been forgotten in Europe, but the concept of the androgynous Krishna or Buddha or a Sufiyana that blurs and transcends gender remain familiar to this part of the world. There is here a different dialectics of the feminine and the masculine. Those who know how to build on these traditions will be socially and politically more creative than those who borrow respectable ideas from respectable Western universities.

2 | Sulak Sivaraksa

Sulak Sivaraksa was born in Bangkok, Thailand in 1933 to an overseas Chinese–Thai family (with an aristocratic background on his mother's side). He was educated at the Elite Catholic School in Bangkok and later studied liberal arts at Lampeter University, Wales, and took a law degree at the Middle Temple, London. He was a Buddhist novice during the Second World War.

His main areas of interest are engaged Buddhism, inter-religious dialogue and human rights. He is well known in the international community among thinkers and activists who search for new alternatives to the present mainstream approach to development and globalisation. Engaged spiritual activists of all faiths are inspired by his commitment to social justice and ecological sustainability. He worked at the BBC in London in the 1950s and, on his return to Thailand, edited several journals during the 1960s that awakened young Thais to social justice, democracy, the environment and cultural values. He is co-founder of the South-east Asia Study Group, the Asian Cultural Forum for Development, and the International Network of Engaged Buddhists. He serves as a board member of many national, regional and international institutions, including the International People's Tribunal, the Unrepresented Nations and Peoples' Organisation, and the American-founded Buddhist–Christian Dialogue. He has received a number of prestigious awards for his mission, including the Right Livelihood Award in 1995.

With his educational background, it was expected that once he returned to his homeland he would gain a senior position in the Thai government. Instead he chose to become a controversial and independent intellectual, a challenging career in the days of military dictatorship. His work had a clear impact on the democratic movement in Thailand that culminated in the first popular uprising, which toppled the dictatorial government in 1973. Over the next three decades his persistent challenges to mainstream development thinking of both the left and the right have gained more and more momentum. He is not only a prolific writer and fine speaker, but also a capable organiser, who has initiated a number of non-profit, non-government organisations working for change in different aspects of society. Through these ventures, he opens up opportunities for talented leadership of civil society to take root and grow. He does not cling tightly to any school of thought but tries to synthesise good points from them all. He advocates 'small b' buddhist values such as compassion rather than competition, co-operation rather than individualism, broad-mindedness rather than dogmatism, living in harmony with nature rather than being masters of nature. He sees these values as common to most spiritual traditions, especially in Asia.

He has written more than a hundred books in Thai and ten in English, including: *Seeds of Peace: A Buddhist Vision for Renewing Society*, *Loyalty Demands Dissent: Autobiography of an Engaged Buddhist* and *Siam in Crisis*.

PRACHA HUTANUWATR: How do you analyse present society in Asia?

SULAK SIVARAKSA: Every country in Asia has a form of government that is an imitation of the West. I think most people in the West would agree that Western governments no longer function adequately. At a recent South–North Network meeting in Brussels they said that 27 per cent of people in the North are not in the political mainstream, and the 73 per cent who are in the mainstream are sub-divided as left, right, green, republican, and so on. It is encouraging that even some of the people in the mainstream are leaning towards alternative politics and questioning political structures. The 27 per cent who are not in the mainstream are challenging the political set-up in Europe and North America. This is happening because the systems are too complex and have been there for too long. The British parliament may have been wonderful in the nineteenth century, during colonial times, but it doesn't work effectively any more. It is an old-fashioned and wasteful institution. Why do we need an army to promote the arms merchants and the arms trade? In these days of modern communications why do you need embassies and consulates? Why do you need the cabinet? What are all the law courts for? If you look at any country, the law courts only want to maintain the status quo. They never make adjustments for the poor or the deprived.

An example is the Bhopal gas tragedy in India, where there was a huge industrial accident that killed several hundred people, and many more continue to suffer. Union Carbide is the multinational corporation in control of Union Carbide India Ltd, who were the organisation responsible, yet the latter say that it is the subsidiary company of the big company and you have to sue in America. Of course this is out of question. These days judgements always seem to favour the ruling classes rather than the common people. Lord Peel invented violent structures, such as the police, and the standing army was invented by Napoleon. The more you have these big structures, the more oppressive the state becomes. Now nation-states are controlled by the multinational corporations, which has made things much worse.

PRACHA: You mentioned that all countries in Asia are following the Western government system, even though they have liberated themselves from colonisation. Why can't they go beyond all these Western set-ups?

SULAK: This is why we need to look into alternatives to consumerism. Unfortunately not only politics, but also economics in Asia are Western-based, especially since the dissolution of the Soviet Union. It is either Marxist economics, or capitalist economics. Since the age of enlightenment the supremacy of Europe known as Eurocentricity has meant that Europeans have arrogantly claimed that without the European model it was not possible to develop. Now the European model has been superseded by the Americans and economically by the Japanese, but they are both based on a Western model. Unfortunately human beings, once trapped by certain models, do not go beyond them.

During the Ming period [1368–1644] the Chinese felt threatened by the West and came to the conclusion that Western civilisation is evil. They considered it an aggressive and arrogant civilisation that can be compartmentalised without spiritual or humanistic dimension. At that time the Chinese wanted Western technology, but at the same time wanted to maintain 'Chineseness'. Unfortunately they failed, and the Japanese too have failed in the same way. All that is left in Japan is a little bit of kimono. Outwardly, Japanese women have maintained much more than the men, but much of this is oppressive oriental culture. Of course the oppression of women is universal and also happens in the West, where women are by and large rebelling to obtain equality, and yet have not been successful.

When you look at alternative politics, you must look at alternative relationships between human beings and nature. This is also true in the case of the relationship between North and South in the global political arena. And it needs to be understood in terms of distinction between classes and sexes. This is where some of the books written by women are very important. It shows that women maintain the feminine, which comes back to the harmony of yin and yang. In the East we tried to maintain harmony, but once we embraced Western culture and superstition the harmony was destroyed. In Korea yin and yang was part of the national flag but it hardly exists now. It has been replaced by a very arrogant and aggressive culture that is not only Western, since most Asian rulers also had that tendency. Buddhism was against this, whereas Hinduism as a ruling socio-political ideology promotes aggressiveness at all levels while maintaining a certain harmony, usually at the expense of the weak. Of course it helps the stronger to be kind to the weaker but also maintains a clear hierarchy with the supremacy of the stronger. The male above the female, the father above the children, and so on. It has certain merits, but I do not like that model.

At first the Asians did not like Western aggressiveness. Now Buddhism holds that you adopt what you dislike unless you try to understand yourself properly and harmoniously. If you hate your father, you will act exactly the same as your father and if you hate your boss, you will act exactly the same as your boss. The Japanese did not want to open their doors to Commodore Perry from the US in 1854, but once they did they realised that because they were weak technically and militarily they must compete with the West. They believed that the West then would accept the Japanese as equals. Although they failed in the Second World War, they now have an entirely capitalistic Western economic system and consider themselves equal and in some cases superior to the West.

If you look closely it is all an imitation of the West, which no country has managed to escape. The Siamese claim to be Thai, but they have been influenced by the British and Dutch colonial systems. The so-called 'democracy' is based on a Whitehall model, and the new Thai constitution reflects even more an American model. It is much easier to take models from abroad.

On top of that, most of our leaders and social elite were brainwashed by their Western education. The Western universities do this. They felt so superior going to universities like Oxford, Cambridge and Harvard. Only one person I knew who went to Cambridge really questioned the education system. He went to Cambridge as a very bright teenager, and later told me that he did not realise the hidden curriculum at Cambridge until he was 50. The purpose is that you learn to write like us, speak like us and think like us in order to go and rule over the bloody buggers in your country. Even Gandhi, who tried to be Indian, went along with Western models when studying in England; his model was transformed by socialism, but it was still Western.

I see this development as the attraction of power and materialism. This is where the West claims to be superior. Since the Enlightenment it has been the era of *cogito ergo sum*, which follows a very rational and intellectual approach with scant acknowledgement of the spiritual. The West is beginning to question this model of development. It is the right time for us to look for alternative politics and alternative education. It is recognised in a modern society that a clever person need not be good. Unfortunately, people become corrupt in the West as much as in the East. Singapore claims to be honest and Western, but it is the rule of Western fascism with a democratic front. If you want to go beyond that, you have to change inwardly and unify the head and the heart. That is why I consider that there is a need for something spiritual.

PRACHA: This Western model is so widespread in Asia and in other parts of the world. Are there any good aspects that make it attractive and acceptable to so many countries and people?

SULAK: The good aspect of it is that it appeals to the ruling classes! It helps kings, prime ministers and cabinet ministers to have and remain in power. These people pass legislation, so the law supports the same people. They are the lawmakers and the benefactors. It helps the rich to keep their power and money. They also control education, which is a way of brainwashing the people. As Tom Paine said very clearly at the founding of the United States: societies are good, though not perfect; people are good; but all government is at best a necessary evil. Most governments are evil and bad, and there is not a single good king in all history. I did not believe this until recently. This sort of system is good for the ruling classes, who brainwash people, telling them that if you follow us you also could come to the top. If you develop like us, you can become like us Americans. Consumerism tells you eat, dress and drive in a particular way, and so on. Education teaches that you are nobody. You have to be able to read and write and for that you must go to secondary school and then university. Your university of course is not as good as our university. You do not have first class honours and you don't have a Ph.D. We are being brainwashed thus all the time. There is an aura around people like professors and doctors, yet for me it is all brainwashing. Other people would not have the courage to say so, because they have been conditioned not to empower themselves.

PRACHA: What about values like freedom, respect for human rights, democracy and equality? These are also the products of the enlightenment.

SULAK: Rhetorically this appears so, but if you look carefully, you will see that human rights are not available to everybody in the West. Look at Western Europe, Canada and the USA, which are supposed to be democracies. Human rights are available to the white middle classes and to the male more than the female population. You go anywhere in the USA; most people in jail are black Americans, or Mexican Americans or American Indians. There are fewer American Indians because there are fewer in the population, as most of them were killed long ago. And most of the whites in jail are from poor backgrounds. The same is true in Europe. In Australia and New Zealand there are many Maoris and Aborigines in jail. Until recently in Papua New Guinea there were no jails, but when the West came with beer and liquor jails soon followed. The West was very capable at that. The Chinese never smoked opium until the British came. They wanted tea in exchange for opium, but now it is guns. I dread the West so much because when they are successful it is always at the expense of someone else. The Chinese realised this and that is why they used gunpowder not for weapons but only for scaring evil spirits. They had that wisdom. The West, before the age of enlightenment, also had that wisdom. This has been lost in the era of knowledge for knowledge's sake. In this era, you do not have to be aware of moral consequences, which is why we now have hydrogen bombs that could destroy the world more than one hundred times.

PRACHA: So you consider that these basic values are positive and cannot be applied universally but only to a particular class? Is that your argument?

SULAK: It has not been applied appropriately because the ruling elite is so selfish. They are very clever and most people are not aware of this. In the American Declaration of Independence, a statement like 'All men are created equal' looks very good. Yet in this context all men does not include women. All men is only white men, not the American Indians, not the black Americans imported from Africa. Even among the whites it is only the landowners. This kind of statement is hypocritical. If you are not careful you can become very cynical. People have only recently realised this and very few have said it. Kirkpatrick Sale's book, *Rebels Against the Future*, shows that the Luddites were revolutionaries, yet society generally makes out that the Luddites were mad, ridiculous people. Of course the media, education systems and the churches propagate this. So the Luddites were defeated, and yet I believe their ideas of preserving farming lifestyles, arts and crafts are revolutionary. It is sad that farmers' rights and local crafts were destroyed with the expansion of capitalism and the empire.

All the textbooks said wonderful things about the empire. Gandhi believed in it until he was chucked out of the first-class carriage in South Africa. This is why you have to confront suffering, otherwise you would not know. Yet most educational systems avoid the confrontation of suffering. The better the university, the more beautiful the campus. In these institutions what you learn is unreal. This is why Graham MacQueen, who is now director of the Peace Study Centre at McMaster University in Canada, said in his Harvard days that the motto is 'truth above all else', and you live with 'truth' so much that you do not care about the Vietnam War. Samuel Huntington, who was at Harvard when MacQueen was a student, seriously proposed to the American administration, 'let us bomb all the countryside of Vietnam, so that the Vietnamese will go and live in the city and be much easier to control'. Nobody ever questioned Huntington. Even now, Huntington proposes, in his 'Clash of Civilisations' thesis, that the Arabs are the enemies. This is because the enlightenment needs an enemy. This implies you can promote arms. When the communists were in power they supplied the rationale for so much money to be spent on arms. Now the communists are gone. Huntington is quoted everywhere, yet most people are unaware of the implications. The state and the ruling elite are very clever in using education and the media. Sometimes education is very hard. The teacher beats you and treats you very badly. You always blame yourself. Only few people see that the teachers are badly paid.

William Blake, who was very bright although considered mad by many, said all universities were bad. Oxford and Cambridge serve only the church and the state, which always come together to condemn the people. In England you have the freedom to study anybody. It is very interesting that people study Blake, and the university educational system says that you will study Blake for the beauty rather than the content, as he was mad. George Sainsbury, a great professor of literature at Edinburgh University, said that in the study of literature one learns style, grammar, and how to polish your writing. That is how to read Blake. There is little to read and learn from his content because he is mad and not good. But Blake's message is wonderful! Similarly with Milton you study *Paradise Lost, Paradise Regained* and the sonnets but you do not study Milton on education or censorship. You do not study his hidden messages, that he was against controlling people. The education system is very clever and they do not set examinations for you in that way. But why should you consider it? You want to get a first-class degree and to do that you toe the line. The same with Shakespeare. Shakespeare is read much more than Milton because he is very harmless and on the whole with the ruling class. Many of his plays are mere propaganda, although he is a beautiful poet. He is admired for his poetry rather than the content. Plays like *As You Like* it and *The Merchant of Venice* are beautiful poetry, but there is nothing in them. *Hamlet* is great, but it is more an illusion, without real depth of meaning.

PRACHA: You have mentioned Gandhi and his search for alternatives. You have also mentioned communism. Mao Zedong is another great leader who tried to search for Asian alternatives. Another is the Islamic model. At the moment Islam is trying to find something outside the Western model. What do you think about these three models in Asia?

SULAK: I do not know very much about the Islamic model but what I know about the Islamic states is dreadful. They do not take the best from Islam; they take the worst. You must realise that all religions have two main aspects for analysis: one is tribal, the other is universal. Considering one's own model as best is very tribal. For instance, thinking Thai Buddhism is best or Judaism is best. Even in the Bible the God of Israel is a very, very angry God. Yet if you go to the base of all religions there is a universal God or universal love that is not tribal. Islamic states are very tribal in propagating things like 'my country is the best', 'men are superior to women', and 'you have to dress this way'. All this leads to fundamentalism and this promotes a monoculture, which in my opinion is dreadful. Even worse is the monoculture of consumerism, which stimulates greed to induce you to do certain things. In religious fundamentalism you may not like to do something but you have to do it because you are afraid of sin and hell, of dictators and inquisitors. The best has not yet emerged, though I think what Abdurrahman Wahid (see p. 226) has been doing in Indonesia as a leader of civil society is encouraging. The works and activities of the Just World Trust in Malaysia are remarkable. These two experiments appeal to me; we must learn from them. I am not very well informed on other Islamic initiatives, although I understand that some are trying to apply Gandhian concepts to Islam in either Egypt or Pakistan.

Mao Zedong tried to be Chinese, but his entire concept of Marxism was underpinned with Leninism and Stalinism. This is not an alternative but the worst kind of fundamentalist dictatorship, where if you challenge the ideas you are a revisionist. It is wonderful to dress in a Chinese way, but he forced everyone to do the same. Mao killed all his friends and seems to have possessed an evil and egocentric character, like most emperors. This is why I never admired him.

PRACHA: If you put violence aside, Mao had a genuine intention to develop something different from the Western capitalist model. He wanted to go back to the Chinese way.

SULAK: You must realise that Mao Zedong was a man of great contradictions. He used Chinese literature and philosophy for his own ends. He distrusted many Western Marxist intellectuals and admired right-wing Western oppressors like Nixon. He claimed to admire Chinese medicine and said that, together with language and literature, Chinese medicine was one of the three great contributions the Chinese have made to the world, yet he never used it except to promote his sexual stimulus, which he believed would give him immortality. He always had Western medicine, except dentistry, because with his Chinese peasant background he believed that brushing your teeth every day was decadence. He was a very complex personality, but if you look deeply he was full of evil. He was very egocentric and would do anything, including sleeping with any woman of his choice. Most emperors did that but at least the emperors had the culture to support it. Mao is much more hypocritical than the emperors as he claimed to be proletarian and a monogamist. Of course he had wonderful meaning for the masses but not for the individual. He loved the masses but could not stand the individuals. This for me is typically Western. Robespierre and Danton loved the masses but they killed each other, which was the tragedy of the French Revolution. I admire the Gandhian model partly because Gandhi never ran the state; if he had he may have followed the same path.

PRACHA: Before we discuss Gandhi could you share your impressions about Ho Chi Minh?

SULAK: Well, Ho Chi Minh was much more beneficial than Mao Zedong because he never ran the state. He started with the party and when the country became independent he withdrew himself to remain as a kind of guide and philosopher. While he had power he did not play around with it as much as Mao. He lived in one room, which in my opinion is a wonderful way to live. He was content with a simple life. There were no sexual abuses. In comparison Mao lived a fancy lifestyle in a big palace with numerous sexual conquests.

As a personality I have admiration for Ho Chi Minh, although his approach involved some violence, which is not my way of thinking. His ideology was entirely Marxist, with little Asian influence. Like the Japanese, the Thais tried to learn from Western technology although we wanted to keep our own philosophy and culture. Of course Ho Chi Minh tried to maintain a little Buddhism and a little Confucianism too. The supreme ideology was, however, an adapted Marxism and for me this is Western.

PRACHA: Let us keep personalities aside. Both Mao Zedong and Ho Chi Minh have created societies that have at least some kind of decentralisation.

SULAK: Decentralisation? Never!

PRACHA: In the sense of commune and the community, which has more autonomy?

SULAK: Yes! The communes were forced to be that way. This is why they are all destroyed now. If it had been a genuine alternative they would still be here. The people were forced to adopt a barter system and not use money. If they had used a democratic means through which people could choose not to use money it would have been truly remarkable. It may have taken longer, but it would have been much more genuine and lasting. They employed so much propaganda. I have visited China six times and seen that changes always came from the top and never from the bottom. The Chinese believe that God Himself sent Mao Zedong. It is like the Catholic Church, where you pay the Pope to bless. Of course Mao Zedong and Ho Chi Minh were patriots and wanted to have their own national identities, but they see no other alternative than Marxism. But you cannot tell me that these are Asian alternatives.

PRACHA: Now can we talk about Gandhi's ideas? Why is he different? Why did he fail?

SULAK: Gandhi is very different and I do not consider that he failed. His ideas are unpopular now but I think Gandhianism will come back in a big way. Gandhi had difficulty partly because of the huge Asian weakness of hero-worship. Buddhism has been challenged in the same way, with the Buddha becoming so great and sacred that you give the image a crown and jewellery and worship him rather than follow his teachings. It is same with the Gandhians, who worship Gandhi but do not follow his teachings or his way of thinking, his approach to simplicity and his challenge to hatred and inner delusion. Another weakness is that Gandhi did not recognise the evils of capitalism. He felt that by being good you can convince the capitalists to be good to you and others. He died in the house of the second richest family in India, and he felt there was nothing wrong with that. Of course the Buddha did not consider there was anything wrong with that either, although it was different in the Buddha's time. He saw Hinduism as both a tribal and universal religion, and his strength was when he advocated the universal values of love, chastity and goodness. Gandhianism is simply wonderful when understood in any tradition, but can fail when applied to Hinduism in a tribal way. Gandhi interpreted the *Bhagavadgita* in a universal way and gained recognition all over the world. He said that in the *Bhagavadgita* the gods came to earth as human beings to destroy violence, greed and lust rather than each other. Gandhi used much from Buddhist teachings and even from Tolstoy, and is admired by many, including Christians.

You can also criticise Gandhi for his male chauvinism and his dealings with the untouchables. He said that if you are born into a Hindu caste and if you are a Brahman you must remain so and if you are an untouchable you remain so at least until you are reborn in the next life. But we all have weaknesses, and apart from these few minor mistakes I think he was truly wonderful. I particularly admire him when he returned to India and went straight to live with the poor and share their sufferings. He would not wear a traditional long shirt, as many did not have a shirt to wear. He would calculate what poor people needed to eat and would not eat beyond that. I think this is simply outstanding.

PRACHA: How come he did not see the evils of capitalism?

SULAK: He saw and felt them but thought that the Asian spiritual perspective was enough to overcome them. Gandhi felt that the rich in India could use their wealth for the poor, but he did not yet know how to tackle the system. Perhaps if he had been a bit more Marxist in this aspect it may have helped him. I acknowledge Marx on the issues of structural violence and class analysis.

PRACHA: In which way? Is it from a religious point of view? How did Marx help?

SULAK: He mentioned the oppressor and the oppressed which most religions never talk about. The religions tend to say, 'oh, the poor are so poor that we should help them'. That is why Helder Camara, an archbishop in Latin America, said, 'we should be generous to the poor, they have not a cent'. They called him a saint but he responded, 'Well, the poor should demand their rights! They should have dignity similar to us. Our riches have come from the deprivation of the poor.' Then they called him a communist and I think this is where the religious leaders should learn from the Marxists, but in a non-violent way. Gandhi's tremendous effort and contribution towards non-violence was the greatest in this modern period, but he did not tackle structural violence. If he had more time, and had the Congress Party believed in him more than it did, the result would have been quite different.

PRACHA: When you are talking about awareness and changing the structure of capitalism in a non-violent way, do you mean what the social democrats have been doing in Europe in their respective countries?

SULAK: No, what you have to realise is that social democrats do many good things on social welfare but one thing they lack is spiritual strength. Capitalism is so strong that you start compromising without restructuring yourself and society. To be effective you must have a good understanding of structural violence and how it relates to your inner self. This is where Chogyam Trungpa, the Tibetan spiritual teacher who founded Naropa University in the US, is wonderful. He said that structural violence is there in each individual. Buddhism can contribute here. If you can change the structural violence within, you can also change society. If we can see this clearly perhaps we can get somewhere, but it is not very clear yet. It is a great pity that Chogyam Trungpa died so early, owing to excessive alcohol.

PRACHA: In approaching structural violence, at least to make capitalism a lesser evil, there is something we can learn from the social democrats. Is that what you are saying?

SULAK: You have to learn from their strengths and weaknesses. Their strengths have made their societies liveable-in. The Labour Party in the United Kingdom after the Second World War, Germany under Willy Brandt, Sweden, Norway and Denmark are good examples. However, there are several weaknesses. First, the social democrats only work within the state. Second, at that time the North had little idea that they exploited the rest of the world. Third, they do not really decentralise as they claim to. Last, they are devoid of spiritual dimensions. This is why privatisation is being introduced in many European countries, which is practically destroying the entire labour movement. I doubt whether Tony Blair can revive labour, and he is very nervous about bringing social democracy into Britain. In Britain the socialist movement was destroyed by eighteen years of Tory government. Devolution in Britain may help the Welsh and Scots, provided they understand the evils of consumerism and capitalism. This is very difficult, as Rupert Murdoch has great control over the media and he is an evil man. The media are a great enemy, and this is why we need to understand consumerism to understand the present modern state.

PRACHA: Will this kind of social democratic ideology be able to cope with globalisation, because now, on the one hand, we are stressing that the state should have less and less power and, on the other, the multinationals are becoming more and more powerful?

SULAK: I am quite doubtful. The social democratic system is almost finished now. We must look for alternatives. This is why groups like the Greens have become more established in the North. The Greens go beyond the social democrats, who have never seriously taken environmental issues into account. The West reinterpreted the Bible wrongly, cultivating attitudes that men are so supreme and that natural resources must be used to serve men. Darwin and Spencer confirmed that the strongest must win, and so on. I think this damaging trend is now slowly moving away. It is encouraging that more than 27 per cent of people in the North are looking for alternatives. I think there is a chance to move away from the 'progress'-oriented development that we have seen with the Renaissance, the Reformation, the Enlightenment, the Industrial Revolution and now globalisation. We must get back to the roots. In regard to our search for roots, I consider the South–North dialogue as a very important step. Europe must go back to the roots and the roots must be before the Renaissance. I do not propose that you actually go back, but you must understand the roots and their meaning, as Europe has increasingly been cut off from its roots. The Age of Enlightenment had cut off all the roots as it was felt that the ties would strengthen the church. They did not realise that it was the church as an institution that was so bad rather than Christianity. Then they threw out Christianity. They threw out the baby with the bathwater, and that is why they have lost everything. They made God so powerful and even male-chauvinistic. They later killed Him. Now God is coming back as Her. God even comes back with Gaia and this is wonderful, but you have to be careful or it will be a superstition. The New Age people are full of superstitions because they want to maintain consumerism. Many so-called Buddhists are also New Age people and want Buddhism to make them feel happy whilst they are acquiring what is known as consumerism. This is what we need to tackle.

PRACHA: It is assumed that the Japanese model, which also follows the West, has helped to solve the problem of poverty in this Asian country. Do you agree with this view?

SULAK: This model has helped the Japanese to overcome material poverty, but it has made them much worse-off in terms of spiritual and cultural poverty. It has more or less made Japan a monoculture country. Most Japanese are not happy and they have no time to think about it either. There are only a very few who escape through meditation. This is very dangerous and, like the social democrat model, it is also at the expense of your neighbours. The Japanese are much more ruthless than the northern Europeans, who, although deprived of Christianity, still have Christian ethics. Although belief in the spiritual dimension has disappeared from Christianity, this ethical dimension – that we must also care for the rest of the world – remains. They are poor and inferior but we must care for them. The Japanese never care beyond the Japanese islands. The Chinese taught them so much civilisation but they went to China to occupy.

The Koreans taught them so much and they went to Korea to occupy. They have learnt so much from the West and now they want to occupy the West. Siam is now following this very bad model. The Thais think that they must be successful in neighbouring countries such as Laos, Cambodia and Burma, copying what they perceive to be the Japanese role in Siam. We must work to change this paradigm.

PRACHA: At least in Japan they developed a model of capitalism that cares more for the workers.

SULAK: Again you must recognise that it only looks good on the surface. The American occupation forces dictated all these changes. When they abolished feudalism they initiated land reforms. The Americans reduced the gap between the rich and poor, which they could not do in their own country. The president of a Japanese company could only earn up to 20 per cent more than other employees, whereas in America they earn ten thousand times more. What Americans could not do in their own country they managed to do elsewhere. In this respect the occupation helped, socially and economically.

PRACHA: Do you mean to say that this has not developed from Japanese collective consciousness?

SULAK: There is some collective element, but the structure of society is Western. MacArthur and his crew did it all. I even know the people who drafted the Japanese and the German constitutions. The German social democrats also came from the American occupation forces. This cannot be disputed although it is rarely stated. Apart from that, the Japanese became successful owing to the Korean and Vietnam wars. This was because the Americans bought things more cheaply in Japan, and they also wanted to help the Japanese economy to recuperate. Something similar could have happened in Siam if it had been occupied by the British or Americans. It is all outside influences and not indigenous culture at all.

PRACHA: When societies, for instance Siam, follow the Japanese model of economic growth, why do we fall faster than Japan?

SULAK: You used the word 'faster'. I fear Japan is collapsing and also Europe and America. All these models are coming to an end. This is why we must look for alternatives. In some respects we are faster. We have already discussed Gandhi and Ho Chi Minh; I would now like to mention Pridi Banomyong. At 33 he was a Thai leader. He was put out of power at 48 after only fifteen years. Before the Second World War he dreamt of a regional system. He supported the Indonesian, Cambodian, Laotian and Vietnamese liberation movements. He did not dare to support the Malaysian and Burmese movements, as he was afraid of the British. I do not know how much he admired Gandhi but I do know that he was very perceptive. Buddhism for him had a political dimension. He always sought truth and explored alternatives to the Western model. That is why he was chucked out. Pridi was the best ally in the Second World War, yet people thought he was a communist. To some extent he was a socialist, but I believe he was looking for something beyond socialism.

In Siam the long and painful destruction of our spiritual tradition was instigated by the process of nation-state building, whilst in Europe it was destroyed by the philosophers and the intellectuals. The feudalistic approach, and more recently consumerism, have had a deep effect on the Sangha, the community of Buddhist monks, who are now very timid. Buddhadasa, the reformist Thai monk, was the only one who attempted resistance. A nation-state without a soul or a spiritual dimension is bound to fail. In Vietnam they have Ho Chi Minh as a soul, even though there is still some oppression. In China they have had Mao Zedong as a soul, though he was a bad one, which is why China has become so difficult now.

In Siam we lost our soul when Pridi was thrown out and the military used the King to legitimise their power. Even though the King did allow some democratic processes, when Sarit Thanarat came to power he destroyed democracy and only used the King as a model. This was supposed to be our own model but Sarit was a sinister and dreadful person. If you read the document he issued during his rule [1957–63] you can see he praised the monarchy and the monkhood and it even says that we do not need the damned Western democracy. He used all the Western gadgets like the Western dictatorships did. Eastern dictatorships do not have all those gadgets. Siam became the underdog of the Americans, politically, culturally and educationally. All these were accelerated and promoted by the Vietnam War, consumerism and capitalism. The Thai elite do not yet see the danger.

PRACHA: What is the difference between Vietnam, when you say that Ho Chi Minh is the soul of the nation, and Siam, where we have the King but no soul? Are they both symbols for the ruling elite and the system?

SULAK: You have to be careful with the word 'soul' as it is a Christian word, and in Buddhism we do not accept it. The word 'soul' here is *jai* in Thai, which means heart, so we are talking about the heart of the nation, which is the most vital force. There must be an element to bind the people together. Well, the dilemma is that the King is not a leader. Although we changed to a democratic regime, the King was put on a pedestal. Ideally we should not develop the soul of the nation into hero-worship, but unfortunately we worship the King and the monarchy, which I believe is wrong. Thais do not worship Chavalit as most, unlike myself, think of him as a damn fool. The King and Ho Chi Minh were

69

successful in making the people believe in their worth, but this is the dilemma of the nations.

The Crown Prince of Siam is greatly praised in Thai society, yet he is a swindler, a liar and he treats his wife very badly. I try to point out this and other truths but they do not want me to. This is why our Spirit in Education Movement teaches people historical truths, and I am constantly questioning the effectiveness of my own work. You have to question all the kings, as most of them are dreadful.

PRACHA: In Burma, Sri Lanka and Cambodia there used to be experiments in a kind of Buddhist socialism. I understand these experiments mostly failed. There are also many people in the West who consider them as alternatives to the present system. What happened to these initiatives?

SULAK: It depends how skilful you can be in applying Buddhism. Luckily it failed, or it would be something like the Islamic state. It would have been awful. In Burma U Nu was a wonderful yet weak person and for him Buddhist socialism was a practice of mindfulness. To be fair, many of the politicians were clean and not corrupt but the top leadership was always very weak. Sometimes they felt that affairs of state were too much and they went for a week of retreat, during which time they were unavailable and nothing was decided. This might have been fine if there was someone able to make decisions in their absence. The leader thought of Buddhism with a capital 'B' and wanted to make it a national religion, without realising that a lot of Christian ethnic minorities would object to this. The army used this as a criticism in the 1962 coup. Things would have been different if Aung San had lived and supported this action. They thought that the British parliamentary system with a Buddhist approach would be nice and kind, but it did not work. I think Buddhist socialism must really go deep and you must understand the *sangha* properly.

The same is true in the case of Sri Lanka, where they also wanted to make Buddhism a state religion. Bandaranaike, who wanted to use Buddhist socialism, was assassinated by a monk who said that it was not Buddhist socialism but capitalism. Bandaranaike wanted to make Sri Lanka like Singapore as for him Singapore is a socialist state. He saw nothing wrong with capitalism under the socialist banner. So it is all misunderstood. Again in Cambodia, on an intellectual level Sihanouk wanted to see Buddhist socialism, but on an emotional level he was a playboy with many wives and a passion for drinking wine. He was not in real control of the country. Cambodians, especially patriotic ones, were not really with him, as they saw him as a stooge of French imperialism with his French education and so on. Most of the countries failed because of internal fighting, and none of them had a real group of patriots or intellectuals with spiritual advancement to help them.

PRACHA: I would now like to ask you about alternative world-views and philosophy based on Asian spirituality. Maybe you can start elaborating on your remark that 'if you want to apply Buddhist socialism you have to understand the *sangha* better'. What do you mean by that?

SULAK: In Buddhism the trinity is the Buddha, the *dhamma* and the *sangha*. The *dhamma* is the path of love and understanding. If you understand this you can get rid of selfishness. Without attachment to the self you can get rid of greed, hatred and delusion. You can become enlightened. The Buddha founded the *sangha*, and this can be seen as a form of socialism and a model for an ideal society with social justice, in which each individual would move from being selfish towards being selfless. Those politicians who wanted Buddhist socialism never really examined the *sangha* in this way. They saw it as being for monks and not lay people. Historically, in South-east Asia we have accepted the two-wheel theory, the wheel of the *dhamma* and the wheel of the state. This means you can use the Hindu idea of force and punishment. If you just use the wheel of the *dhamma* then the *sangha* can help to tame you, from being too aggressive and violent. I think it is a mistake with the traditional *sangha* that you cannot include the laity. This is where the Mahayana school of Buddhism changed the idea of the *sangha* into *mahasangha*, which includes laity. If you want Buddhism close to socialism you should co-opt some of the Mahayana concepts of *mahasangha*. This means that the state could really be the *mahasangha* state. You do need to be careful and use skilful means. The state otherwise could become a puritanical state. This is where you could become similar to the Islamic model of the Iranians. With certain compromises it can become a theocracy like Tibet, where they are now experimenting with a new form of democracy. This Tibetan model comes from their own unique roots and is very experimental.

In South-east Asia the state has generally used the Hindu model with Buddhist influence. If you look at politics beyond the state you find an imperfect Buddhist socialist model. Historically in Siam the society model is more or less socialism, with the notable exception of Chiang Mai, where you have priests who were autocratic and Hindu-influenced. I think we should pursue this as we look at the *sangha* as a model. The *wat* (monastery) was at the centre of a kind of socialist or indeed communist society with a very clear ideology, which we have now lost. The ideology of the *sangha* is that we live together harmoniously, respecting each other and all sentient beings for the main purpose of overcoming our selfishness, greed, hate and delusion. To do that you have the *vinaya*, the monastic rules and regulations, which were laid down by the Buddha. If you adhere to these rules, every fortnight you can examine yourself to know whether you have followed the rules. If you break a minor rule you must ask for forgiveness and if you break a major rule you are expelled temporarily. When you are really sorry and have changed your consciousness you are re-admitted. Certain rules are not so significant and expulsion is not mandatory, but confession alone is not sufficient, as you must also get rid of things which made you to break that rule. If you have more than three pieces of rope, you must try to own them jointly or give them away. If you have too much money, you must share with others or give the money away. If you adhere to that strictly, then these rules help you. Every year you must live together for three months and this is a very good experiment as at the end of this time you ask the people in the community to advise you, guide you and criticise you. Then the larger community will imitate and support the *sangha* and the monkhood. The monkhood supports the people through spiritual, political, social, ethical and health guidance. The lay community helps them with material things and so on. Both monks and lay people support environmental balance. If the monkhood lives harmoniously for the three-month period the lay community offers robes. The purpose is to show care, respect and goodwill of the community for the monkhood.

There are many scientists trained in the West who think ordinary people are stupid, but they are not. Unfortunately during the last one hundred years the people have begun to internalise this self-doubt. It is the process of education and the model of development that has made them feel insecure. This is why I feel that if you want to have Buddhist socialism then you must empower people spiritually. You do not go back, but you must bring the ancient roots into modern society. When Bhikkhu Buddhadasa, the monk who reformed Thai Buddhism, ordained this, it was the reason one remained a monk. Once a farmer was asked, 'why do you grow rice?' The farmer replied, 'to offer to the monks'. Growing rice to offer to the monks is a primary motive in traditional Thai society. It is good for cleansing and generosity, although you may have bad motivation and just want to go to heaven. Growing rice was so joyful with song, dance and collective activities, but the first motive was to offer it to the monks and to perpetuate a model of society that we must all imitate. Rice is for us to eat, to offer to the gods and to our neighbours, and what is left over is sold. There is nothing wrong with selling, but it must be the last thing you do. The first concern is spiritual, then cultural and then material survival. Generosity is the main motivation and profit the last concern in this sustainable and ecological way of organising things. This model worked in Siam for hundreds of years and still works in a few villages, although sadly it is dying out. When I was young it was everywhere, and even my mother-in-law, who came from a fairly rich background worked in the fields like anybody else.

PRACHA: You mentioned the model of *mahasangha* as alternative politics. How is this different to the Theravada *sangha*?

SULAK: The Theravada *sangha* is purely for monks and nuns (Bhikkhu and Bhikkhuni); they prefer not to include lay people. The Mahayana *sangha* is more inclusive as it includes lay people as well as monks and nuns. In this day and age lay people should have a bigger role, some monks and nuns could be more spiritual, some monks and nuns could link more with the social and the environmental aspects but not the political. Whereas some lay people may be entirely spiritual, some may link with monks and nuns and some may be involved with social, environmental as well as political aspects. Whatever the form of the *sangha* we must stress the spiritual element, otherwise we become compartmentalised and overly intellectual.

I think being spiritual means linking mind and heart through meditation practice, and this results in inner harmony and planting seeds of peace within. This would be a kind of *samadhi* or *citasikkha* and would help *silasikkha,* which means an ethical norm for each individual, at the same time embracing social justice within society; it could develop into *pannya* or wisdom. Wisdom and understanding have three dimensions. As each individual has special potential to be enlightened or to be awakened, the first step in cultivating wisdom (*sutamayapannya*) could embrace reading, listening, seeing; the second dimension involves imagination, artistic and cultural aspects (*cintamayapannya*). One then moves further to understand the ultimate truth, overcome personal suffering and to really awake by practising deep meditation (*bhavanayamaypannya*).

The more you have the *sangha* established as an alternative from the bottom up, or even 'no up but bottom', as Gandhi said, the more it will be an equal relationship – no centre or periphery. This would be very Buddhist: interrelated; individual to individual – village to village. If a village has special potential to produce something, for example food, medicine or clothing, they could specialise in these areas and exchange in a barter system or through local currency. You can have a co-operative movement, credit union and all kinds of things using less power. There is power, but power should be exercised with compassion. Instead of building jails you use justice and education. Justice is a way to improve the one who has done wrong. Instead of killing the person or putting the person in prison, put him in good surroundings and the *sangha* can help him or her to a personal transformation from greed, hatred and illusion into generosity, compassion and understanding. I think that would be ideal. I am not talking out of the top of my head. This is the whole history of the *sangha*, particularly the Theravada *sangha*.

When you join the *sangha* you join the community. The two main objectives are to train yourself and to train the community to be less selfish. At the same time you have similar rules and regulations to govern the community (*gihivinaya*). Nowadays the *vinaya* has to understand structural violence, the TNCs, the mass media and so on. I think the *sangha* used democratic means such as consensus, majority vote and others. This approach was detailed by the Buddha 2,500 years ago, and much is still relevant; we may have the opportunity to introduce more that is more relevant to the modern world. The whole concept and procedures of the *sangha* are wonderful guidelines, and on top of this is the procedure of the *vinaya*. The Buddha also recommended the seven principles of *aparihaniyadhamma* or *Vajjidhamma*, the conditions for societal welfare, and that of course is the real core for political entities as well as community.

PRACHA: So you think the Theravada *sangha* model is not very different in its basic assumptions from the traditional village community in Asia where a village is also a lay *sangha*?

SULAK: The word *sangha* was never used to include lay people in the Theravada tradition. The traditional village in Buddhist countries was modelled after the bhikkhu *sangha*. If the bhikkhu *sangha* was strong spiritually, strong in their *vinaya* with a harmonious and simple lifestyle, this will influence the villagers. At the same time, both the villages and the *sangha* would collaborate and the village would incorporate some of the noble tradition of the *sangha* into it. Sometimes this is negative and sometimes positive. Animism, shamanism, traditional medicine and so on are mixed. I think we should bear this in mind. Local indigenous wisdom should not be ignored, but at the same time it should not be romanticised. It should be used appropriately in a Buddhist context. We use skilful means – *upaya* – appropriately if we have a deep meditation practice and we know that we use these means not out of greed, hatred, fear or love – we get away from the four prejudices.

You can apply modern technology in the same way, bearing in mind that modern technology on the whole is much more harmful than traditional law and local wisdom, because people believe that the most modern things are the most effective. Most are not appropriate, and modern technology in fact is not neutral. The more advanced and complicated the technology, the more it is beyond our control. It would be in the control of the transnational corporations or some superpower, which I think would be much more harmful; we have to be aware of that. At the same time you cannot ignore or not accept it at all; if you do reject it all, you have to understand the full consequences.

My point is that in the Theravada tradition lay people are treated as too lowly, and the monks are too exalted, and I feel they must now be much more equal. The laity have been playing a larger role in teaching the *dhamma* and meditation. In the old days only monks were literate, but now lay people are more literate, particularly in computers. I feel that the monks should not be left behind, but they must limit their role and not be involved with greed or have anything to do with commercial transactions and money. Unfortunately they do a lot of money transactions these days. Likewise they should not be involved with politics. Unfortunately a lot of monks do that too.

PRACHA: What about the structure above and beyond the village level?

SULAK: Without modern communication and modern technology the villages were mostly left to themselves. There was taxation, and you had to compromise with the state, but the governance was largely influenced by Buddhism. The rulers did not want to oppress the people, and did not mind getting less tax. They wanted to be caring and loved rather than being known as oppressors and disliked by the people. This is why many South-east Asians do not hate the oppressor or the King, whereas in Europe they did. In Europe, with feudalism, the lord of the manor was very oppressive and supported by the church. Farming and taxation were very direct because the land was regarded as more important than the people. In most of South-east Asia, partly because of the Buddhist influence, the people were regarded as more important than the land. There was little need for oppression. That is why in Siam, Cambodia and China the farmers were taxed. I'm not quite sure about Burma. When the Chinese taxed the farmers some of them were excessive but on the whole they had to be fair, because if they taxed too much the farmers could appeal to higher authorities, and the officials were punished and removed.

When Prince Damrong first came to the ministry of the interior, the whole ministry had only about 28 employees. But when he left after about 25 years there were 2–3,000 employees. Now each province has several thousand employees working for the ministry of the interior. I think this is wrong; the state should go back to employing fewer people. Nowadays the state is so bureaucratic and there is so much corruption.

A recent meeting in Brussels on South–North dialogue discussed the mechanisms of state, with all agreeing that the state does not function any more. I think that people are going to resist more and more because they feel that the state controls them rather than the local borough. In Europe the local borough is more related to the people. Although you can talk to your MP they do not have much power. That is why Scotland wants to separate from England and Wales, because they feel Whitehall is so powerful, and now Brussels is going to overrule Whitehall. The European Union is like a new kind of colonialism with the Central Bank of Europe over the Bank of England, and the Bank of England over other banks. Now there is the World Bank, the IMF and the multinational corporations who have control over the union of Europe and so on. More and more people are realising this, and, as I said earlier, 27 per cent of people now want alternatives. 'Alternatives' means decentralisation and autonomy at lower levels. From a Buddhist perspective you must use the *sangha* model. The *sangha* is a real fraternity where you stay together for liberty. Liberty here is not a capitalistic liberty, which suggests that I can say whatever I want and have as my property anything I want. Liberty in the Buddhist sense is liberation from greed, hatred and delusion. There is also harmony and equality, and no formal hierarchy like the state system. The *sangha* model has been working in this country for at least 800 years. Of course we should not go backwards, but we should consider something that worked for so long, which has vanished only during the last century, with the real destruction taking place in the last 40 years.

In Europe they now want to go back, beyond the Renaissance to Saint Francis of Assisi. The bad thing in Europe at that time was that the church became so powerful and stood too close to the feudal powers. In this country the *sangha* was never powerful, and even now when it has been co-opted by the state, it still remains weak. So I think the positive aspects of looking back at our roots carefully and critically outweigh the negative.

PRACHA: Why should monks not be involved in politics?

SULAK: The monks should be shining examples and have less and less to do with greed, hate and illusion. We lay people have no other choice; we have to deal with it and sometimes we are on the losing end. We have to realise that when you are involved with power, you are involved with commercial transactions and with mass communications. Unless you practise deep meditation you can go wrong. The monk's job is to reach the stage of *nirvana*, so they should have less to do with power, money and sex. Monks should not be involved with these things. But of course they could be involved indirectly. If something dreadful happens, monks can make a statement, carry out a symbolic action, or guide in a non-violent way. When King Naresuan wanted to put all the generals to death, the monks would come along to stop him. When the King of Burma and the King of Siam were fighting, sometimes the monks would be the mediators to reconcile the two. That is possible. You see the role the Buddha plays in the fighting between his father's clan, the *sakaya* and his mother's clan, the *koliya.* The idea is reconciliation, raising consciousness or stopping violence. Like the Japanese monks beating their drums all around the world to call for peace and reconciliation. I think that is perfect. I would call that direct political action. It is political. Siding with the poor, creating consciousness among the middle classes. I think this is useful. Again, if people want to have a barter system without money, the monk can help to explain the principle. Involved only indirectly.

PRACHA: In this case you are against the Tibetan model, where the monks are directly involved in the power.

SULAK: The Tibetan model has been developed since the fifth Dalai Lama, and I think that if the Tibetans reclaim their country the monks will have less and less to do with politics. Right now in Tibet the monks have been trained more than lay people, and have been involved with politics. Those involved with politics are wonderful monks. You have to be careful if you have monks who do not have good meditation training, as they could be corrupted by politics easily. The Tibetans know that. His Holiness said that if he had a chance to return to Tibet he would give up being head of state. He would be head of the *sangha*. I am sure that Samdong Rinpoche, who is now the Prime Minister of the Tibetan government in exile, would be the first to prefer to have a long retreat. After a long retreat he may want to help with teaching Sanskrit, Tibetan philosophy or how to apply *Buddhadhamma* into politics. I don't think he wants to be directly involved, but he has no choice because the tradition has been going for the last few hundred years. If they had a choice I think they would do something else.

PRACHA: What about the monks who are part of the parliament, as in Bhutan?

SULAK: I don't think it is appropriate. In Cambodia there is a monks' parliament. The English also have the House of Lords. If it is cultural and not to debate politics then maybe this is possible, but if monks are elected and election involves campaigning, then I think this is very bad for the mind. Once you campaign you have sides; monks should have no sides at all. Among political parties they should not choose the Greens or the reds. They could help the Greens to become more aware of being more moderate. They should not join the existing party.

PRACHA: Before we go further I would like to recall what you said earlier about the theory of the two wheels and the Tibetan model. Do they have their roots in Buddha's teachings? Or did they develop later?

SULAK: If I am not mistaken they do not go back to the Buddha's teachings. The two-wheel theory started from Ashoka, and the Tibetan experiment in theocracy started with the fifth Dalai Lama. However the *sangha* was always very strong and there were many spiritual leaders called lamas. The fifth Dalai

Lama was also the King, so he also had the power to persecute Buddhism. It was the same with the Emperors of China who sometimes severely persecuted Buddhism and sometimes supported Buddhism, according to their own purposes. This is why Buddhism never had a political dimension in China.

PRACHA: Historically speaking, did Buddha ever express or imply the kind of state which is appropriate in the Buddhist ideal?

SULAK: Buddha admired the *sangha* model and used it for his own community. Indeed the word 'sangha' was used for certain states. He saw something wrong with absolute monarchy. So the model is the *vajji* model, which is very similar to his *sangha* model but appropriate for lay people. He said that as long as they do not lead luxurious lives, the *vajji* state will be able to survive. You cannot help admiring Chinese communism when many leaders chose to live a simple life although they were very wicked in many other ways.

I think people must learn to lead simple lives and try to resist consumerism. The monks used wooden pillows, so I think they were on the right track. This is why those of us who have luxurious lives go back to a simple life with a hard bed, no food and no sex on the full-moon and half-moon days. This is also in the Jewish tradition, as every Sabbath they stop everything. I wish I could do this and have one day a week without work or food or even thinking! I think this is essential to recharge your spiritual batteries.

PRACHA: Now let's come to the lay community, the *sangha* community of course is quite well established by the regulations from the Buddha's time. But to come back to the lay *sangha*, one issue would be that we are working and confronting ownership. This new idea of private ownership of wealth becomes part of the exploitation. How does the new *sangha* deal with this concept of ownership?

SULAK: Well you have to go step by step. Ideally, Buddhism is very communistic in this sense. The monks themselves don't practice that, so ideally we should have the monks as a model. If you own, you own the minimum. Ideally the community owns, rather than the individual. At the same time if you cannot attain the ideal state, then if you own something you should own it for subsistence – enough land to till, and so on. Ownership of the river, the canals, the sea should be more open, but of course you must have regulations even for the sea and the rivers and so on. Fish must have enough time for breeding because traditionally it was observed that way. So you have to use local wisdom, traditional wisdom in the world; at the same time you have to use regulations, for example governing the minimum mesh of a fishing-net . I think that it should be done that way.

PRACHA: What about companies running, producing and selling things?

SULAK: Well I think even some TNCs are now changing and becoming involved in social venture networks. Many companies are now learning. Those who are executives feel that they should be more humble, should have more time for meditation and should not exploit themselves merely for profit. They should learn to be harmonious within themselves and with fellow colleagues, and at the same time they should not be exploiting the labour force. They should learn perhaps to have representatives of the labour force on the executive. Similarly, they should not exploit the consumer, the purchaser. In fact some should be invited to have a say in the company. Lastly they should not exploit natural resources. Actually some companies are changing that way, and once they start to change they realise that the company exists not only for greed. If you want to change greed into generosity, a certain amount of profit should be for the poor, not to keep them poor but to empower them. Companies should get together and force the government to change the laws and regulations for those who have private ownership: the more land they have the more they should be taxed; if they have more cars, they should pay more tax. If they use electricity less, and use alternative power instead, they should not only pay less tax but perhaps be given a bonus, which should not be monetary, but rather some form of recognition, and so on – everything should be done outside money, outside power.

PRACHA: So the company itself should function in a kind of *sangha*?

SULAK: Yes, I think everything should be *sangha* and less hierarchical. You may need to have a president of a company, but the presidents can take turns. As Mahatma Gandhi said, any sensible woman could become the President of India; she need not be even literate, as long as she is good. So anyone in the labour movement could also become the president of the company. And of course you have to realise that in the US, presidents of companies sometimes get paid 800 times as much as the labourers. That is not possible in the idea of the *sangha*. Ideally you should be paid because of your needs not because of your position.

PRACHA: What about the idea of scale?

SULAK: Well I think small is beautiful. If you get too big it gets impossible. Companies should be made small. Consider Gandhi's idea of the village republic: all villages are small and link together mostly in a horizontal way. The same with companies, they should be small and linked horizontally. TNCs control almost all fruit in the USA. This is not the way. Food should come from local farming. Let local people cook. It is much more sensible and people would enjoy themselves.

PRACHA: How can we move from the existing structure, with all these TNCs, to the ideal without political power?

SULAK: Well I think we are moving. The NGO meeting in Seattle was the first time the NGOs made themselves known as a global force. Even *Time* magazine and *Newsweek* regarded NGOs seriously for the first time. Since Seattle I think the NGOs have become much more powerful. People like Walden Bello are very well known worldwide. Food First is his small foundation. Of course we need Food First, but I would say Breathing First. Breathing First then Food! Focus on the Global South, another of his organisations, is well known, and he has people like Bumroong Kayotha, who cannot speak English but convenes an NGO farmers' union around the world with the help of an American peace corps. I think this is wonderful and very positive in contrast to Mr Bush and the response to 11 September and Iraq and so on.

For me the negative things will not last, because if they do the whole world will be destroyed. If you look at the positive things NGOs are doing internationally you can see that even the TNCs are now listening. Shell admitted they were killing people in other countries, and I think that they now regret it. Changing. For the first time the World Bank is visiting the poor. The two books came out: *The Voices of the Poor.* Of course you can't change things overnight, but they are changing. I am going to consult the World Bank next month in England, and they put me on the panel, The Sustainable Community for a Global Vision for the 21ˢᵗ Century, and you have people like Swami Aggranivesh representing bonded labour. I think that some people may say this is superficial, but of course if you use skilful means you can change things – if you use the Buddhist concept of 'we all have Buddha nature'. I talked with Mr Mike Moore when he was still in charge of the WTO. He talked with me about globalisation, although he was defending it. I was against globalisation. He talked to various bankers in Morocco and said that it was the first time that he had heard something very meaningful, that we people should not think so much of profit but have more time for nature, more time for meditation, more time for enjoying simplicity in life. So I think the message will get home.

PRACHA: When you talk about your vision, it seems that to move into that vision these organisations like the World Bank and WTO need to dissolve themselves.

SULAK: It depends whether you mean ideal or practically. They won't dissolve easily, but we can show those who hold power in those big organisations what is right and what is ethically possible. For example, if you think the present Thai government of Mr Taksin is a very bad government, we can criticise him and his cabinet. But in some way we should have dialogue with them. At the same time we should have demonstrations to change the unjust things, and if they are smart they will change in order to survive. If they are smarter they may even make the government machinery smaller. In the Buddhist context conditions have to be right. This is the concept of *upaya*. I feel that we can put all these conditions together if we are wise and non-aggressive, and network with like-minded friends. I will be at Canterbury next week; one of the people on my panel is the former president of the IMF. This is the Quaker idea of speaking truth to power.

PRACHA: This means maintaining dialogue with power, and at the same time go on protesting when necessary and building alternatives and networks among ourselves?

SULAK: That's right, but you have to be careful; NGOs could also be corrupted. The good thing is that they cannot be corrupted too much, because they have no power. So I think the way is not to make them powerful in the financial or political sense but in the ethical and spiritual sense. So they will be humble, they will have flexibility like water, which is strong but not solid. And we can do the same with TNCs and governments. If they could become something like NGOs, with less power, they could be more effective. Instead of the state running everything, let each province run things, and in the province, let each community do things, so there would be no concentration of power. I think that would be easier to realise. The American model is a very bad model, one man deciding not only for a country but for the whole world. I think that is wrong.

PRACHA: If we have this kind of diversity, how can we develop a standard of ethical or basic values. How can we make it standard if different NGOs and different communities claim their own truth and morality?

SULAK: I think that if people are trained to be less selfish they will agree. Now we have a common global ethic agreed by most people. It was drafted by Hans Kung in consultation with people like me, Buddhists, Confucians, etc., and came out of the World Parliament of Religions in Chicago. It is obviously not ideal but it is accepted by most people and encompasses the basic five precepts – to abstain from killing, from stealing, from sexual misconduct, from false speech, and from intoxicants causing heedlessness – minus number five because in the West alcohol is part of the culture. The four precepts really deal with the three root causes of suffering – the craving for sensual pleasures, for existence and for non-existence. I think every religion seeks to change the three root causes of suffering into generosity, compassion and wisdom, but they use different languages. I think that will be enough, but we also have the Earth Charter to help you understand the Earth. This of course is done with collaboration from all levels, and Steven Rockefeller is the main key. He happens to be from the Buddhist tradition. Hans Kung is from the Catholic tradition, but it doesn't matter which tradition you come from if you want to do something for the whole world, for the universe. It has to be accepted by most people, and if you do it conscientiously, with less attachment to your own tradition, your tradition may help you to be more skilful. I think that is perfect. I think that will come about. The Universal Declaration of Human Rights is a wonderful document, not perfect, again, but the point is that the governments, the superpowers, are so hypocritical. They say they are for greater human rights but they sell arms more than anybody else. So I think we must learn to be less hypocritical, particularly governments and companies, which of course consist of people like you and me.

PRACHA: Another aspect you have mentioned is social justice. But the concept of social justice is very Western. What does it mean in Buddhism when we say 'social justice'?

SULAK: Whether it is Western or not, social justice is the same. It means you do not exploit yourself and others. In the book *For the Future to be Possible*, edited by Thich Nhat Hanh, it relates to the five precepts. Most of us do not practise the five precepts in the best sense.

PRACHA: What is the difference between the Buddhist concept of social justice and the Western concept of social justice, which is more or less from the socialist tradition?

SULAK: According to the Buddhist tradition, each individual must also examine himself or herself all the time. You must have personal transformation as well as social transformation. I think that the West wants only external transformation. They do not care about the internal development; it is considered to be a task left up to each individual. Of course, if you become socialist in the Western manner you move against spiritual development, as spiritual development is felt to make you tame and without courage. This is why Western political scientists have attacked the Christian model. In Christianity, if they slap your left cheek you give them the right cheek to slap, and the more they are against you the more you offer yourself to them. You go back to the book of Job, and God tries you and punishes you. This model has been condemned and misunderstood in the West, particularly in the Age of Enlightenment.

In Buddhism we also love the enemy, but not in the same way as in Christianity. At the same time, the inner strength required for this will give you courage to be active in society. Of course the ideal society must be entirely non-violent. This is why we have to discuss whether we need the two-wheel theory in lay society. Ultimately we do not need violence, and this is where Gandhi becomes highly important.

PRACHA: By violence do you mean jail, courts and all those related things?

SULAK: Yes! But you may not need that everywhere. In many places there are no jails. This is the case in Guernsey, a small island with a population of around 6,000 people. It is part of the British Isles. In this kind of community people live closely together, although I am not sure how consumerism and joblessness will affect this in the long run. If you set up a society that is socially just, you do not need mechanisms to punish. In the *sangha* model the worst punishment is expulsion from society. We have to think clearly what to do in lay society. Perhaps the idea and perception of a jail could be changed to a place where you go to be educated. Unfortunately re-education is misunderstood, as this was the name given to forms of torture by the communists. The implication is to persuade people to follow a certain ideology, but these schools could be for personal redevelopment and transformation. Nowadays many jails in the West have a Buddhist meditation master to help them, and they benefit from it. We do not even do this in our own jails.

PRACHA: How can we move our society in a certain direction without developing a certain ideology? You mentioned re-education as the method by which the communists tried to convert people into one ideology. If we want to develop a society to go in a particular direction, we also need a frame of reference. This would take more or less the form of an ideology.

SULAK: It depends on what you mean by ideology; you must be careful when using Western words. In our own concepts and tradition the word education is akin to Western 'ideology'. With education, unlike ideology, people must have the liberty to challenge your concept. The Buddha welcomed challenge. *Tribhumipraruang* was a model of Thai ideology, which slightly adapted Buddhism although based on Buddhist principles. Some Mahayana sutras are also distorted, although they have Buddhist roots. In some sutras, written at a later stage, you get situations where two Buddhas are talking. It becomes an ideology because most of the Buddhists in those schools believe in the authenticity of the texts. For those who question these texts, there can still be a good set of guidelines. There are both positive and negative aspects, depending on how you use it. The contribution will be more positive if you use it more skilfully and non-violently. Gandhi used the *Bhagavadgita* on the side of non-violence, and it became very positive.

PRACHA: Again, how does this differ from ideology in the Western sense?

SULAK: In the Western sense you cannot challenge an ideology. This goes back to the whole concept of God whom you have to believe. Once you have decided that God is in three parts, then it has got to be the trinity. If you challenge the trinity, you are condemned. Father Tissa Balasuriya was excommunicated because he said that Mary, the mother of the Lord Jesus, was not a virgin.

In contrast a Buddhist has the liberty not to believe that the Buddha walked seven steps as soon as he was born. A Buddhist can choose whether to believe in the law of *karma* and rebirth. There is no strict ideology, and this is why most modern Thais do not really believe in *karma*. This has led many Thais to become very agnostic, worldly and consumer-oriented, with little spirituality. This is both a strength and a weakness of Buddhism. I do think there is a great danger in not believing. The question is: how do you believe all these things in our modern times? We have to bring the message through reinterpretation rather than ideology. In my understanding you must be able to reinterpret and transform personally as well as transform society.

PRACHA: You say that the state should have less power. If we believe in the Western democratic process, the parliamentary system and presidential democracy, the state is to some extent accountable to the people. What about the multinational corporations?

SULAK: I think there is a move to make multinational corporations accountable. This is why there is a need for new paradigms, because the laws of each state deals only with that state alone. Even international law is archaic, without any laws functioning on several issues. So we need a new paradigm, but I believe the first step is to decentralise. What is realised by few people is that even the worst states are heavily influenced by the West. The word '*rattha*' in Sanskrit and Pali means 'people'. The people have come to live together and then if you go back to Aggannya Sutta you just elect somebody to do something. I think if we go back to Cakkavattisihanattha Sutta, it is clear. But most politicians do not take this seriously because our language is mystical and poetic. The essence is there. But now the political treaties must be entirely rational and logical. Ours is not that way. If you read the Sutra, non-violence is the main thing and the Cakkavatin; the emperor is right because he is righteous and non-violent. If you read the twelve points of the Cakkavattisihanattha Sutta it is all about non-violence. The King of Siam was supposed to be a Cakkavatin whereas the King of Chiang Mai is Pradesh Raja. This is why they have autonomy and we do not interfere. Likewise, the Pradesh Raja of Chiang Mai did not interfere with the villagers. If you use the Cakkavatin model then you may have international law where the Cakkavatin can deal with the multinational corporations. But ideally we should dismantle or dissolve the multinational corporations. It would not work otherwise. You can have a united Europe or united Asia, provided they have no seat of power. The European Parliament is a good model, as it has no real power, although it can side with the people and sue the state. However, many people do not like the power in Brussels, especially since they have set up the European Central Bank, which may cause the whole European Union to malfunction under one currency. We must remember that this could be very dangerous, and that these people work closely with the World Bank and the IMF. I believe that all these bodies should be dismantled and decentralised. We should also disenfranchise the multinational corporations. Many people will criticise this as going backwards, but I believe they have no moral legitimacy. We must dismantle the multinationals in the same way people dismantled the Soviet Union.

PRACHA: People like Chandra Muzzafar used to see the state as one of the evils of modern times, although later on when he saw the coming of neoliberalisation and multinationals, he thought the state had a function: to counter the multinationals.

SULAK: Well, you play into the devil's hands. I have been at many meetings with people who want to make the state stronger in order to counter the multinationals. I do not agree with this view, although I concede that if you use it as a skilful tactic then it may be possible. But it would not end there. I think every seat of power should have less and less power. Giving the state more power is not the non-violent way. I feel that we must make each individual strong, with a good concept of community, and each community should have a good concept of other communities. Communities should relate, in what I call fraternity and equality. There should be no nation-states, no rich and no barrier due to languages and ethnic differences. The Thais should regard the Burmese as brothers and sisters, and we must protect their well-being as much as we protect our own. At Kanchanaburi, on the Burmese border, the local people should protect the Burmese and it is the same in north-east Siam with the Khmer and the Laos, we should consider them as our brothers and sisters. This is the approach I advocate and I think we will win.

PRACHA: You mentioned finding our 'roots' and this is very much a catchword now. What do you mean by that, especially from a Buddhist perspective?

SULAK: Many people in the North are now agreeing that we should look back to our roots. This is why American Indians and indigenous people such as the Karen and the Kachin are very important. We have been taught to look down upon them as primitive and uneducated, which I think is wrong; but while we should understand our roots clearly, we should not idealise indigenous cultures. We are interested in the future. I believe that our roots generally have more positive than negative elements and we should acknowledge this truth. If this is not true, how have we lasted so long?

PRACHA: When you talk about back to the roots, what are the positive means that will allow us to move into the future?

SULAK: I mentioned the *sangha* as our best model and, to put it into the Thai context, the community is based around the *wat* (monastery) and the *ban* (village). Everyone is a relative and you call everyone *pii* or *nong* (younger and elder sibling). *Pii* and *nong* apply not only to human beings; even the animals and the trees are our brothers and sisters. It is very important that people live with trees and rivers in this way, as whatever one does becomes meaningful. Everything is poetic and everyone understands what you are doing. Work becomes joyful and you also realise the beyond-this-world aspect of the truth, to worship the Buddha and the *dhamma*. Life is approached holistically, with meaning and joyfulness at the worldly, other-worldly, sensual, and less sensual levels. When you lose this, life becomes fragmented. Our lives can become more meaningful by learning simple and relevant *dhamma*.

Dhamma alone is not enough. If we want to move towards *dhammic* socialism there must be fewer private cars and more public transport. We should decapitalise Bangkok and send the King to Ayuthaya. The government can go to the provinces. In 40 years, the ministry of the interior should have only 48 staff. I do not consider it a dream. We have to go back and produce only what is essential. As Gandhi said, you produce your own clothes, food, medicine and so on. This is simplicity, and once you have that there's something beautiful you can produce. This means more home-made and less machine-made. Ultimately we may even throw away most of the machines.

PRACHA: When you use the word 'holistic' what do you mean?

SULAK: Not fragmented. We are trained to be fragmented and we remain so. My daughter is going to a camp entirely for mathematics. She will deal only with one section of mathematics and she is going to be very clever at that, but she has no other ideas. I was at a science and technology seminar in Chiang Mai. All those scientists know only their own particular area. 'Holistic' means that you understand yourself and you are not selfish. You are selfless, know who you are and understand your community. You love yourself and other beings and recognise that we are interrelated and everything has meaning. A fragmented perspective would consider a sheet of paper as only for writing on and then to be thrown away. With a holistic view you see the paper, tree, rain and sun as part of the universe. Everything is important.

PRACHA: Can we claim that all Asian cultural traditions are holistic at large?

SULAK: All cultures, until the Age of Enlightenment in Europe, were the same. Saint Francis of Assisi called the sun his brother and the moon his sister. It is the same vision of the world. When the Pope becomes an emperor at the Vatican then of course the church becomes less and less holistic. That is how the church destroyed itself in Europe. The new church leaders are the scientists and the media communicators who serve the multinational corporations. It is not holistic, because they only want you to buy. They see people as consumers or employees. In a holistic view, buying and earning money are the least important things. Being holistic is like the farmer who wants to cultivate rice just to give to the monks. Then he would feed himself and his family. Later he would also offer rice to his friends. The monkhood is an ideal in this society, for instance, and your own son could join the monkhood and may become the enlightened one. If not the enlightened one, he will at least do less evil, or he may do more good. It is very important to support this kind of idealism. Supporting all sentient beings as well as yourself is holistic. Most modern lifestyles are very fragmented.

PRACHA: Regarding what you have said about Saint Francis of Assisi and his holistic view, you consider the moon, sun, trees as our brothers and sisters. It then comes to the point of how much we can make use of nature for our own benefit. In order to survive we have to make use of the nature around us. What is the criterion for making a decision as to what is appropriate and what is right?

SULAK: This is why I said that you have to go back to the roots. The Karen and the Kachin have lived in the mountains for many generations and they do not deplete the mountains. Of course they take some of the trees and some fish, but they never take all the fish or cut down all the trees. They preserve the trees. When you turn to your roots you find out the ancient and local wisdom. This is what Helena Norberg-Hodge tried to tell people about Ladakh. If we miss this point we become more and more fragmented. There is also destruction on the large scale. If you live a simple lifestyle, the scale of destruction is also small.

A monk sees social justice as not damaging the land or cutting down the trees. You have to accept that only a certain group of people can do that, but we can follow their example and try not to kill or upset the land or at least be aware of it and do it as little as possible. If you do not destroy the land too much, then nature will ensure that from seeds the trees will be reborn. This is why Rabindranath Tagore said that the whole of Indian civilisation rests on the forests and the rivers, whereas modern Western civilisation is based entirely on brick and stone. Unfortunately countries like Siam are now opting for the Western model.

PRACHA: What is the philosophy behind this attitude towards nature, taking just enough to survive.

SULAK: You have to go through the whole ideology. If you merge with nature that is holistic. The Taoists are harmonious with nature and the Hindus say that you join Brahman. In Buddhism you go beyond this, but of course you are with nature. I think the truth is something beyond, but while you are here you must create harmony without exploitation. If you have to exploit, there should be less and less exploitation. I think it is very clear once you accept this.

PRACHA: From this perspective of 'holistic' and 'harmonious' how do you see industrial civilisation?

SULAK: Industrial civilisation destroyed all these visions of holistic development, as Kirkpatrick Sale said very clearly in *Rebels Against the Future*. In the name of advancement and technology, the industrial revolution has destroyed people and the environment. Yet people have been conditioned to worship advanced technology. Of course it brings some benefits, but it does more harm than good. It also concentrates power into very few hands. It used to be just the British industrialists, then it was the empire, and now it is the multinational corporations. The most advanced technology is military technology, and this is where the computer came from. That is why things like e-mail are so cheap, as they have something much more advanced that we do not know about. It is very dangerous, and, as Sale said, within two decades most of the middle class will have no jobs. This is true! If you do not have a holistic approach you get the money out with your credit card from any machine. It is convenient, but how many have become jobless because of that machine? I never use a credit card and ideally we should not use banks but start our own local currencies that may not be based on money.

In Siam we did not use money until the reign of Rama IV [1851–68]. The ruling elite considered this as very backward. I, however, believe that money shows oppression, as it removes you further from a holistic society. Food is real, fish is real, rice is real but money is not real. Nowadays you are brainwashed by being told that with one credit card in your pocket you can go anywhere. Rich people do not even keep accounts, they just look at a computer to see how much money they have. If you think holistically, the more money you have the more you deprive other people. If you overeat it is bad both for your health and for those who do not have enough to eat. With food you cannot eat much more than three or four meals a day but with money there is no limit. People are not stupid, but they have been fooled. I think this is where right education can help, particularly teaching people alternatives in the North and the South. I am pretty sure we can help people realise this, perhaps sooner rather than later.

PRACHA: You also mentioned that we should not produce more than what is essential. This is very similar to Samdong Rinpoche's ideas. Surplus is evil.

How can civilisation function without a surplus? People like you and me, intellectuals, live on the labour of others, who produce more than they need.

SULAK: You have to realise that monks and lay people are different. For the monks the basic need is only the four requisites. Lay people can have a bit more than the four requisites, which is the minimum. But we need also to set the maximum. I mean, for example, ice cream is a luxury, but it is acceptable, provided you don't use that chemical stuff, and don't exploit the cows, and so on. My friends in Holland produce ice cream with a wonderful result of respect. I think that is the sort of ice cream we should have. Some perfume is OK; of course monks don't use it; but for lay people it should not entail killing animals. If you want to eat meat it is OK, but it should be kept to a minimum, and no cows or pigs should be slaughtered in a cruel way. We can learn from the Tibetans. They ask for forgiveness. In Bali, when they kill chickens, they ask permission from the chicken, and the chickens enjoy themselves while being raised. So I think the whole concept would change if you do not worship endless surplus, and settle for what is enough. You have something extra, but not too much.

PRACHA: Can we return to the concept of power, as now we are talking about politics related to power? What is the difference between this alternative concept of power and the power that the modern state uses now?

SULAK: In the *sangha* model the power must be non-violent and based on *dhamma* and justice. The Dalai Lama and the Thai monk Buddhadasa had power because we respected them. They are spiritual beings with real humility and compassion. In the future we need more like them, among lay people too. Parliament needs people like them, who do not tell lies and who keep the five precepts. The assembly should hold together and reduce individual selfishness. They are all so cunning that this seems impossible. The whole process is so corrupt and many politicians are backed by the multinationals.

PRACHA: In your view what are the basic characteristics of a good and sustainable society?

SULAK: I have already mentioned the *sangha* as a model, and I think it must be examined more seriously. Traditionally the *sangha* is a minimum of four celibate people, and we could start small, with four families. The maximum requirement is twenty, and these members can do everything, including re-admitting an expelled monk. In a *sangha* each of us must take a strong stand, that we are together in order to transform ourselves into better human beings. Buddhists use this to reduce selfish desire and work towards selflessness, and I do not think many would reject this. The *sangha* has very clear rules and regulations that we can study and adapt appropriately for lay people in the coming years. If we go back to the roots, we can see that this has been used in this country effectively for centuries, and is still used in some areas, although it has been widely destroyed in the last few decades. The key ideas in my concept is the *ban*, the *wat* and the *sangha*. After ordination you become a learned person; this should be open to women too. I think we need that in order not to have a male chauvinistic approach.

So the simple life means contentment in oneself and in society, and each society would be unique. One village may be expert on traditional medicine and another on weaving. Every village would have the means to be self-reliant. These would be basic knowledge on how to produce medicine, how to cultivate rice, how to weave and how to build a house. Some may have more artists, but this is not essential to livelihood, rather an extension of life for beauty. When I was a novice monk there was a lay leader living in the temple, and people paid him to mend watches and shoes. These items were never thrown away. If each village has someone like that, we can reduce the need for machines, many of which are not essential. That is what *Resurgence* magazine is proposing with decentralisation, and what Maurice Ash was talking about when he said that the county should be the biggest level of government.

PRACHA: So this is the *meuang*, the small town.

SULAK: This is the *meuang*, although updated, and without ruling or hereditary power. These days the *meuang* must be democratic, and only for one hundred *ban*, each with a representative to discuss business and so on. If necessary you can have a big hall where all the *ban* can get together every so often, perhaps on market day. This is just like the boroughs in Great Britain. When I went to Lampeter University in Wales they had market day every Tuesday and the cinema twice a week, and that was enough. Television should be localised or perhaps made by the *ban*, or at most the *meuang*. There should be no multinational corporations running television and no advertisements at all.

PRACHA: What about structure beyond the *meuang* level?

SULAK: It is the same. If they have one hundred villages for a *meuang*, then one hundred *meuang* could be a state or a province. This could become regional and we could take turns in electing somebody who has no power. Someone like the Dalai Lama could become the head, as he is a nice person, and in a crisis you would consult him. As Costa Rica is attempting, we should do away with the army. Ideally you would not even need a police force. The police force in Siam is less than 100 years old, and originally all the heads of police were Danish or English with most members imported from India.

PRACHA: If you do not have police and an army how do you deal with the criminals and the mafia?

SULAK: Once communities are strong enough they will manage. If you curtail the multinational corporations, the drugs business will decrease. That illegal drugs are the most profitable trade shows up the hypocrisy of the whole profit system, in which the drug mafias need the support of corrupt politicians, which is why the mafias need to support the politicians. The whole drug business should be an open market. In Holland they are much more effective now in dealing with Aids, but the European market will not look at Holland because of prejudice.

PRACHA: If we have all these small *ban* communities each developing their uniqueness, would there be a chance that they would develop some kind of narrow tribalism, and feel superior to the next *ban* in a way that could cause quarrels?

SULAK: There may be a little tribalism. If you look back, the Mon refused to pay the Burmese and the Burmese refused to pay the Mon, but on the whole they lived together. The wars were always organised by the King and never the people. In Kashmir before the British came, there was no trouble: the Muslims, Hindus and Sikhs lived together peacefully. It is the same in Siam, with the Muslims and Buddhists. At the Thai–Malaysian border area Thais speak Malay and Malays speak Thai. In Kashmir and other indigenous areas most people speak three or four languages quite naturally. This ability to speak many languages is lost when the state gains control and promotes only one language. Now, because of the multinational corporations and the arms trade, they are all fighting. They do not seem to realise why, although they seem to think it is a religious and ethnic conflict.

The point here is that living should always have a dimension of self-improvement, rather than selfishness and self-centredness. In Siam, this has been killed only in the last few decades. Imagine if there was contentment everywhere and nobody showing off their riches. Other members of my family are very wealthy but they do not display it. Their silver is tucked away in cupboards and they use it when need be, but you can come and borrow it. This way of thinking is ideal for the community. The English word is 'trustees', and the Christian concept is trust. We look after things for future generations, and we inherit from past generations, so we have respect for past generations and this is why there is ancestor-worship. When you worship rightly it means you are grateful to your ancestors and you care for future generations. Nowadays we want to use everything for this generation and this is wrong.

PRACHA: As we definitely cannot go back to the past, can we take some values from the past and make them appropriate for now and the future? If we do this, will the standard of living change, as people always want more comfortable things?

SULAK: You have to educate people to control their wants, as they will adopt consumerism in wanting more and more comfortable things. I use air-conditioning because of this tape recording and for foreign guests. I do not use air-conditioning in my room. The way we live should be simpler rather than more comfortable. You have to look to the tribal, go back to the roots and see how they survived. Generally, simple food and simple living is good for your health, while comfort and excess is bad for you. If you drive a car all the time, in 20 years you will hardly be able to walk. In Europe, bicycles and walking are gaining popularity, and even in Chiang Mai bicycles are more popular. We could do this in Bangkok if we put our minds to it. We have to realise that if you want a sustainable society it must be a just society. If everyone has cars the whole damned world will be destroyed. What will happen in two decades when there is no oil? England has now run out of coal, and soon all the gas and oil will be gone. Now they want nuclear energy, but this is all wrong. Solar energy and wind energy, which are renewable, are much more appropriate and sustainable. They should charge people much more for using non-renewable resources. People should also be charged 1,000 baht [about £15] per television programme to encourage them to switch off. It makes you feel powerful to have the television on all the time, although you may not properly watch. You switch on with a remote control, and people do not realise that technology has taken the place of superstition. Technology serves superstition and science serves technology; this means that science serves superstition.

So science should be something very clear, to which everyone should have access, in the sense of having information to be able to decide, not only by standard Western logical thinking, but also through emotion and meditation. People should know how to become less selfish and how to restructure their consciousness. I think every individual and community has the potential to do this. The need is to travel less and spend more time with nature.

PRACHA: In this vision of a new society, is there a function for the state and parliament, and so on?

SULAK: No. The point is that I do not want to be a Plato, who planned everything for people. I feel that once people decentralise, you can have village republics, a hundred *bans* to a *meuang*, a hundred *meuang* to a borough or whatever, and they can decide for themselves what is essential. I think it is wrong for philosophers to plan everything when people can decide themselves. The people in Chiang Mai may want to collaborate more closely with the Burmese than the Bangkokians do. Once you have no nation-state, the rules change, whereas now you fight over prestige. If the Shan want to join the Thai, there will be a fight. When there is no economic or national interest, there is no reason why northern Malaysia cannot separate from Malaysia, or Kachin State or any other ethnic group from the rest of Burma. In Siam we spend 1 per cent of the national budget on arms. This is very dangerous, as it supports the arms merchants and the politicians who are linked with the multinational corporations. The UN declaration of the Decade of Non-violence could be helpful. We could begin with a reduction of arms. It is going to be hard, but I think it is possible, since people are beginning to realise and understand that violent structures do not work.

PRACHA: It seems we have a clear picture of what we want to achieve. Now the point is how to go from here to there. What are the steps?

SULAK: For us the centenary of Pridi Banomyong's birth is relevant. It is an opportunity to bring his ideas into the contemporary situation. My next step is Buddhadasa's centenary. These people who are no longer with us are important because of their relevance to our lives. We should keep their ideas alive. The Spirit in Education movement should build upon the grass-roots leadership training we have done with the ethnic groups from Burma. These three-month courses include raising awareness of the negative effects of development, techniques for sustainable community initiatives and exposure trips to NGOs tackling issues such as poverty, Aids and pollution. We should run similar courses for the Thais, targeted at all levels. I think it is very important to start by empowering the poorest and get them to sustain their empowerment so that the *sangha* could be established. We should think regionally and involve people from Laos and Cambodia, perhaps running joint projects. We should invite Buddhist monks and nuns and lay people to this kind of training to work out how to revitalise the *sangha* at community level. We can use the concept of *sangha* and include praying, meditating, eating and learning together as integral parts of the training. It is not surprising that the seeds of vision can come from only 30 people. We need more experimental communities like Wongsanit ashram, where spiritual practice and community living are part of everyday life. We should not let frustration and failure put us off. We should link with alternative colleges like Schumacher and Naropa, and think about alternative media. Perhaps we can spread our ideas through a television or radio network as well as publications.

PRACHA: In your view, who will be the main agent of change?

SULAK: All of us. I went to a meeting in Oregon of the US Foundation. US not meaning the United States: US meaning us. Usually people point a finger at Chavalit, the Prime Minister of Thailand when the economy crashed in 1997, but three fingers point back to us. We can all do it. We start with ourselves and our friends who understand. Then those who do not understand and think we are mad will eventually start to see the light. You start with five, then ten and then one hundred. Like Buddhadasa and Pridi, each village can have their own heroes for the *sangha* to celebrate. Meditation is not something to be too serious about, and the *wat* should be a real community place full of joy and liveliness, which is what it used to be, and still is in many parts of Burma. The *wat* could be a useful place where old people live and young people have as a playground. We should bring this joyful community centre back to life, and we can start with just a few people.

PRACHA: We talk a lot about the grass roots. Do you feel that they can play a role in the future, or be at the forefront of the movement?

SULAK: The grass-roots are essential because they still live with nature. All those who have been removed from nature must learn from those who live with nature. Those who live with nature have been persecuted very severely and have managed to survive, so we must give them credit for this. Like all of us, they may have something nasty inside, and we have to help them to change that. We are all alienated, and I think if you live close to nature you are less alienated than if you live in an air-conditioned room where you have no contact with nature. The people at the grass roots are so important as they are confronting suffering directly. The middle classes are quite unconsciously influenced by the media and consumerism. They are kept away from suffering. This is why we have to go back to confront suffering. You have to relate to the causes of suffering, which are authoritarianism and egoism. I think they can learn from us, and we can also learn from them. I think it is very important that we do not teach each other but learn from each other. Once they realise this truth it will be more useful. I do not want them to think that Sulak knows all the answers. If I live with them for a few days they will learn that Sulak does not know anything, not even how to cook.

It would be good for us to be humble enough to learn how to cook and cultivate rice from them. The best student goes to Harvard; the best student must go to Pak Moon Dam. I think this is where Mao Zedong is right in his concept, but he misused it. He had never encouraged any real democratic participation. Sending urban people to the countryside was a wonderful idea, but he thought it up by himself without any consultation. The poor people in the villages suffered because the people from the city had no idea how to do anything, and the villagers had to feed them even when they themselves were starving. The idea is good, but the idea must be challenged and debated, and the villagers must also agree to have you. Mao had many brilliant ideas, but mostly for his own survival. The Cultural Revolution, when millions died, was designed to get rid of his competitors. We cannot afford that. It must not be violent, it must be only through non-violent means.

PRACHA: What about the local NGO movement, which seems to be dying, and those from abroad are also disappearing?

SULAK: Once we train them they can survive. The NGOs will be challenged if they remain middle-class, and find that deep down they want to opt for consumerism and social security, with land and a house somewhere. This is more hypocritical than the people in big organisations. If the NGOs are really working well with the people you do not have to worry about social security. The monkhood does not think of personal and national security, as they know that the people will support them. If the NGOs have a simple lifestyle they will be respected. That is why Ajarn Cha asks, 'how can I take a car from those people who do not even have a cart?' If the NGOs can understand and learn from that they will not die, and even if they die they will be resurrected.

Self-sufficiency is also important. Ariyaratne in Sri Lanka has preached self-sufficiency since 1956, and it took him 40 years to be self-sufficient. Anyway you cannot blame him because money keeps coming and he kept receiving prizes. This is another model we should look at, and its strengths and weaknesses. I find there are more weaknesses than strengths. I may be being unkind. We should also look at the Gandhian model, which I think has more strengths than weaknesses.

PRACHA: I think the Gandhian movement is dying, even though it was very successful once all over India.

SULAK: They still survive as a community, and it has become a *wat* in our sense now, with Gandhi as a Buddha. They still survive eating vegetarian food, most of them not using Western medicine, and so on. The Gandhian movement is not dead, but of course we are all dying. In the Buddha's instructions, as soon as you are born you begin to die. I may die tomorrow or next year or in a few years. Our job is that, if we think anything is worthy as a model, we should do what we can. I think this will be one resolution at our Alternatives to Consumerism meeting. We must put our heads and hearts together as we need to survive. Every story has its successes and failures, strengths and weaknesses. Ajarn Buddhadasa's model also has many weaknesses. We must learn from other communities too. I take Gandhi very seriously. In my view, if one applies Gandhi's concepts skilfully it is possible to challenge the transnational corporations and consumerism in a similar way as Gandhi challenged the British Empire. I want to share this message, but I have not worked out quite how to do it yet.

PRACHA: In my opinion, fighting the British is easier than fighting the multinational corporations.

SULAK: Well! Fifty years ago nobody thought that Gandhi could do it, but he did it with strong resolution and righteous conviction. When the British wanted to fight in the world war, he withdrew; he would not fight. If your opponent is so weak, you must bow to your opponent. I think we should do the same with the multinational corporations, as we must realise that many people working within the multinational corporations and the World Bank are with us. So I think we have some very good friends, although you have to draw certain norms so that they could join us. Ashis Nandy's book *Intimate Enemy* is wonderful. Gandhi gained success because on certain issues he did appeal greatly to the common British people, and this is very important. It is possible to succeed against the multinationals with determined resolve and commitment.

PRACHA: Is there anything to do at the upper structural level?

SULAK: The upper structure will change when the grass roots change. If the middle class joins the grass roots, the upper structure will either change or move out to live in another country. They were ready to go when they were threatened by communism. The Thai royal family is now sending a lot of its money abroad. Either they should change or they will not last in this country. In the long run you must educate upper-class people to be clever for their own survival. Most politicians have no understanding of this, so we have to educate other people to understand.

PRACHA: What do you think about the Green parties in Europe, which are trying to make certain changes at the grass roots and at the upper level as well?

SULAK: There is a need for a lot of rethinking and synchronisation within the Greens. They fight amongst themselves and accept the present structure too much. That is why I feel that the Buddhist approach is right. You must restructure your consciousness. Petra Kelly was a wonderful person, but she felt that only she had all the answers. That is why she got killed or she shot herself, I do not know. You burn out. If you want to look for alternatives you must not exhaust yourself. You must sleep soundly and have *sanuk* [fun]. *Sanuk* is very important; if you do anything without *sanuk*, it is not worth doing. People can learn this from the Thais but these days the Thais themselves are losing their *sanuk*. In the old days even a cremation was *sanuk*. When it is not *sanuk* you wonder why you do anything without enjoying what you do.

PRACHA: In your vision you talk about a situation when the nation-state is no longer needed. Now the nation-state everywhere is very strong. When will nation-states gets weaker? How do you see the process of change?

SULAK: The process of change is like that for the individual, you change greed into generosity, hatred into compassion, illusion into wisdom. The present nation-states are the embodiment of *dosa* [anger]. TNCs are greed. If you look at Europe, the nation-state has become less and less important. The EU is replacing it.

PRACHA: What if the EU becomes a super-nation-state?

SULAK: You have to be careful. Right now, the EU's first interest is greed, not power; they will not fight among themselves any more.

PRACHA: They will fight with other blocs?

SULAK: If need be, this is where the British and the Germans are different. The British want to link with the Americans to fight the Arabs; the Germans don't want to because they were defeated twice in the world wars. They remember that. The Germans are afraid at this stage that they will be regarded more as greedy. This is where NGOs can help, and NGOs here include the churches. The church has become mostly useless or ceremonial, or not up-to-date enough. The church should have a role in politics and economics, like the *sangha*, an indirect role. A spiritual guardian giving ethical input, as Bacon said of the British monarchy. The church has the right to warn, the right to encourage, the right to criticise; I think we need that. This is one model to look at. We can use this model for change.

Of course the nation-state is only 200 years old. In the case of the Thai kingdom it is less than 150 years old. How we functioned previously was not ideal, but at least there was no nation-state. The King of Ayuttaya had more power than the other city states, but there was not just one. The people lived their own lives, and this is where the *sangha* comes into it, the church, the temple. But of course we have not empowered the people enough politically, although the people were empowered spiritually and culturally.

I gave you one example in the European community, and Thailand in the past. Modern Thailand has Mr Taksin, who feels he is very strong because he uses the democratic model and abuses it with money and power. If we built enough strength at the grass-roots, in the middle classes, in the NGOs; if the *sangha* becomes stronger and the church is stronger I don't think Taksin can challenge us. I even say, if he starts the gas pipeline in Songkla that will be the end, as we can rally all the Muslims around the world against him morally. So I feel that the state and so on is ultimately a moral relationship. To go beyond that you need spiritual guidelines. We are now working with the ethnic nationals in Burma, and we can do similarly with the Khmers and the Vietnamese. I think that will make the grass roots strong. This is why I think the dictatorship in Burma will melt. The other model is Ajarn Pridi's model of the league of South-east Asian nations, although his vision was that the govern-

Sulak Sivaraksa

ments represent them. I would like to see a league of South-east Asian nations represented by the NGOS. I think if we can do that without power, without money, it is really a moral force. With spiritual guidelines I think it would be something people look up to.

We can also help the parliamentarian. That is why I am involved with E-parliament, to link the parliamentarians to be aware beyond the nation-state. To care for environmental issues, social justice issues, human rights issues without boundaries. I think the prestige of parliament will come back through E-parliament. Jacob Van Uxell is trying to implement the future World Council, which is the dream of His Holiness the Dalai Lama. If you really care for the future of the world and for the generations to come, the nation-state will become much less important. That is why His Holiness is willing to go back to Tibet. Tibet does not want to become a nation-state; Tibet just wants to be an entity free of violence, where you have environmental balance, spiritual growth. I think that is why they are talking to the Chinese now. I think it is possible.

PRACHA: Can the weakening of the nation-state happen in one country before every country?

SULAK: I think you can see that Indonesia is not a real country. India is not a real country, India came into being because of the British, Indonesia because of the Dutch, and the USA used to be two countries, north and south, and Lincoln forced them together because it helped the Yankees. I feel that states like California or Texas could be countries. The Texans would love to have their own country. So I think smaller is better.

PRACHA: When you talk about the dissolving of the nation-state, can we compare it to the reducing of greed, hatred and delusion? It is workable for the individual. For example, if you want to reduce your greed, your hatred, you have to develop your *sila* and you meditate and get wisdom, because you see things as impermanent. That, for an individual, is quite clear. How can this relate to a nation-state?

SULAK: This is where the social venture network is a good model. They don't want to have maximum profit; they want to have maximum spiritual growth. Something for themselves and for their colleagues and their buyers, and they also want more environmental balance. They know that this is for survival for seven generations, they know that. There was a meeting where His Holiness the Dalai Lama, the former Dutch prime minister, and an adviser of Mr Tony Blair were present. That meeting made it clear that we have to change competition into compassion. Some people are ready for that, so people are not all that stupid. Of course a lot of the mainstream is not changing quickly, but if you have, as Margaret Mead said, a small group of people changing, they will follow.

In the USA there are more people meditating than in our country. Why? Because they suffer much more and they have been under the illusion of the mass media much longer than we have. They are under the delusion of materialism much more than we are; that is why they are sick. Of course, by seeking change they may be trapped by spiritual materialism. As Trungpa Rinpoche said, we have to grow beyond this. I see human potential in changing things, because the nation-state is only 200 years old. If Napoleon had had his way, there would be no nation-state, but he failed, and Bismark had *his* way, and that is how Germany came into being. In England the English fought to subjugate the Welsh and the Scots, and now even the Scottish and Welsh are freeing themselves. Not much, but better than before. Northern Ireland also wants to be free. I see that in the Buddhist context everything is impermanent, but when you confront *dukkha*, when you understand the sense of lack, then you overcome that and you see yourself as ultimately *sunyata.*

PRACHA: How can a country, a collective like Thai society, understand the sense of lack?

SULAK: Well, you have to teach them. The Thais right now don't understand that, despite the fact that they claim to be Buddhist, because the Thais don't confront the truth. We are hypocritical; we think our history is great; we think King Chulalongkorn is great, but he is the one who destroyed our culture. He centralised; he used education to brainwash people and force to control people, yet he is seen as the best king in history. You have to get things right first. Get the truth first. That is why the four noble truths teach the understanding of suffering. You can understand suffering when you understand the truth. Our mass media are full of lies. You have newspapers with full-page articles on monks involved with superstition, but none on monks who really deal with the *dhamma.*

PRACHA: When we start on the path to reduce our greed, hatred and delusion, do we start with the right view for individuals? How can a collective change their view to a right view?

SULAK: Well, once they see they are in the wrong view, I think they will change, and this is why David Loy's perceptions of the West, in his *A Buddhist History of the West: Studies in Lack*, are wonderful. We can have the Buddhist perception of success, which encompasses the balance of the whole environment. What is regarded as successful now is destroying all indigenous people. Telling lies is regarded as successful. As I mentioned, even the World Bank is now listening to the poor. Once people listen to the suffering ones, I think they will change.

3 | Helena Norberg-Hodge

Helena was born in 1946 and grew up in Sweden. She studied philosophy, psychology and art history at universities in Austria, Germany and the UK, then went on to study under Noam Chomsky as a linguist at MIT. She speaks seven languages, including Ladakhi.

In 1975 in Ladakh, a high-altitude region in the far north of India, she started the Ladakh Project, which became the International Society for Ecology and Culture (ISEC) in 1991. Its mission is to alert people in both the North and the South to the threat that economic globalisation poses to traditional communities, democracy and the natural world, and actively to promote economic localisation. ISEC has initiated many international campaigns and grass-roots initiatives, as well as producing many useful educational tools for conscientising people in all parts of society. She travels extensively around the world to give talks and participate in discussions on these issues. Helena is a passionate speaker and activist, with a warm personality, and is a key player in raising awareness of the root causes and effects of globalisation. She supported the Ladakhi people in organising the successful Ecological Development Group (LEDeG), and together with them she received the Right Livelihood Award in 1986.

Helena is one of the very few thinkers and activists in the international arena who work against mainstream modernisation and globalisation and for the empowering of local communities. She has a deep understanding of Asian cultures, especially those related to Buddhism. Her decades of first-hand experience in Ladakh have given her deep conviction about, confidence in, and great sympathy for traditional communities all over the world.

Her book *Ancient Futures: Learning from Ladakh*, an inspirational classic, is very popular among indigenous people around the world, as they can clearly identify the sensitively shown negative aspects of development. The book and/or the video have been translated into at least 42 languages. ISEC's recent focus has been on mobilising communities to strengthen local food systems. They have developed an educational tool-kit – including the book *Bringing the Food Economy Home* – which outlines their enormous social, ecological and economic benefits.

The Interview

HELENA NORBERG-HODGE: There is something inherently wrong with having one economic system dominating the entire world. This highly centralised global economy is attempting to plan, structure, and assimilate every economic system on the planet. It is completely unsustainable, particularly in social terms, because it is leading to growing fundamentalism and divisiveness as it robs people of their ability to govern themselves.

SULAK SIVARAKSA: What about the Greens? Are they an alternative or not?

HELENA: The Greens have made an attempt to provide an alternative, but today they are considerably weakened in Europe as a movement. This is partly due to their failure to stick to their original policy, which was to say that their

Helena Norberg-Hodge

political direction was neither left nor right but 'straight ahead'. It is my belief that this direction should involve a respect for ancient and non-Western traditions. This was the reason that I chose to call my book *Ancient Futures*. Unfortunately, the Western Greens have been caught up in a Eurocentric industrial world-view. But I wouldn't want to criticise all the Greens, as I do feel they are making one of the more hopeful attempts to work for change in the West.

At present the economic system in the West is leading towards a rapid increase in unemployment, poverty and environmental breakdown. I think it is vital that all movements integrate social and environmental issues into a more holistic and spiritually founded understanding.

SULAK: I feel that the Greens will fail like the Communists before them, who had a wonderful agenda, but were full of anger and violence. The Greens have no spiritual dimension and no time to meditate and cultivate loving kindness. They don't have to be Buddhists; the best in Christianity and traditional European pre-Christianity should come out. This is not to follow a superstitious way but to add a spiritual dimension.

HELENA: I don't think that the spiritual aspect alone is enough. During the last ten or twenty years there has been in the West an increase in interest in the spiritual dimension. The Western mind and experience has, however, been so separated from the natural world that spiritual traditions have tended to be interpreted in a purely personal way. Hence they are rendered quite apolitical. I feel we need to think in a really integrated way about developing a spiritual economics and politics.

SULAK: This is my main criticism of the Western Buddhists. They take Buddhism to be something wonderful and peaceful. They say, 'I'm all right, Jack'. Then they become goody-goody and accept any kind of system. The important issue is that you must have peace and love, but must not remain goody-goody alone. You must know how to analyse the present structure, which is full of violence, helps the rich and destroys the natural environment. Once you know that, with good will and peace we can work. So far the Greens are weak on that, and if they are not careful the movement will end up as Green capitalism.

HELENA: Absolutely, we are faced with political and economic structures that are inherently violent and antithetical to the values of wisdom and compassion. They are based on a very narrow and reductionist view of the world, an assumption that we can conquer and control nature and people. Essentially, they are based on exploitation. If we are Buddhists or spiritual people in any way we need to examine those structures from the viewpoint of wisdom and compassion. If we decide that these structures are against our spiritual and moral values, we must reject them. We can't accept them. I feel there can be a mental trap in Buddhism. We are taught to accept the flow of time, the changing cycles of life and death. Many Western Buddhists, and maybe even oriental Buddhists, confuse that acceptance of life with the acceptance of an exploitative economic system. So they respond to the building of a new nuclear power plant or a super-highway which will destroy local agriculture with the attitude 'we are taught to accept; we must not be attached'.

SULAK: In Burma you can see this clearly. Burma has many meditation masters who teach *vipassana,* teach people to be kind and have peace, yet they don't question the dictatorship that has been there since 1962. The dictatorship has got worse and worse and commits atrocities. Since 1988, Burma has opened up to capitalism and now they have both evils. This is where Buddhists so far have been weak. To have peace is important, but peace in the Theravada tradition is only *samatha* – to be calm; you need *vipassana*, which means to develop critical self-awareness. This should include criticism of your own society, political movements, economic set-up and even your own Buddhist tradition. The Buddha said that you could even criticise him and his teachings. They have made the Buddha too sacred. I think we should come to terms with that.

HELENA: One way of doing that can be to start with yourself and be consistent. If you buy food in a supermarket you should know how it has been grown, using dangerous poisons and slaves on the other side of the world. It also implies harming their health and the health of other sentient beings in the process. It's just not Buddhist to go along with that. You have to scrutinise the impact of your various behaviours on all sentient beings. You have to take responsibility in a consistent way.

SULAK: You have to take the law of dependent origination seriously and not only internally. As you are from the West, can I ask you, does democracy in the West work now for ordinary people? Or does it work only for the multinational corporations and the 10 per cent of society?

HELENA : I really think that democracy has become only a word. I grew up in Sweden, a country that considers itself very democratic, yet we are seeing increasing secrecy on the part of government and a manipulation of public opinion. It is tragic that economic growth has become the dominant imperative, which translates into an unquestioning support for trade. This means actually subsidising the trading bodies, such as the transnational corporations, with taxpayers' money. A lot of this has been done in ignorance, with many people genuinely and well-intentioned supporting the growth of trade. That means investing billions in building more roads and infrastructure to facilitate more trade. In the process governments have actually been subsidising huge corporations that are outside their boundaries and their control. This amounts to a serious erosion of democracy, since the corporations have more power, effectively, than our elected governments. We have a situation now where out of the 100 largest economies in the world, 51 are corporations and 49 are countries. When you subsidise these trading bodies they move offshore. They know how to avoid taxes, so we have this huge structure of about 500 corporations actually running the world behind the scenes.

I think the tragedy today is that more and more people are angry at their governments about unemployment and food shortages. They are not looking at the power of the corporations influencing their governments from behind. They are not looking at the larger picture. This is slowly beginning to change. One of the main problems has always been that the media are very much in control of this situation, and as a result there is very little informed critique or discussion about the power of the corporations.

SULAK: The worst trade is the arms trade and unfortunately the first world is selling around 87 per cent of its products to the third world. The irony is that people feel that we in the third world need arms to catch up on development. In Sweden, when I received the Alternative Nobel Prize [Right Livelihood Award], another recipient was Carmel Budiardjo, an English lady with an Indonesian husband. She went to the Swedish foreign office and asked the under-secretary of state to influence his government not to sell arms to Indonesia as those arms will be killing Indonesians and East Timorese. His response was to say that Indonesia needs development and therefore needs arms. Without arms you cannot have national security, and with national security you can have free trade and commerce.

HELENA: This world-view and the paradigm it represents is based on the belief that competition is the basis of life. In contrast, most spiritual traditions are based on the understanding that life is an interdependent web of relationships, and to survive you must be part of that web of relationships. The Western belief that you can conquer and dominate nature and other people is like the belief that you can destroy harmful bacteria. The bacteria always return even stronger. *Karma*, on the other hand, wisely teaches that every action has a reaction.

I believe that it is only through co-existence and interdependence that we can have relatively happy, fulfilled and sustainable lives. If we look at the literature in the West it tries to justify military control. It is also directly linked with a world-view that developed with the rise of modern science. This view talks in terms of controlling nature. Adam Smith and John Locke talked about trade as something that will benefit everybody. If you actually look at what was happening at the same time as these great men were writing these ideas, you see that this particular culture was growing beyond its own land and resources and moving across the entire planet to enslave people and transport them in order to produce more for Europe. Interestingly enough, at that time the same elite pushed their own people off their traditional lands to become cheap labour in the cities. I am not saying that everyone in the West is evil, but if you look at the historical roots of development it is clear that it is an evil system that has to be rejected.

SULAK: There are two points I wish to add to what you have already said. Two years ago I was on television in Bangkok with the former Thai Prime Minister. He was supposed to be Mr Clean, a technocrat and very able person, a product of Cambridge, where they still teach Adam Smith and so on. Firstly, the prevailing law of education and thinking is still very much on that Locke and Adam Smith level. Secondly, this man, Anan Panyarajun, agreed with what I said about spirituality and non-competitiveness but accused me of being in a dream world, and said that, unfortunately, in the real world you have to depend on arms and trade. This goes back to Darwin's *Origin of Species* and the survival of the fittest. For him democratic capitalism is the least evil. He admits that it is not an ideal condition but possibly the best that we know. What is your response?

HELENA: People often cite Darwin's 'survival of the fittest' to justify the current economic system. But what most of them don't know is that Darwin actually based his theory on the economic paradigms of Adam Smith. So to justify Smith's economics using Darwin is not correct.

Unfortunately, the historical memory of Western culture, which in a way means that of the whole world, is very short. Most of our data, statistics and beliefs start after colonialism. You don't hear about how people were living before the colonial powers arrived. Generally speaking, it was these Westerners who travelled across the world who started defining and describing the rest of the world. One of the tragedies is that it is hard to get information and hard data about what was there before they arrived. There are now some very interesting Southern scholars who are looking at the initial reports of the Portuguese and Spanish when they first arrived. There is growing evidence that these were peaceful societies living in abundance. The reports describe the existence of democratic systems and the most remarkable high yields in agriculture, for example ten tons per hectare in India. We must not idealise these societies and say they were perfect. There was also violence and warfare in these societies. However, they were vastly more sustainable and peaceful than what came afterwards. What we need to recognise, particularly as Westerners, is that our culture and civilisation is based on robbing and theft. We can't glorify that and make it into something to be proud of. Above all, we can't export it as a model. After all, how can you conquer the entire world, plunder its resources, become rich and go around telling the people you have conquered them, and then also insist that 'you can be rich too'. For example, you have a group of ten people and ten oranges and one person takes nine oranges and asks the rest to follow his example. It is simply a joke, a hoax.

SULAK: Francis Fukuyama said it is possible in history. You don't have to go back to the big Spanish or British empires. You can become like little Japan and get rich, and after that you have the four NICs – Taiwan, Hong Kong, South Korea and Singapore. Of course, my own country, Siam, wants to become the fifth tiger. I think this model is still very appealing. Men like Samuel Huntington said that when we can get rid of the Muslim fundamentalists the world will become more beautiful. These names are well-respected in academia. What is your response?

HELENA: I would respond by insisting that we look honestly at our history. When a centralised power invades a local economy, diversified production for local and regional use is destroyed and often local and regional trade is forbidden. Countries are turned into 'banana countries' or 'coffee countries' or 'sugar countries'. Economic dependence completely destroys their systems. The ability for self-government is also destroyed. You can't separate economic and political power. The process is a homogenisation of diverse economic production and cultures to create one unit, where there has been more regional control and trade balance. So even when the centralised colonial power leaves, what you are left with is not freedom but the creation of a new elite which controls and tries to extract resources for the larger global economy. This economic model is not working now in the West itself, and I think it is vital that we examine this.

SULAK: If it does not work, how come the European Union (EU) is doing just that? They say what France and Italy should grow. The global experiences have now been transferred to Europe and these people are supposed to be the leaders of our generation. I agree with you, but tell me why?

HELENA: There are two major trends developing in the world today, one towards integration and another towards fragmentation. They think of these as separate trends. They do not understand that the so-called integration is actually an attempt to amalgamate every economy into one centrally controlled system, and it is precisely this that is leading to the fragmentation of social, community and individual identities. Nearly all the symptoms we see of environmental and social breakdown are the consequences of an economic system that does not respect and understand the diversity and interdependence of life. Ironically, it is an interdependent economic system that is destroying the interdependence of life. It is precisely this reason why many spiritual groups confuse the teachings of the interdependence of life with the message of the interdependence of one economic system. In reality this simply means having a few monopolistic corporations running everything.

SULAK: If it is that bad, why has Sweden joined the EU recently? There was a national referendum.

HELENA: Having worked in those campaigns, it was very obvious that losing one's democratic control, identity and language does not naturally appeal to people. I have worked in many of these campaigns, for example: NAFTA in America, the Maastricht treaty in Denmark, and the question of joining the EU in Norway and Sweden. What happened in all these countries was that public opinion was clearly working against the government, and as a result there was a major media blitz from government and industry telling people that they would lose their jobs if they did not say 'yes'. People voting in the referendum for Europe were also told that they would be responsible for the breakdown of Europe, creating a kind of Bosnia on a pan-European scale, if they chose to stay outside the EU. Another tactic employed very often is that treaties are rammed through in secret, as happened with the GATT treaty. In India, parliament would not go along with the intellectual property rights clause, so it was removed and parliament voted it through. Then the President restored the rejected clause by decree. In Spain there was so much opposition that they had to hold a parliamentary session in the middle of the night to get it through. There is a good reason why Reagan, Bush and then Clinton talked about 'fast-track' policy. This means not even allowing Congress to scrutinise or debate, and the President can rubber-stamp these treaties despite popular opposition. There is a growing gap between government and people. There is more secrecy, and if only people understood the implications of what is actually happening there is absolutely no doubt that they would vote 'no'. The result of all this secrecy and manipulation is that people, especially in the West, think this process is somehow evolutionary. They are confusing evolution with economic policy. We have this perverse situation where people can clone sheep or think that they will put an end to ageing through modern technology. But they cannot stop an economic treaty, because that is 'inevitable' and 'evolutionary'. It is a complete reversal of reality that the natural world should be subject to every manipulation that man can conceive of, while the man-made culture of globalisation is somehow perceived as immutable and inevitable.

SULAK: What you have said is important. People feel that they have become helpless. The disillusionment is common not only among the ordinary people.

I am reading *Faith and Credit*, a book by Susan George on the World Bank. You have directors and vice-presidents of the World Bank who also feel hopeless. They are technocrats who are linked very closely with the multinational corporations. The World Bank is supposed to help poor countries, but the money goes to the big multinational companies. This is the reality. How can we get out of this?

HELENA: You are right. It is interesting to talk to the heads of large corporations, presidents and ambassadors of these countries. There is a sense of not being able to control 'it'. Leaders in Europe made similar statements to Bill Clinton, who said at a NAFTA conference, 'The world is changing and we have to move with it. We can't stop it.' This is like the story of the emperor's new clothes. These people are pretending that this is the way things are and we have to move with it. They are not looking at their own responsibility in shaping the system. There is a secret underpinning in the relationship between free-trade treaties and sophisticated technologies. People at the top have difficulty seeing what is actually happening in the world. There is a structural problem due to the distance between the decision-makers and the impact of their decisions. By means of technology and the international economic system you can sit in New York and be a very nice Buddhist, meditate every day, be good to your family and yet destroy the world. You don't even have to know you are destroying the world because on paper you have said that economic growth is good and it will help the third world. To increase economic growth you have to increase trade, you are doing all those things that you sincerely believe in. When things fall apart in the world you think it is because of tribalism, fundamentalism, poverty, overpopulation and all other things that have nothing to do with you. Hence you are absolved of responsibility. This reality gap is a big problem.

SULAK: In Buddhism we call this *moha* or *avicca*. It means you think 'you know, but you don't, because you only use your intellect. You never bring compassion and wisdom together. Your knowledge is not wisdom because it is very arrogant, intellectual and compartmentalised. You are subconsciously controlled by greed because you want to make more money. You want more power and you are controlled by delusion because you don't really know.

HELENA: The reason we need human-scale units, and human-scale connections in the realms of power and economic activity is because you can't be a good Buddhist if you can't employ compassion and wisdom at the universal level. You can't have compassion if what you do has a bad effect on the other side of the world. So human-scale units are necessary to be a Buddhist. We need to promote the move towards the small-scale. Decentralisation and localisation of development, we need to promote.

SULAK: Maurice Ash, the administrator and writer from Dartington, said that a county level of government with grass-roots democracy and full consultation is more appropriate than a national government. Politicians say this is not possible, a daydream, and argue that the world is moving in the other direction. The former Thai Prime Minister agrees with what I say but asks how it can be achieved.

HELENA: The real power is in the economic dimension and that is where the big changes need to happen. If governments and corporations can sit around the table and sign the GATT treaty, then they can certainly sit around that table again and sign another treaty. This is not dreaming. This is how these economic forces come about in the first place. God does not ordain them.

I think we need to work at an international level if we want to make a rapid transition away from where we are today. We need new global treaties. Instead of signing over power to multinationals, the governments around the table should come forward to support sustainable small agriculture, small businesses, and allow people to gain more control at the local level. This treaty could begin to reduce trade so people can produce more of what they need for themselves. In other words, we want a balance between trade and self-reliance.

SULAK: Are you dreaming or do you think this is possible?

HELENA: I think this is possible, but for it to happen we need a clear strategy to work with the social movements, the environmental movement, the spiritual movement, the peace movement, the women's movement. These well-intentioned communities around the world, which unfortunately, until now, have not looked at the economic situation from a spiritual and ecological foundation, are starting to unite. This is what we are trying to do in our organisation. We are linking movements across the social and ecological sector not just at the national level but also internationally.

Together we can pressure and inform our governments. There is a lot of ignorance among people in positions of power, because they are out of touch with the realities. From below we need to inform them about what they do. They are not getting that message because unfortunately much of the grass-roots work remains unknown. We need ambassadors from the grass roots who can articulate another theoretical framework, then inform and explain it to the movements, which can communicate directly with the governments. This could create the pressure that is much needed. I think this can happen. There is greater understanding and appreciation of alternative perspectives today. It needs to coalesce. My worry is whether it will be in time.

SULAK: On the hopeful side, I like to recall there was an ASEM (Asia/Europe

Meeting) held in Bangkok a few years ago. Before that there was an international NGO meeting. We told them that ecological, social justice and human rights issues were missing from their agenda. I think this was only a beginning. They were to meet in Europe next time. Unless, as you say, we can articulate well, they will not take us seriously. Then if they take us seriously, it's against their own interests. If the government takes human rights seriously then they can't sell arms. If ecological issues are taken seriously it will affect industry. If we care for the poor and elderly it will disturb the national budget. That is why in the UK they are getting rid of the National Health. In America Bill Clinton's plans for social welfare were defeated. Why?

I find Susan George's book very sympathetic. Europe was more or less controlled by the single church before the reformation, and by several churches after. Now the economic set-up has become the new church. The World Bank and the IMF together represent the new Roman church, and its article of faith is growth. Most political leaders adhere to this. This is also linked with the multinational corporations. The greed for money and consumerism in the long run will destroy the ecological balance. If you have faith in the new church of economism, the technologists will come up with a solution. It is a blind faith and there is no other faith except dogma that goes beyond that.

HELENA: Susan George has taken a long time to look at globalisation and free trade, and almost completely agrees with our analysis. When you take the argument further, you should also be recognising that the real power is with the World Trade Organisation. It is quite dangerous to criticise only the World Bank as it is seen as working hand in hand with governments. This is the difficult situation we are now in, as governments have been very much involved in creating this exploitative and very destructive system. They have signed away their own power.

The system is top-heavy and so destructive that there are almost no winners. It is no longer in anyone's interest to keep the system alive. The Conservative Party in Britain is suddenly waking up to the fact that you can't have sovereignty, in other words rule by the government, and free trade. Until very recently they believed in both and now they no longer think so. The party is beginning to split. The Labour Party is also starting to split. What we are seeing is a significant development, but not yet the development of a coalition. At the very least what we should be talking about is an integrated eco-social agenda, rather than in the typical Western way, switching from anthropocentric to ecocentric. We have to care about humans as part of the natural world, which also means a care for the natural world. The problem of dualism is a real danger in the West. Some Greens have overcome this, whilst others have remained more anthropocentric. This more holistic, integrated, spiritually based understanding is still quite rare.

Today, things have gone so far that there are almost no winners in continuing this system. Even heads of government are beginning to realise that to continue in this direction could mean losing their jobs. There will be no role for the nation-state or for the government. Even if you are the head of the biggest corporation in Britain, British Petroleum, you are still not big enough and your job is threatened. You still have to merge with Mobil. Mergers mean job losses. We are getting to a point where even top executives feel insecure. What we need is a big shift in terms of world-view. This requires a different analysis and description of what is going on, to move people beyond this infantile assumption that somehow the world is moving forward and we are 'progressing'.

SULAK: How can we get rid of the new article of faith in trade and growth that you said some are now questioning? Even when questioned, how can it be shifted? A lot of people are now feeling unhappy in the World Bank because technocrats run it all. How can you get out of it?

HELENA: The first step is to raise awareness and I believe that this can be done effectively. The point of view that we represent is also reflected by most ordinary human beings, based on their experience of everyday life.

SULAK: It does make sense to me but I still shop in supermarkets, as it is cheaper and more effective. I agree with you intellectually, but out of my own habits I still go to Safeway.

HELENA: Where analysis is concerned, even the Soil Association, which promotes organic agriculture, has been working from a fragmented perspective. They have not looked at the whole fabric and understood the need to support local initiatives. In our organisation we are trying to work with other organisations and movements to get a broader and more holistic understanding.

We are highlighting to people the fact that supermarkets are cheaper because they, the people, have paid for it with their taxes. They are paying for the roads, the packaging, and the university research that is interested in transporting food long distances rather than growing healthy food locally. They are producing monoculture for healthy trade instead of producing polyculture for more local markets. In other words, we are showing that fresh, local food is naturally cheaper and more abundant. We are researching to show that local diversified production is more productive. The need for diversity is very important, and urgent.

SULAK: I agree with you, but what happens if I live on the 60th floor in Chicago or a condo in Bangkok? How can I grow my own food?

HELENA: No, you don't have to grow your own food. This is what is so good

Helena Norberg-Hodge

about the schemes that are already starting to happen. We have been supporting them. It has to do with shorter food links between the producer and the consumer. Many people who live on the 60th floor of a high-rise block are starting to buy local, fresh food from what are called local food link projects, community supported agriculture. What happens almost overnight when farmers market locally is diversity, because people don't want sixty pounds of carrots. They want different vegetables.

The pressure is to diversify, which requires far fewer chemicals. This is a wonderful experience: the pressure to diversify allows you to move away from chemicals and monocropping. Small is beautiful. In many cities in the West there are long queues of people signing up for local produce. There are cities with not enough farmers to fulfil this new demand for local food.

SULAK: This is wonderful! We have some similar experiences in Siam. Green Net is an organisation that encourages farmers to go back to traditional farming, without chemicals, and at the same time to educate others to eat non-chemical food. The farmers are also going back to traditional medicine. Not only medicine, but also spiritual things, such as curative and preventive measures. It is wonderful to return to protecting the forests and the rivers. We must have alternatives to consumerism and mainstream politics. Alternative politics means consultation at grass-roots level and empowering people spiritually.

In Siam people have been blindly following government propaganda. The government is blindly following international propaganda. Farmers have been growing three crops a year using chemicals, with the result that they are more in debt, as the chemical fertilisers are very expensive. The chemicals destroy their land, as they are poisonous. The environment too is destroyed and rural people can no longer eat frogs and fish. They are already suffering. They are even selling their daughters to prostitution and their children to slave labour. Things are now beginning to change in a big way. There is a real hope in my country. I think we need this hope in Ladakh and in the West.

HELENA: In the West too there is hope. There is a growing movement towards local, economic, environmental, spiritual and social renewal. Local farmers are supplying organic food. Local and organic together are vital for a holistic understanding. This also stimulates a sense of community. The social and economic benefits are coming together, and you can combine that with a spiritual understanding. You get a 'deep ecology', spiritual connection with nature and you get beautiful projects. Some people work with prisoners to produce local, organic food. The prisoners' sense of humanity and spirituality changes when they get into contact with the land. There are projects with juvenile delinquents working with wounded animals, and almost overnight they become different human beings, when they learn to nurture and to care for other living creatures. For the economic survival of small business, an economy that values life and the spiritual dimension within a local society are quite essential.

In medicine there is also a definitive trend towards alternative, holistic and spiritually based medicines. Recently a survey in *The Times* said that the majority of British people would pay higher taxes for a better health system. Whilst many of those people would not be looking at preventive medicine, it is still encouraging to see that even in these difficult times in the West values have not been lost.

When people feel that their identity and way of life is really threatened they become frightened. Intolerance grows out of that fear; they soon become intolerant of people of different races and traditions.

SULAK: We must also understand the fundamentalists. They become fundamentalists because they are so afraid to lose what they have. The free-trade people and the multinational corporations fear them, but arms and drugs sales are very lucrative. We must not use violence but should awaken the people and challenge them in a non-violent way.

HELENA: I feel very strongly that many people, including myself, are able to love people trapped in this ignorance and this system. I do feel concerned towards these people. I have family and friends in these high positions, and the real culprit – as Buddhism so wisely teaches – is ignorance. We must try to spread awareness about these issues. We must try to share our understanding in a loving and compassionate way. This can be very confusing: people can start loving the systems and the structures rather than the individuals. The corporation is a structure, an artificial and evil structure, but as for individual people, including those working within these structures, we must love them and treat them in a compassionate way. It is fairly simple, the difference between an individual and a system, but many people don't see it that way.

SULAK: We must make clear distinctions. I equate the present multinational corporations and free trade with the former British Empire. The British Empire crumbled because of Gandhi's spiritual strength. His spiritual strength was based on his own tradition and his interpretation was in the best possible way. Hinduism could be very dreadful and class-oriented, but he did not interpret it in that way. Gandhi was also influenced by the best traditions of the world. He can relate to Buddhism and Christianity. This is why the best people in the West supported him. He attacked the whole British Empire and questioned its legitimacy to rule. But comparatively speaking the British Empire was doing much better than a multinational company is doing now.

The Thai national corporations now have no moral legislation at all. I believe you need a spiritual force. Unfortunately, in India, Gandhi was a one-man show. After him there was not much to say. Gandhi was revered so much and it all became too goody-goody. I think we need a spiritual direction and spiritual depth, but not that kind of charismatic leadership. The Dalai Lama is a truly wonderful spiritual leader. He openly states that the Chinese who destroyed so much in Tibet also need love. Aung San Suu Kyi has been under house arrest for nearly a decade now, but she has cultivated loving-kindness towards her enemies. To me this type of love is essential. But we must not only rely on the leadership, we must have a real movement.

HELENA: This may be too simplistic. But I feel there is a very important point in all this that is not widely recognised or understood. It relates to the levels on which this movement for change must function: at the global and at the grass-roots levels. In order to change this centralised power structure, where a small elite rules the entire world, we need to think in terms of different structures, different forms of analysis, and different ways of articulating. This is what I call 'counter-development' – countering those centralised forces. I believe that grass-roots movements alone are not enough and that to some degree we must work through centralised activities. It is vital to use all the centralised media, television and computers at our disposal to get out a message to the world about how this anti-ecological, anti-spiritual and anti-democratic structure does not work. To articulate this, one needs to understand those structures and to know about GATT. To be able to deconstruct that power structure requires a different kind of understanding from the grass-roots work of decentralising, rebuilding the fabric of community and learning how to live.

In terms of the grass roots, how we live can never be determined centrally. I don't think the media will help us very much with that, because how we live has to emerge from our diverse communities and local environments. We must sit down together to decide how we can live, how we can respect each other, how we can build, how we can grow our food and how we can survive. This means extreme decentralisation and a participatory grass-roots approach. May be I am polarising this a little but it is very useful to think in those categories: the 'big picture' work that can function effectively to attack these centralised structures on their own terms, and the grass-roots work to find local, life-affirming alternatives. I see people confusing the two, and to create change at the political level they start getting too concerned that every local person should be involved. They start saying it is anti-democratic to work any other way. They say there should be no leadership, and the result is a complete inability to act. Several movements for transformation suffer from this problem.

SULAK: This is precisely what is happening in my country. In October every year the anniversary is commemorated of the Bloody Coup [1976] that killed so many people and burned many books. Luckily I was out of the country, otherwise they would have burnt me alive. Now they want to commemorate the event to teach democracy to people, but they say that democracy means that everyone has to decide together. I think your point is well taken. I had started a new movement called the 'Spirit in Education Movement'. This is for the heart and the head to synchronise. We want people to have time to meditate and we are teaching in natural surroundings. But we must also teach subjects. We have people coming to tell us about the World Trade Organisation and GATT and how the UN and the World Bank operate. I think we need that. At the same time we need people like you, or Satish Kumar or John Lane to tell us about life, arts and a spiritual dimension. We need both.

HELENA: In our organisation and in my life too I am trying to integrate the spiritual and the political. We should recognise that separating the two can be dangerous. The people who travel around the world as analytical spokespeople criticising the large structures are quite different from those who sit in a circle in a small village. These two kinds of people need each other. They need to be connected.

SULAK: What you say is very important. People like you and me travel, but we need to listen to those people. Since we can't spend a long time at a stretch with them, we must go to them every now and then. We need to recharge our batteries in a spiritual and ecological way. At the same time they also need people like us to convey and carry the message. Everyone has a role to play, but we must examine our role regularly. We should do this not for our ego, for great achievement or recognition. We do it because this is the role we are more at home playing. At the same time, whatever role we play we must have time for nature, for trees, for people and particularly for listening to others and questioning our own thoughts. This will help to build our lives on the basis of wisdom and compassion. I think this is essential.

HELENA: One of the most important things to remember is that the globalisation of the economy is possible only if people are forced to seek things that they do not actually want. When you speak to leaders and to corporate heads about these issues, you are made to feel so powerless. They shift the responsibility to the people. They say that this is all happening because people want to move into the cities and accept these changes. In fact, this global economy is fuelled by the vested interests who are using the most skilled psychologists, advertising and PR teams to influence the common people. Consumerism is not a product of innate, natural human responses. Children in Thailand – and even children in America – wouldn't dream of Barbie doll or Rambo with a machine-gun, but they respond to them when they are presented as the only way to have self-esteem and be loved. People are of course fallible and vulnerable, but we must recognise that they are also being victimised. We need to be alert about the extent to which cultural changes come via children and how much spiritual destruction goes on via the young. When vulnerable and impressionable young people are made to seek things in order to feel loved, the very fabric of society where previously people felt loved, felt heard and felt part of a whole is destroyed. Even as children they are made to feel they must have brand-new-label shoes, and later new technology, a car, and so on. They acquire in order to be loved, to be seen and to be admired. It actually separates them and creates loneliness and a sense of alienation that they then attempt to dispel with more and more consumerism. It's a vicious circle. When people are robbed of the love they need and are no longer seen as the spiritual and loving beings they potentially are, they become very unhappy and often very angry.

For women very often the anger turns inwards. This is why we are seeing an increasing number of women around the world trying to be valued and find self-esteem by being something that they are actually not. In China women are operating on their eyes to look more Western, and in Africa dark-skinned people are using dangerous chemicals to lighten their skin. In Ladakh, I have seen the beauty ideal for women radically change in the last ten years – now women want to be taller, have bigger noses, Western eyes and a lighter skin – an ideal to be somebody they are not. It all creates self-hatred that leads to self-destruction. In Sweden, where I grew up, people are taller, have bigger noses, blue eyes and blonde hair, yet hate themselves even more than in Thailand or Ladakh, because they have no community left, no healthy environment in which to develop a secure identity. The process of breakdown has been going on for so much longer in the West. I would actually say that they are worse off. In the West women go so far as to starve themselves to death. In Sweden, England and Germany girls as young as 6 years old already hate their bodies because they think they are not slim enough. It is vital to understand that this self-hatred is a fundamental component of the consumer culture.

With young men often this self-hatred turns to externalised anger. Today, almost everywhere in the world, from the streets of London, New York and Bangkok to Leh and Kathmandu, there are young men who have been uprooted from their identity and the web of relationships where they feel connected, loved and have responsibility. Uprooted from where they have a connection to place, nature and animals. Alone in the city, they struggle hard to buy a car, blue jeans, and try to look different from what they are. They lash out at anybody who is different. In Ladakh I saw young men getting angry and beating up Christian and Muslim Ladakhis and increasingly showing anger towards Westerners. This violence is growing very rapidly and creating gang warfare.

In the West, the violence takes an even more brutal form, where young men have even taken babies and murdered them for pleasure. I feel that we Westerners must recognise that this could never happen in traditional Thailand or Ladakh. This is something we must really look at. Do you know of any instance that teenage boys could take a baby and murder it for pleasure in a village in Thailand? You can't comprehend the deprivation, the anger and the confusion that leads to something like this. What gives me hope is my conviction – and there is evidence for it – that the same boys who murder babies for pleasure can in a very short time rekindle their spiritual selves, if they are given responsibility to care for a young baby or an animal that is wounded. I believe that almost without exception, given the right conditions, trust and responsibility, in a very short time they can change. Obviously it doesn't happen overnight and the whole phenomenon can be very scary. It is as if the light has gone out of these boys. But I do believe that the spiritual light is never extinguished completely.

Here we see some of the root causes of violence and fundamentalism that occur when people are subjected to a combination of psychological pressures, self-rejection and loss of community. There is no longer a daily experience with living role models. Role models become distant, unidimensional, media-generated and impossible to live up to. In attempting to live up to them, you have to continually acquire more money and goods. The whole system is fuelled by having to buy more and more consumer goods.

The economic pressures that breed the consumer culture are also urbanising. The psychological and the urbanising dimensions of consumerism need to be articulated and spelled out much more clearly. When you remove people from rural areas you immediately remove them from greater community. They may not always be wonderful communities, they may be poor, run down and intolerant, but there is at least a kind of community fabric. When people are pulled into an urban centre where there is no connection with each other and a dependence on distant forces, you are creating powerlessness and loss of identity. The urbanising forces are also centralising political and economic powers. As people feel more and more powerless, their anger grows. Almost everywhere this anger is directed to the local and immediate enemy: the people you see in the street who are different from you or the government that is immediately above you. These angry people don't look at the system, the finance market, pension funds and the structures behind the scenes. This combination of a very real loss of political power and impoverishment through the imposition of an urbanising consumer culture, alongside the psychological pressures, is an utterly unsustainable disaster. It is no coincidence that I see racism growing in Sweden and America. In Ladakh, Bhutan and India these differences are becoming the cause for, at best, political competition and, at worst, bloodshed and violence.

As far as we know the world has never been completely peaceful. There has always been death, violence and friction. However, we are talking about a very dramatic increase in conflict. This is why it is vital that we look at the psychological and structural pressures of the system. If we look for solutions it is very obvious that people need community for survival. They need to have human bonds, where their identity as a child growing up is shaped by living role models, by values such as compassion and wisdom and where love is the most important value. This could be construed as romantic, but in structural and economic terms these at best can be described as the need for decentralisation and diversification.

This is a problematic topic for the urbanised West. When you talk about community being long-term and connected to place, Westerners often think of this as fascist, linking it to blood-and-soil Nazism. It is therefore vital that people from the South remind the people from the North that roughly half of the global population still lives in rural communities, in close connection to the land. We cannot talk about humankind in terms of the urbanised section alone; to do so is nothing but Eurocentric. Our theoretical framework, our values and our recommendations have to respect the living experiences of the rural people who remain invisible to Westerners.

I believe the village structures must be strengthened by bringing appropriate development to them. If they need greater comfort, then through renewable energy sources you can bring small-scale power that is very benign and much cheaper in comparison to mainstream energy sources. If people can be self-reliant in this way they have much greater control over their own lives. This is not happening because of large vested interests in the petroleum industry and the associated corporate consumerist system. These organisations don't want small-scale energy projects, as they threaten their livelihood. Shell International has two scenarios in its forecasting of the future. First, everyone goes back to the local; this is the most horrible, depressing and dark scenario. Second, the bright future is when everything and everyone depends upon Shell International. There is a need to move away from global dependence on a few remote power centres to local interdependence.

PRACHA: You talk about the destruction of community in the West, where people have lost their sense of identity and hate themselves. What about Sweden, where, compared to Thailand, there is a greater scope for participation in politics? There is more decentralisation of power and politics. Why do you still say that people have no sense of power?

HELENA : It is not true that, compared to Thailand, Sweden is decentralised. Compared to the modern structures in Thailand, we are decentralised. But in Thailand, you have 60 per cent of your population still working on the land and this is truly decentralised. This is because when people are close to the land they have real power, as they have relatively more control over and access to food, water and their direct needs. Even if you have a kingdom or government that exerts a lot of power, in terms of your daily needs and economic power you still have far more power than anybody in Sweden. In Sweden, if someone at the centre turns off the tap, you would not have anything to eat. No one has the skills to feed themselves. They don't even know where their water comes from. It is very important to remember that. In Sweden you have political decentralisation without economic decentralisation. There is the appearance of local control but in fact the economy has been highly centralised for many years. Effectively, political decentralisation is meaningless without economic decentralisation.

Our system is so centralised that even the money granted to clean up the social and environmental problems created by the centralised modes of production is from top-down sources. This is not decentralisation, and it is not an effective long-term solution. We need structural change. You cannot be compassionate if you can't see the consequences of your actions. There has to be a decentralisation of the economic system. This does not mean that everybody has to produce their own food. It means you need to have some sense and real knowledge about what is being produced and how. Even if you do not see it every day, there has to be more visibility and accountability. The gap between producers and consumers must be decreased. Small-scale and decentralised production should be encouraged.

The left has neglected this. The ecological and spiritual base of life has been disregarded. This means that the scaling up of production into larger and larger units, more and more specialisation and monoculture is never questioned. What the communist countries did was to scale up government so that it could then divide and hand things out. This is the role of a centralised political power to deal with a centralised economic power. They have not realised that centralisation creates a much bigger gap between ordinary people and the centres of power.

SULAK: This is where the Congress betrays Gandhi's hope. Do you have hope in the present political parties in India?

HELENA: I do have hope. Everywhere you look you see that the dominant system is not working. More and more people are beginning to recognise this. Ironically it is the breakdown itself that is the primary indicator that the system is not working. The natural response to this in every place on the planet is that some people are beginning to do things differently, beginning to create a new system, new paradigms, new developments – in medicine, in spirituality and in human relations. Until now many of those efforts have not been holistic enough, but this approach is becoming more widespread and holistic. I feel that the growth of these smaller initiatives combined with the breakdown of the dominant system means that there is still time.

The mystery of this world is that it can heal itself. The human spirit cannot be so easily destroyed. The hope for new culture lies in this spirit.

One thing we are saying in the globalisation forum is that to continue in the same direction is impossible. The system cannot continue forever, as it is based on destroying life and cultural systems of people. You have to build even bigger roads and energy installations and centralise even more. There are fewer and fewer jobs available now. It is impossible to continue even in purely practical terms. It is not a question of whether it will break down, but more a question of when.

SULAK: The prevailing powers control the media. *The Times* being taken over by Murdoch made things much worse. The television set is the new pulpit and it makes us become more greedy and violent. Are you optimistic that people will resist brainwashing by the media? How can we get out of this dilemma and the powerlessness?

HELENA: It is so sad to see so much destruction in the less developed world. It is heartbreaking to see people's way of life being destroyed.

SULAK: They have been brainwashed to believe that their life is no good. A friend of mine in Munich, Michael Vanbrook, spoke of the holistic life in an Indian village, but within one year of the television satellite coming in the whole community was destroyed.

HELENA: At a recent meeting, Michael Harishis was saying that we should stop the transport of goods but the transport of ideas is beneficial. Satish agreed that ideas don't pollute, but the transport of goods does. I disagreed, and said the transporting of ideas is one of the most polluting things today.

SULAK: Yes, because it is a one-way traffic.

HELENA: This one-way traffic of ideas flowing from North to South must be understood as Eurocentric. Everyone in the world is speaking English and wearing the same clothes.

SULAK: The irony is that the EU says that it likes to respect the Asians, but it respects only those who mirror the European image, the Asian who feels that human rights and spiritual dimensions are not important. They say they know Asian values, but they never consult the majority of people in Asia.

HELENA: In the West, many people, including those in the movements, are guilty of this. It is very hard unless you have really been outside Western culture. We just expect people to look like us, speak like us and be like us. In a way it is the responsibility of people like you from outside to unmask this Eurocentricity. Westerners are often so resistant to this message and some even become angry when you tell them.

SULAK: When people get angry it is a sign that they are weak. The Chinese are now so angry about the Tibetans. The Tibetans are so gentle, truthful and full of compassion and wisdom. The angrier the Chinese become, the Tibetans become more beautiful.

HELENA: I must tell myself that!

SULAK: In Buddhism you must take everything with skilful means and become positive. In our private conversation you said you had hope in the Green Party in India? The West regards them as very fundamentalist.

HELENA: I had a conversation with a senior functionary in the Tibetan government-in-exile. He was saying, like Vandana Shiva, that the BJP in India is actually the best party, although most Westerners don't understand that. Most Westerners don't realise how the media feel threatened by this. Of course, there is a growing intolerance and some people are not good, but he was saying there are some very good people. Again we must talk about understanding the causes of fundamentalism, rightism and fascism.

I believe we need to recognise that this is a natural, quite automatic reaction if your identity, your way of doing things and your ability to control your own self is threatened. Your reaction is to protect, and that protectionism is seen at the outset as fundamentalism. This view is further propagated by the media who completely promote free trade. Anyone who opposes free trade is seen as selfish and fundamentalist. We have to be very careful about how we interpret the media. Everywhere in the world there is a need to protect real democracy, which is the ability to be yourself. To allow this on an international level, everyone must control their own economy on an international scale. This is why I feel that it is important that the attempt be on an international level. If it comes from only one country then they are accused of being fundamentalist, being nationalist. If all the nations and peoples of the world speak at the same time they cannot be ignored. This is partly what the Unrepresented Peoples and Nations Organisation (UNPO) is about. It is not just the Tibetans who are threatened. There are many people who want their independence. It is not just 'Free Tibet'; the need is to free the entire world from the yoke of the same system that won't let anyone have their own freedom. I believe we must articulate it in this way so that we can't be rejected as being nationalist or fundamentalist.

PRACHA: I would like to dig a little deeper into what causes self-hatred? It seems to be deep within us, especially in the modern sector. Do you have some different ideas as to the cause of this?

HELENA: I feel that my understanding of this is very much from seeing it in Ladakh and also reflecting on my own experience. I can now see how I was influenced by these images from the outside world. I thought that I was not slim and beautiful enough. I feel I can empathise with the young Ladakhi children in whom I have seen such a dramatic change, from being self-confident and secure to being worried about appearance, school performance and becoming more and more like Western children.

Western academia never attempts to comprehend the whole system and the interconnectedness of all things. It functions within a paradigm that teaches you to see yourself as nothing but a material atom. You are trained to experience your own self through the intellect alone, causing a split between heart and mind, an alienation from the body. You are separated from place in terms of your feeling and relationship with the earth. It is very important to realise that in a traditional culture the vast majority of people are closer to nature, even those who live in a city. In a pre-industrial situation you have much closer contact with the nature, rivers and animals.

I often think of how different I feel in Ladakh than I do in the West. I only recently realised this from waking up in the morning, hearing animals, seeing running water and feeling the wind in the trees. I also hear people singing as they work. I don't hear any machines or anything that drowns out my experience of being surrounded by other sentient beings. This process of cutting myself away from that life means I am cutting myself off and becoming diminished in terms of how I experience the world and relate to it. It is so Orwellian, that people in Ladakh are now watching television in a plasticised house sealed off from the smell and the sounds of the natural world. They are being imprinted in terms of who they are.

In a rural, traditional society, when you interact with animals you are responsible for them and they are responsible to you. There is a greater sense of living and sharing. If you think of a child learning to take responsibility for other living beings it can only increase humanity. They are part of human relationships. You are looking after the younger children. All your life you have also been closer to older people. Hence you are looking up to and emulating older people and being cared for. You are also nurturing the younger ones and being a model for others. You are part of this web, the cycle of life.

When you are cut off from the circular relationship of caring and being cared for and teaching and being taught you are suddenly stuffed into a concrete box with only children of the same age. This unnatural condition is rather like the battery hens in a coop – you start pecking at each other. You can't co-operate and you are not physically able to achieve co-operation. If you have a room full of one-year-old children, how can they help each other? They are all clumsily trying to learn to walk, so their whole universe becomes competitive, frustrating, angry at the age of one. As they get older they are kept together in age groups. You have a group of five-year-old children and there is a sudden pressure to be the same, to be as good as the other. So if another five-year-old can run faster than you can, you feel inferior. This pressure to be as good as another makes you reject yourself. Whereas before, when you have had a combination of one-year-old, five-year-old and six-year-old together, no one ever thought one should be the same as the other. No one ever had that expectation. This is a very important point. The mixing of age groups gives you the freedom to be accepted for what you are.

These points suggest that the modern system does not accept individuals as they are. Whereas the other cultures allow each and every one to be accepted for what they are. I wrote about this in *Ancient Futures*. I asked mothers in Ladakh whether they were worried when their children did not walk at one year old. They thought this was the most ridiculous idea, like worrying whether spring will come if it has not arrived on the same day as last year. They know spring will come after winter and will not worry if it has not come by the first day of April. But this is what we are doing to our children. If they are twelve months old they should be walking. This has to do with the very early structural shaping of society into competitive units. Competition seems to be the law and the only way to survive. Before, you had structural ways of creating co-operation within the fabric of the society, economy and family. It is no longer the same in Ladakh now. In the early days people lived and worked together. It was a beautiful way of living with grandchildren and grandparents going together to the water channel. It was not a paradise, but it was certainly a very rich culture. They were so happy together.

SULAK: How can we get this condition back, or look forward to moving beyond the present powerlessness?

HELENA : This is where we need to work on a more theoretical framework. When people go to Findhorn on an 'experience week', they open up to community, and many people simply love it. The problem is that many people do not translate this into a political and economic framework. They do not understand the fuller implications of their actions and responses. It is still very encouraging, however, as it shows what people ultimately value and want – community and co-operation. Our organisation has 20–30 community groups in local areas. These groups meet to discuss, interact and start building community and making changes. We encourage the groups to do this at a personal, spiritual, and intellectual level. At Schumacher College, where we run courses, we use a community approach. The tragedy is that these are people who come from all over the world at great expense, when they go back they are on their own. I believe we should encourage this group approach where people are actually living. There is nothing more powerful than working together with local groups and helping to explore how they can support each other in making local change.

We need to think about how to promote the idea of 'small is beautiful' and how to encourage people to slow down. It is paradoxical, but the promotion of many small-scale units of people coming together can become a real power. An antidote to consumerism is connection to the cosmos through more spiritual practice and connecting with one another through community. I believe that the way ahead is to get people to do these two things.

SULAK: I agree with you in principle. First, it is essential for consumerism that it is the prominent world value. It is therefore necessary for the media and educational establishments to make people feel they are powerless. Second, violence is encouraged, which is why the education system promotes Napoleon and Alexander. People in my country even question the existence of the Buddha and the possibility of overcoming lies with truth and hatred with compassion. This is very much an export from the West. Are you saying that we should organise alternatives that are spiritually based and grassroots-oriented?

HELENA: The number one issue for me is whether the half of humanity which still lives close to community and place is allowed to survive. I believe this is an issue for the West as well as the East. If industry and our governments use all their wealth to urbanise the East, destroying the community and the ecological balance in Asia, you can say good-bye to the biosphere. You should also speak out against people talking about 'equity', meaning that they have a right to use petroleum the way Westerners do. It is a standard thing to say that until we stop we can't expect them not to use it. This is a very dangerous way to look at it, and is exactly what the corporations want us to say. From their point of view it is not so bad if the West talks about cutting down on fossil fuels. They also know that it is not going to happen so quickly because the West is so dependent. But the corporations do not want anybody telling the other half of humanity, not yet caught up in consumerism, 'don't get caught in the web'. If you say that, you are considered a fascist and hypocritical. I keep saying to Westerners that it is they who are hypocritical, since they are using ten times their fair share of resources and then go around preaching to others that they can do the same. That is a real hypocrisy. If I am part of a society and against my will using more than my fair share of resources, but I am working to change it, then I have every right to warn the people on the other side of the world how powerless they will be if they become dependent on using these resources.

SULAK: I was speaking in Amsterdam, and a Chinese girl mentioned her right, indeed the right of every Chinese, to own a car, and asked why only Westerners should have one? I responded by telling what my friend Ivan Illich used to say, that the best invention in the world was the bicycle. She pointed out how much I flew round the world, and how it was different for her and her colleagues. I told her that if we all fly around and all have a car, the world will not survive. Her final comment was, 'okay, if the world won't survive, we will all die together, but now I must have my car'. I feel this is a fairly powerful argument. The Chinese suffered during the Cultural Revolution. All had to wear the same dress, and they were very poor. Now they want to become rich. What is wrong with the Chinese wanting to become rich like you?

HELENA: What is wrong is that it is not happening. We have around 20 years of good statistics that show this won't happen. In every country the gap between the rich and the poor is growing. A recent UNCTAD report shows that due to the process of globalisation, polarisation has sharply increased both within the individual countries and between the North and the South. Only a tiny elite is benefiting.

SULAK: If you talk to them they will agree with you intellectually, but emotionally they will ask why not?

HELENA: I don't think they would even agree intellectually. The big problem is the West. The Westernised elites and even people in the villages have been taught that wealth is created through technology, so they just look upon technology as a cure for everything. They forget about the water and the food. There are real limits to natural resources.

PRACHA: The problem here is that the real limit of the resources is somehow not seen in the process of growth. In Thailand, the gap between the rich and the poor gets bigger but on the whole everyone gets richer and has more consumer goods than before.

SULAK: The point is that this affluence is due to selling their daughters to become prostitutes, selling their children to become child labourers. Part of their family has to work in the slums of Bangkok and Saudi Arabia. This richness has come from their own human suffering. At the same time they have this hallucination, fuelled by television, that you must buy food, soap and shampoo rather than make it. They become landless labourers in their own land and have to spend half their time in the slums of Bangkok. They may be better off and more affluent materially, but what about spiritually?

HELENA: It is amazing how quickly spiritual, ecological and social poverty comes. You now have mental illness in a way that was not there before. You have teenagers committing suicide because they are not doing well in school, hating themselves because they don't look fine, and families breaking up. It almost comes instantaneously. It would make a huge difference if we were on Thai television even a quarter of the time the other propaganda is on. We could present a real view of what is happening to people and their culture.

PRACHA: There are two points here. One is the spiritual and the other is cultural poverty. On this I agree with you. However, when we argue about the impossibility of this consumer lifestyle, it is very difficult to convince people. In Bangkok more and more people have cars and TVs.

SULAK: You have to ask them if having more cars makes their lives better. The image of car-selling is so convincing. The car is a status symbol, and even a sex symbol but this is all an illusion. In Bangkok the Mercedes Benz is a best-seller yet the locals know they cannot move their cars in Bangkok. The Japanese call Bangkok the biggest car park in the world.

HELENA: What keeps things going in Ladakh is the strong belief that the West is a paradise, even though people in Leh and Delhi know it is crowded, smelly, and work is getting harder. There is still a belief that the West is superior. They are taught in school that the reason society is not working so well is because they are bad, undisciplined and not ambitious enough.

SULAK: The return of the British Empire!

PRACHA: This is how I was taught to think when I was in high school.

HELENA: In my international experience people everywhere are starting to blame themselves. Even here in England, very typical Brits are blaming their failing economy for not being as good as the Germans and Japanese.

SULAK: This is what we call the law of dependent origination. The Japanese feel they are superior yet culturally they feel inferior to the West. This is why they have Western concerts, have to dress in the Western style and their cars must be more punctual than those of the West. They have that hallucination of 'catching up' which is linked to competition and violence. We want to switch off violence and then consumerism. It is an hallucination. The Buddhists call this a *maya*. And this is what is dominating the world now.

PRACHA: In China, the multinationals are entering in a big way and the economy is now booming. Temporarily at least, many people will get richer, and this effect will also trickle down to the poorer people.

SULAK: Well, you have to qualify your statement. The media makes it look that way. My friend George Wong comments that every city in China is worse than Bangkok, which I regard as a terrible city. Ten years ago cities like Shantou were beautiful, and now they are full of ugly, modern buildings. Of course with the arrival of the multinationals, those who work for them get more money but the majority of people are bound to be much worse off. This is because in the old days you ate simple meals and drank tea. But now you have to drink Coca-Cola and wear dark glasses. There is more crime and prostitution. Earlier you were controlled by only one force, the force of dictatorship, like Burma. Now you have the force of consumerism, which is much worse than the dictatorship. You at least hate the dictators, but love consumerism. This to me is the dilemma. I believe consumerism will work as long as the *maya* is alive. The hallucination is that you will feel better only when you get a Mercedes Benz. You think it is wonderful but you must also have a Volvo. If you have a condominium you must also have a villa.

HELENA: Today you are taught to compete with others. It goes deep into the family, so brothers and sisters compete against each other. I have seen it in America where, sadly, family and friends can't support each other. Addiction is another way of looking at what is happening in our society. We are becoming addicted to consumerism. This is separating us further from each other. There are many addiction groups, starting from alcohol, drugs and going on to other things. The first step to de-addiction is to reawaken the spiritual dimension, not only God as a separate thing, but a strong connection to a community and a group. A good mechanism for getting off an addiction to consumerism is getting together in a group, introducing the spiritual dimension and also very consciously building community. I believe this is very much a part of the spiritual dimension. In the West our addiction is perpetuated through keeping secret the private sphere, such as fears of weakness or feeling ugly, or a strong sense of insecurity. Exposing weaknesses in a supportive group releases this terrible fear because underneath it is the fear that drives you. Competition is driven by fears like the fear of not being loved, the fear of not being seen and the fear of not being somebody. I think we have a very powerful tool in helping people to get together in community like this. So far the groups we have in America are very encouraging and now have the strength to start doing activist things like getting involved with local agriculture.

SULAK: I think that particularly in the Alternatives to Consumerism Project we need three dimensions. First, we must expose consumerism as the new demonic religion in every way. Secondly, we must try to tell the stories of those working against it in Ladakh, in India, and so on. Those which can remain alternative must have a spiritual dimension. Third, as Helena said, this spiritual dimension alone is not enough; it must be linked to a political and economic movement. Otherwise we remain goody-goody. I think we must do something more.

From the Buddhist perspective whatever you do must be meaningful, whereas with consumerism whatever you do is related to your desire for more money and goods. In the Buddhist view you enjoy doing whatever you do, because you relate to the earth, trees and to your neighbours. We are now alienated because we relate only to machines, like television and computers. Computers make us feel powerful as we can control them. We need to relate to nature and animals and the whole spiritual atmosphere. In Hinduism they call these spiritual forces gods and goddesses. I think this is something we should understand.

HELENA: What is really exciting in Ladakh is that the people who left their secure government jobs to head the Ecology Group are now heading the new local government. It is exciting that there is a Green government in Ladakh, and the leader of the Ecology Group is still the undisputed and admired leader of the Ladakhi people. He is a Rinpoche by birth, although he has now left the robes. He has great influence, and I believe rightly so, as he has so much integrity.

I hope that he can receive help by staying away from the mainstream. People in Thailand and Ladakh now have unrealistic expectations and are under extreme pressure. They have been led to believe that the only way to progress is through the consumer culture.

SULAK: We can invite the leader of the Green government in Ladakh and a few other people to come to our country. UNICEF has asked us once to show eight people from Bhutan who were visiting Siam the alternatives in our country. Then we can see what is positive and negative in our culture. My country is a real Buddhist kingdom and at the same time a wonderful place for consumerism. We also have wonderful viable alternatives. They could meet the supreme patriarch, the mainstream and at the same time we could show them the alternatives.

HELENA: In terms of change in Ladakh, the original idea of the Ecology Development Group was a local body of people determining development policy in Ladakh. At that time the government came from outside, people from Kashmir and India. I am trying to organise more rural women at the grass roots. We now have an alliance of around 3,500 women who are working with Vandana Shiva's farming groups, collecting indigenous seeds and working on alternatives to consumerism. We had a week of turning off the television and discussing its impacts. These vibrant women are wonderful to work with and are having quite an impact on the establishment Ladakhis who are more Westernised now.

I have been working for a long time in Ladakh to start an alternative school. This is difficult, as it must be clearly spelt out that schooling is part of the problem until we look at what the children are learning and how? Otherwise the present system will perpetuate itself. When schools are linked to sustainability they must be linked to diversity, different eco-systems and resources. This means that the content of what you learn will also be linked to different economies and different survival systems. The complete role of agriculture and primary production has to be reassessed. Right now it is the school that is taking everyone out of agriculture. We have an economic system that says we need technology and money and we do not need farmers and the earth to survive. That system is directly linked to schools, and what children are being taught is the skills to survive in a technological society.

SULAK: It is wonderful if you help with Ladakh. I believe that Ladakh has a better chance than Bhutan. Many Westerners do not realise, since they believe that Bhutan is going a different way, but it is not.

PRACHA: How did this movement turn into the Government?

HELENA: The leaders in the Ecology Group were people I recognised as being the leaders of the Ladakhi majority, who were Ladakhi Buddhists. In the part of Ladakh where I was working the Buddhists were 90 per cent of the population. The government was essentially Buddhist, and I was bringing together Buddhist leaders who would influence the government. As things became more decentralised, young men in the urban centres without jobs got very angry and started demonstrating against the government and the local Muslims. They got the leaders from the ecology movement involved in turning this into a political movement for independence from Kashmir, to have a local government. This is happening everywhere now as a consequence of people's unhappiness with centralised power. My life was threatened as the Kashmiri Muslims thought that I had started all this.

What I am talking about is very deep. I am not in favour of Ladakh being politically independent from India, or even from Kashmir, as it is so vulnerable at present. I was talking about economic independence, by keeping their agriculture, their identity and their self-respect. There have been difficult years and some bloodshed, but in October 1995 they were finally granted Hill Council Status, and a new local government was formed that will actually dictate to the Development Commission. It is very significant and it was elected by the Ladakhi people.

PRACHA: When you say the Greens are too Eurocentric, what do you mean by that?

HELENA: It is quite understandable that Europeans tend to universalise from their experience. A Westerner would say, when relating to technology or urban centres, 'human kind has arrived at this point' or 'we have evolved to this point of civilisation'. They forget that most of the world has not arrived at that point. Does this mean that Westerners are highly evolved and other people are a lower species? I point this out again and again but Western people regularly speak like this.

If I try to talk about urbanisation as one of the major issues, they immediately ask how this can change as everyone is urbanised. The majority of people on the planet actually are not. Westerners have a mental framework from the point of view of urban centres and concentrate on issues such as how to green the cities and develop the cities. They also assume that you cannot change the cities away from urbanisation. They forget about agriculture and see it as a peripheral topic. I believe that if we are going towards green economics the most important thing we should be looking at is the production of food. People from the West do not understand this, and when I pointed out the need to concentrate on agriculture, one of the leading environmental economists in England accused me of imposing my special interests. When I told a Western woman about this she suggested that next time we have a conference, we should try not giving them anything to eat for two days, and then if they ask for food we should tell them that we didn't want to impose our special interests.

At a recent conference, I was saying this to Ed Mayo of the New Economics Foundation; he said that he knew an Indian woman who thought weaving should be the basis of the economy. This suggests that cloth has the same importance as food. Why can't people understand that food is something we need three times a day and it has to be healthy? When you have an economic system that marginalises how we produce food, then we are marginalising ourselves. Food and drink weigh a lot and everyone needs to eat three times a day. The transportation of food must also be considered. The understanding that it is more efficient to have shorter transportation of food is just starting to penetrate.

PRACHA: Do you agree that agriculture should be the basis of society?

SULAK: Yes! From the Buddhist point of view to understand what is essential in life, you must know how to breathe, how to eat and how to live. The more natural, the more local and the smaller the better.

HELENA: When I say that we should see agriculture differently from other things I don't mean there should be no other industries. But the overriding values and goals of any other industry or technology should be other than economic growth, and very carefully weighed against the loss of power, identity and happiness.

PRACHA: What is the philosophy behind the agricultural life? Why is it better than an industrial society?

HELENA: Industrial society is based on the notion that we do not need food. If you really look at the working of industrial society you will see that it is destroying the production of food. It is saying implicitly that in the future we will synthesise food rather than grow it. Visions of the future indicate that people in cities cannot afford to waste time growing foods. Rather than growing tomatoes they can make ketchup. There will be huge containers outside the city using chemicals and bio-technology to make tomato ketchup. It is not so much a question of philosophy as recognising that we already know enough about synthetic food to understand that it does not nourish us, and that many of the elements we produce are poisonous.

SULAK: Apart from that, we must recognise that 'agriculture' and 'culture' have the same root word, meaning 'to grow'. We can only grow if we can relate to each other, the land, trees, mountains and rivers. This is interdependence. We are grateful, but at the same time we can produce our own food. Industry is a delusion, and today the word means something technological, chemical and not relevant to an individual. Your life is only to make more money so you can buy things you want. In its true sense agriculture places less importance on money and more importance on trees, rivers and mountains. The pollution of river, forests and the degradation of human lives are all due to the unmindful industrialisation of the economy.

PRACHA: What about the argument that better management can reduce pollution?

SULAK: That is a mirage. In Siam an overseas Chinese company produces all the chickens. We should raise chickens ourselves or there should be a movement of small farmers producing 'happy' chickens. It is an unfeasible dream or hallucination to believe that everyone can have a car or fly around the world.

HELENA: If you are rethinking economics and moving towards green economics then agriculture must be given priority. The goal of the economy should be that human beings are able to produce what they need for their survival. Is there anything that we produce that is more important than food? It is a question of priorities. I am not saying that everybody should be producing food and nothing else.

The argument about clean cars is a separate issue. I believe agriculture should have priority, but we should also have safe, efficient cars used very carefully for certain things. I certainly believe that travelling is a good thing, and would not advocate cars at all because of their destructive ecological, social and spiritual impacts. People don't understand that the car culture is actually making them slaves, as you see in Bangkok. Every city is now getting more polluted. In San Francisco there are studies that show that, due to more traffic, neighbours know each other less and old people and children cannot go out. What kind of a society are we creating?

PRACHA: It seems that both of your visions for a new society are based on agriculture, land and community. How is this society different from a pre-industrial society?

HELENA: From my experiences in Ladakh I believe it is possible to have small-scale hydro-electricity, passive solar energy for greenhouses, water heating, wind power and pumps to make it easier to do some things, without destroying community fabric and the relationship with resources. I feel that it is quite urgent to introduce these small-scale technologies into the villages. This could help to strengthen the grass roots.

One thing we must be careful about is that if we speak to the outside we should not be advocating that they go back. I know my book sounds like that. This is why I feel it is vital to use these technologies in a very skilful way. I think those technologies could be introduced more cheaply than anything else that is being done. The new direction can be implemented more quickly, would cost less, pollute less and be socially less disruptive. I would not say that this is the best alternative, as even a small hydro-electric scheme takes certain things away and centralises more than what was there before. People in a community must introduce these technologies very skilfully, and become aware of the power they are trading off. This awareness won't come as quickly as I would wish. We should, however, introduce these decentralised technologies and encourage such initiatives.

SULAK: The point is that the industrial revolution has been lauded as something great, and people are frightened of going backwards. They don't recognise that the industrial revolution has destroyed community life in England. The industrial revolution came along with the British Empire, as it needed raw materials to feed the industrial plants, and markets to sell the goods. The Americans want to overshadow the Europeans. The Asian industrial plants need more raw materials. This is linked with the multinational corporations, who want to control natural resources. Human beings are encouraged to consume more and worship money and technology. Of course, you can have agricultural produce with chemical mixtures, which is harmful. In its true sense agriculture means to relate to the land, to local wisdom, to the spiritual atmosphere of the whole community. Whatever industry we may have we should not disturb this balance. I don't see anything wrong in going back, but at the same time we need to be mindful. There were also many wrong things in the past, but the damage was not so huge, since the scale and intensity was too little to compare with the present. The King of Siam and the King of Burma may have fought a few wars, but at the same time, when we look at the history, we have lived with the Burmese for 800–900 years peacefully. All those wars put together cannot compare with the killings in the Gulf War, not to mention the two world wars.

People used to know all the preventive medicines and their lives were more holistic. Once you relate to the land there is more respect for other people. The five-year-old kids have some responsibility for the toddlers, and the grandparents are involved in family life. Of course the minor and major wives system may not be all that good, but at the same time you have the extended family. Today at the age of 30 you are still not grown up. You need a bachelor's degree and then a postgraduate degree. The pursuit is incomplete unless you go to Harvard or Oxbridge. You are still nobody unless you get postdoctorate qualifications. People need to be mature and grown up. Once you have a sustainable and self-sufficient lifestyle, life becomes harmonious and not compartmentalised. I think this is what we should learn from the past. We cannot go back, but we must carry all good things of our past into the future. For me this is vital.

HELENA: When most Westerners think about the past they have short memories. They think of the past as an era that began after colonialism and urbanisation. They think of the beginning of the past as being Dickensian London, where people were pushed off the land and into the cities. Their images are of poverty, dirt, disease, and crime in the cities. They don't think of the past as the majority of people living in villages, and they know little of these rural-based societies. They think of the past in the rest of the world as what they see now, countries ravaged by colonialism and underdevelopment. They think of the past as a period of ignorance, stupidity and poverty, with people dying everywhere. These images are very misleading.

Many things about the past are desirable even today. For example, generally speaking pre-industrial societies had a much smaller gap between the rich and the poor. People lived closer to nature and the lifestyle was more sustainable. Usually, despite arguments to the contrary, the water was far less polluted and there were no such things as CO_2 emissions and ozone depletion. Socially there was a much closer relationship between the family and the community. There was more respect for the aged. It is not correct to think we can have all these good things without learning from the past. This fear and ignorance that prevents people from returning to a more healthy system of values and practice is a consequence of modern life. We need a more honest and genuine appraisal of the past.

SULAK: In Europe, there are two reasons why the people are against the past. First, the church was too powerful and made people believe whether they liked it or not. It was an article of faith. They thought they had won after the French Revolution when Nietzsche killed God. What is not understood is how the church has reappeared with the IMF, the World Bank and the multinationals. The article of faith today is belief in free trade, growth and technology. One thing the West must learn is that there has been a switch from the old religions to the new demonic religion, and the blind faith this is imposing.

Secondly, in the West, particularly in Europe, you have a history of oppression. In Britain, after the Norman Conquest, there were Lords of the Manor everywhere oppressing the people. The people thought that once the industrial revolution and democracy came they would be free, but they were oppressed by the new middle-class industrialists. Whereas in our culture the good thing is that we have never had the church. We have only monks who live an exemplary life, whereas priests have some special relationship to the almighty. Now we worship the new priests, who are technocrats and economists, who relate to things we don't understand. Of course the past may not be an ideal, but it is our heritage and our roots lie there. We must understand both the negative and positive elements of the past, and move carefully towards the future with a spiritual dimension.

Japan is heralded as a new model, but it has no ethical or spiritual dimension. Singapore is worse, with only material and technological growth. There are no free human beings and you can't question the system. The technocrats are even worse, manipulating the people to believe blindly in economic growth. The societies they influence have the view that compartmentalisation and violence is the answer. They also make people believe that gadgets and chemicals can prolong life and give you immortality. They make you believe that you can accumulate happiness through consumerism and material wealth. You have to go for different kinds of sex and drugs to become happier. I think it is vital to go back to the basic necessities in life and use skilful means and a holistic approach.

HELENA: I want to add something about the role of spirituality in the past. Almost everywhere there was a deep spiritual belief that linked people together.

Statistics can show us that 30 years ago there was less crime, less mental dis-ease, less violence, less family breakdown and less sexual abuse. Virtually all the indicators of a healthy society will show us that things are worse. This is helpful for people to wake up.

SULAK: Adam Curle, the Quaker and Buddhist peace worker and writer, told me that until 30 years ago his village hardly changed for 500 years. His family was considered a local authority, as they had been to Oxford for five or six generations. He saw the negative side of Oxford that makes you feel like a nobody, and the only good thing he found were two professors who became his friends. In this age you don't even have good friends. In the old times of course the Lords of the Manor and the churches were too powerful, but the villages survived.

The First World War was declared in the name of the Empire, the King and the need to sustain the process of industrialisation. Over one million young English men were killed. This big upheaval caused much suffering. Today everyone is suffering and we must change from the present paradigm.

HELENA: We shouldn't give the impression to the public that we think everyone should be in their village making everything they need for themselves. This has never totally been the case, as there has always been some trade, technology, economics, material production and the specialisation required for this production. The issue today is that blindly promoting specialisation for trade has come to mean that the economic systems and institutions (the transnationals) dominate all of society. Hence spiritual, ecological and com-munity values are subordinated to techno-economic imperatives. We should reverse this so that spiritual, ecological and community values determine our choices of technology and our economic orientations. This implies a greater respect for diversity. The respect for diversity and local wisdom with the holistic approach to development is absolutely essential. All these should reflect the qualities of human compassion and collective social wisdom.

If these are the guiding principles then we may have all types of innovative technological developments and economic growth taking place around the world. There will be a multitude of experiences in business, economic activities and production. Today, we have only one way, which is an impoverishment of options. We should be talking about the kind of growth rather than growth versus no growth.

SULAK: Growth must be holistic and it must have respect for life. The West-ern scholar who wrote fifteen volumes on science and civilisation in China said that the Chinese could have created machine-guns one thousand years ago but they did not because they considered it harmful.

HELENA: I heard from a Swiss economist that the Chinese had developed boat technology at the same time as the Europeans. They also came to Africa but turned round and went back. They did not colonise, perhaps for the same reason as you say.

SULAK: First, the point is that China regards itself as the centre of the universe already, and to show might to other countries is only bad taste. Second, why should they expand? This is interesting, as all spiritual traditions have that limit. This gives human beings both the mundane and super-mundane dimensions. Lee Kuan Yew thought Confucianism would be wonderful to support the state. He made everyone learn Confucianism and invited the best scholars on Confucianism from Harvard and Princeton to teach in Singapore. Deep down Confucianism proposed more contentment. Every religion on one level is goody-goody and teaches you to be obedient to the state, but the best religion teaches you to be above the state. This is the spiritual dimension we need.

4 | Tu Weiming

Tu Weiming, Director of the Harvard-Yenching Institute, was born in Febru-ary 1940 in Kunming, China. He earned his BA degree in Chinese studies from Tunghai University, Taiwan. He received his MA degree in East Asian regional studies from Harvard in 1963, and his Ph.D. in history and East Asian languages in 1968, also from Harvard. He has taught at Princeton and at the University of California, Berkeley, and since 1981 has been a Professor of Chinese history and philosophy at Harvard. Active in many public bodies, he is a member of the Committee on the Study of Religion at Harvard, the chair of the Academia Sinica's advisory committee on the Institute of Chinese Litera-ture and Philosophy, and a Fellow of the World Economic Forum held regularly in Davos, Switzerland. He is a member of the Group of Eminent Persons on the Dialogue Among Civilisations convened by the Secretary-General of the United Nations, a Fellow of the American Academy of Arts and Sciences, and a board member of the Chinese Heritage Centre in Singapore. In 1999 he was awarded the title of Harvard–Yenching Professor of Chinese History and Philo-sophy, and of Confucian Studies. He was given an honorary doctorate from Lehigh University, Pennsylvania, in 2000, and in the same year received the Thomas Berry Award from the Center for Respect for Life and Environment, Washington, DC. He has been awarded visiting professorships at several uni-versities in the People's Republic of China, including Beijing, Nankai, Nanjing and Zhongshan.

The Interview

PRACHA HUTANUWATR: The first thing I'd like to hear from you is your analysis of Asian society in general, from a Confucian point of view.

TU WEIMING: Asia is complex – like Europe or the United States. In some sense it is even more complex, consisting of several major civilisations. There is East Asia, South Asia and South-east Asia. In East Asia normally we include Japan, South Korea and China, sometimes even Singapore, which by another classification is really in South-east Asia. Then there is socialist Asia: that cat-egory includes China, Vietnam and North Korea. These countries are also con-sidered as part of the Confucian world, even though they contain a great deal of cultural diversity. Buddhism, Shintoism, Taoism and, of course, Islam form an important part of the community of Asian nations and cultures. South-east

Asia, for example, is both Islamic and Buddhist. South Asia comprises primarily Hindu culture but also includes, very importantly, major Islamic traditions, such as in Pakistan, Bangladesh and other important countries of the region.

Asia in the twentieth century, at the end of the colonial period, emerged as a very important point of reference for both North America and Western Europe. At the same time, it also presents very differing versions of the modernising process. The modernising process assumed different cultural forms: the Japanese form, an East Asian form in general, a South-east Asian form, and eventually there were many other forms. This means that it is very important for us to understand the role of traditions and traditional influences in modernity, rather than simply looking at modernisation as an economic mode of thinking.

Thus Asia presents a very significant challenge to our understanding of the world, not only in terms of economic–political power relationships, but also as a combination of many different cultural universes, including of course spiritual and religious forces. It is very important for world peace that we develop a dialogue among civilisations, like the one that took place in the year 2001, when I was involved in Kofi Annan's Group of Eminent Persons for Dialogue Among Civilisations. The notion is that if we accept pluralism, especially in terms of culture and religion, as an irreducible feature of the emerging global community, and then if we can engage in a dialogue among the various civilisations in a proper way, then – and this is the only way – we have a hope of developing a culture of peace for the entire world.

Asia broadly defines itself in terms of its cultural diversity, with many different traditions and religions co-existing. Asia, however, has more than twenty countries with a tradition of having devoted a few centuries to Western learning. South-east Asia, South Asia and East Asia in general have been very much involved in learning from the West. Subsequently India in particular, but other countries as well, have recently begun to retrieve their own cultural resources. To really learn from outside you have at some point to retrieve your own cultural and spiritual resources. The depth of their traditional intellectual and spiritual heritage is such that the more we try to probe the depth of Asian mentalities, the more we have an appreciation of the complexities of the entire world. We also realise the numerous ways in which we can configure the world and the ways in which we condition the world.

PRACHA: How do you see Japan retrieving its roots and yet moving forward to modernisation? What is your opinion about Japan's approach since the Meiji restoration and the Second World War?

TU WEIMING: Japan, culturally, spiritually and intellectually, is considered both unique and also an integral part of East Asia. Japan has been successful in incorporating two major Asian civilisations: Mahayana Buddhism, which originated in India, and Confucianism, which traces its roots to China. But Japan has its own indigenous traditions of Shinto and also its own mythology, history, a strong sense of ethnicity, a keen sense of land and a sense of its primordial origins as a defined country. In the modern world, at least on the surface, Japan has been successful in learning from the West. The Meiji Restoration wholeheartedly embraced Westernisation, which means internationalisation, but at the same time the Japanese never lost sight of their own cultural roots. So the combination of internationalisation and localisation actually seems to work in a rather creative way in Japan.

But there was also a certain kind of radicalism that raised its ugly head.

There was a clear statement, particularly earlier in the twentieth century, that Japan wanted to leave Asia and join Europe. In recognising the military power of the European countries at that time, Japan began to learn from Europe about military weaponry, not only from the British but also from France and Germany, and in more recent decades from the United States as well. There was a price that Japan had to pay for its emphasis on total Westernisation, for its mind-set of leaving Asia and cutting itself apart from the Asian community. For a while, Japan became very militarily aggressive against its own neighbours. That created major problems that linger still into the present day, both for Japan and, of course, for Asia as a whole.

In recent decades, happily, Japan has come to the realisation that it ought to become an Asian nation, that it should join the Asian community as a responsible member, in addition to its success in having become in many aspects a part of Western Europe and the United States. Japan is a unique country in Asia in that it has been a member of the G7 (countries with the largest economies in the world), and there is no question about its economic success. Even with an economic downturn in the last decade (the 1990s), Japan is still the second-largest economy in the world. The size of its economy is much larger than those of China, India and many other countries combined. Yet returning to Asia presents a new challenge, and that new challenge is very difficult for Japanese intellectuals and for the academy or the government to cope with.

First of all, rejoining Asia requires of Japan the ability to recognise historically exactly what happened, to achieve reconciliation with its own historical past. On the surface they have apologised many times for the past, but in the deep psychology of the country, the effects of the recent past have not yet been fully explored. That represents a serious problem for the Japanese. The three approaches are: to be Asian; to continue to be global but at the same time to be local; and now to be regional as well. How will Japan be able to negotiate its relationship with Korea on the one hand and with China on the other; or with the other ASEAN (Association of South-east Asian Nations) countries, including India? This is a major challenge that requires some kind of watchfulness from outside observers. We are engaged in a kind of patient watchfulness and at the same time we are engaged with some intellectuals in making it feasible to explore possible alternative answers, rather than continuing to accept the Cold War mentality that continues to shape Japanese politics.

PRACHA: What do you mean by 'Cold War mentality'?

TU WEIMING: Well, I use the phrase 'Cold War' in the sense that Japan was a part of the strategy of the United States during the Cold War for stopping the spread of Communism. For a long time there was no need for Japan to worry about China because China was totally isolated. Japan's relationship with Taiwan in those years, for example, was very intimate. Japan's relationship with the United States, by contrast, was that of a junior partner, and its whole defence posture very much followed the line of the United States. But now Japan needs to look at its own situation by seeing itself as part of a much more complicated network of relationships.

PRACHA: When you say that Japan's way of modernisation exacted a big price, what was it?

TU WEIMING: Japanese intellectuals realise that if Japan wants to mobilise herself, she has an incredible ability to mobilise the whole country to, for example, become more powerful, wealthy and militarily strong. But they know that if Japan goes too far by simply trying to learn the best Western technology, the Japanese might even lose the source of who they are. What does that mean? It means that Japan has been successful for centuries in cultivating a kind of aesthetic sense of the world and of nature. It has crafted a delicate understanding of human relationships and a very affirming understanding of nature, especially of the environment in Japan. It has developed an ability to learn from major foreign cultures and to transform them, to indiginise them, so that they seemingly become typically Japanese. All these helped to develop Japan's process of modernisation. But now the new generation, under the influence of the benefits of an affluent society, seems to have lost touch with these very powerful resources of the country. I think that could be troublesome for the future.

Further, Japan has been very much focused on its own land, and it's difficult for Japanese people to establish themselves in other cultures as an integral participant. They are willing to invite world civilisations to come to Japan, and to transform these civilisations into a Japanese version, but their ability to move out and accommodate different cultures and allow themselves to be an integral part of those foreign cultures is limited. Thailand is very different and China is very different in this sense. There are many Chinese and Thai communities spreading all over the world trying to adjust to their new environments. But in Japan's case, there are far fewer communities in this diaspora. It's as if the mental adjustment involved in adapting to a totally new culture and way of life is just too difficult.

PRACHA: What cultural elements contribute to that difficulty?

TU WEIMING: Japan is culturally extremely fixed with its language, behaviour, ritual and its strong sense of its past and even of its mythology. So that puts it in a very isolated situation in the world context. Within Japan it is almost impossible to replicate the world outside, so Japanese can feel that they are international and yet still feel a tremendous sense of comfort. But it is very difficult for outsiders to penetrate the society and to be accepted by Japanese as full members of Japanese society. It is equally difficult for the members of the community to become adjusted to the outside. Japan is proving successful in some of the globalisation process, to the extent that Japanese *manga* cartoons and some gadgets are very successful. They are also able to allow the outside world to become highly local. They are successful in both. But how successfully Japan would be able to welcome guest workers from the Philippines and other parts of the world, for example, I don't know. The percentage of these workers might not be so high, yet what they represent as interlopers in Japanese culture is very significant.

Japan's sense of herself in terms of ethnicity, history, cultural heritage and philosophic thinking will have to be transformed. How would they do that? I think that's a major challenge for the Japanese.

PRACHA: What about other Confucian countries, like Taiwan, Hong Kong, Vietnam and Singapore?

TU WEIMING: Of all Confucian communities, Korea is the most Confucian. It has major issues in terms of democracy and also concerning the issue of equality between the sexes. The feminist movement in Korea is very powerful. And Korea, among the Confucian countries, has been very receptive to Christianity. Right now 30 per cent of Koreans are Christians. In fact, the Koreans are even exporting Christianity to the United States and, actually, all over the world. Of course Korean Christianity has also been deeply embedded in Korean culture. The Korean kind of Christianity, with family centricity and strong networks of relationships, is quite new to the Christian community at large. In the global world, Korean Christianity is unique. This is a phenomenon that needs careful study. Korea is also intellectually extremely dynamic. You know, Korean students study all kinds of subjects, not just science and technology but theology, political science, humanities and history. They not only come to the United States, but they also go to Europe and other parts of the world. So Korea has become very cosmopolitan in terms of its intellectual development.

This brings forth the whole question about Korean heritage: how might we choose the cultural elements that define what Korea has been striving for over the past centuries? One major cultural issue in Korea is how well the Koreans accepted Chinese characters as an integral part of their cultural tradition. Since the fourteenth century or earlier, all the major writing in literature, philosophy, and history have been written in classical Chinese characters. One question is whether Korea can define its classical tradition as a kind of anchor, like Latin is to all European communities, rather than as a specifically Chinese import. Because of its well-defined cultural awareness and sense of cultural identity, Korea does not want to be totally overwhelmed by Chinese culture.

Yet for some young Chinese today, their classical tradition is also quite alien to them. They are not strongly trained in their own classical tradition even though they may recognise certain Chinese characters that are part of this tradition. How will a Korean be able to recognise his or her own heritage without feeling overwhelmed by another major culture? They want to be themselves. That is a major challenge. It could be done if there is a strong enough sense of cultural identity and yet the people are open to all cultural resources, including their own, when formulating a new vision of who they are and what kind of society they want to become.

China, of course, is going through a major transformation. For me, the big question is whether the re-emergence of China as an economic power with political and military implications is fully recognised as a late twentieth-century cultural phenomenon. This is a very significant turning point. But what is the cultural message we should draw from these changes? How will China become integrated into the larger international community without being perceived as a threat by Western powers, especially by the United States? How will China be able to develop its economy without being perceived by less fortunate countries all over the world as a country that monopolises all the direct investment in the region? How can China not be seen as a threat to the less developed countries? Earlier, China felt it could present an alternative model to that once followed by the colonial imperial powers of the past. Has China abandoned that sense of originality and simply joined the globalisation process? How will China be able to continue to develop its own strategy for modernisation, since it needs investment from the more advanced countries of the West? How can it not be seen as threatening to less developed countries?

This is a major issue that the Chinese need to address. I have a very concrete sense that the way they eventually decide to address it will depend upon China's ability to deal with its own minorities, on the one hand, and with religion, on the other. These are the two important indicators that will be able to show us whether China's leadership has developed a cultural awareness and a cultural sophistication and is able to deal with more complicated issues or not. The officially recognised minorities in China number 56 or 55, and they constitute not more than 6 per cent of the population, but the number of people they represent is large, about 70 million or 80 million persons. This includes the Tibetans and the Muslims, both Chinese-speaking and non-Chinese-speaking. The non-Chinese speaking Muslims are an especially large group. How China will deal with them, and especially with Tibet, is a critical issue. For example, when the Chinese are able to recognise their own indigenous resources, not just Confucianism but Mahayana Buddhism as well, then perhaps they will begin to appreciate Tibet as a cultural resource. They will cease viewing Tibet as just a political problem or a separatist movement or simply as a threat to Chinese unity.

The question of religion is linked to China's relationship not only with minority groups but also with Western countries. This issue has a lot to do with the question of human rights and the question of democratisation. One of the causes of the conflict between Taiwan and mainland China is nationalism and democratisation. There are at least two kinds of nationalism at play here, pro-PRC (People's Republic of China) and pro-ROC (Republic of China on Taiwan). There is also the nationalism of Taiwan's indigenous population. So the larger question is: how will China be able to focus on possible fruitful dialogues between the Han and China's other minorities, and between the state and the various kinds of indigenous religious groups? And can China encourage a vibrant pluralism to emerge?

China has a slogan now touting the Three Representatives (*sange daibiao*). The first is that the Chinese Communist Party will develop the most advanced economy; second, it will help to forge an advanced culture, which will combine East and West, traditional and modern; third, it will represent the interests of the overwhelming majority of the Chinese people. In essence this implies developing a kind of democracy. It means China wants to become democratised and that it will possibly embrace a cultural sophistication able to accommodate all religions. China hopes to develop an economy that will be a combination of agricultural, industrial and even post-industrial systems. Possibly China could develop a model suitable for itself as well as for others.

However, it is almost impossible to fathom now how the major power that emerges from this process will contribute to rather than disrupt world peace. As we know, the rise of Germany was a major factor that led to the First and Second World Wars. After the Second World War, the United States became a superpower. In reality the United States did not represent a major threat to world peace. Well, perhaps in fact the record is not totally clear on that point, but at least we can say that it is a very different situation from that of the countries that provoked the First and Second World Wars. Now, with the emergence of China, we should ask if China will follow the model of warfare as a way to achieve its goals or if some kind of peaceful transformation can take place? The way China conducts itself and how China is perceived by the United

States, by the other powers, and by the rest of the world will all contribute to this process, but it is bound to be a difficult one.

PRACHA: Before we move on, I would like you to reflect on how communism has affected Chinese culture on the mainland?

TU WEIMING: The kind of socialism that China adopted, first of all, was an indigenised version. We can say that behind China's development of its form of socialism, three narratives were combined in a complicated way. The first was the effect on China of the impact of the West. The second was the rise of communism in China, which worked to help China become unified, and the third was the rise of Mao Zedong within the Chinese communist movement. Mao, by choice, never went abroad for study. He worked at a university library in Beijing and was certainly widely read; he even read some English books. With the help of Zhou Enlai and others, he was not simply confined to a very limited universe but rather had a broader vision of the world. At one point, he suggested in one of his poems that Europe, the United States and Asia could be three poles, and China should play a significant role in Asia. He was not simply interested in the idea of China as a super middle kingdom. He had a sense of a pluralistic universe.

Mao also has the feeling that China had to struggle not only to survive but also to flourish. How could China first stand up and then become a prosperous country? Unfortunately the method in use ever since the Chinese revolution in 1949 is very much predicated on the radical transformation of society, based, I think, on two false assumptions. One was that the modern had to be totally detached from the traditions of the past. Thus Chinese society had to get rid of icons that were attached to the past. The second false assumption was that China had to learn from the West while at the same time remaining extremely hostile to Western imperialism. It seemed to Mao that China had to fight against the West. So the model that seemed most appropriate to China was a revolutionary strategy based on a theory that was deeply rooted in the West and yet was intrinsically anti-Western. It was Marxism as transformed by Leninism with the success of the 1917 revolution in Russia.

China really moved away from considering all kinds of possibilities to adopting this particular model, and Mao felt that this model was the only way out of China's difficulties. But the cost of using this model was very, very high, especially from 1949 to 1979. Every five years during that time there was a major disruption: the Korean War, the Great Leap Forward, three years of major famine due to collectivisation, and then the campaigns of the Cultural Revolution (1966–1976). These brought all kinds of suffering to the Chinese people. In addition, there were also natural disasters. So the social suffering of China in the last 30 years was partly the result of Western imperialism and partly the result of Mao's radical policies. It was a total reversal of the Confucian process of harmony, dialogue and communication. It was premised on a total radicalisation in Chinese politics, a struggle for survival while forgetting about most other things, including China's own rich tradition.

Now that forgotten China has re-emerged, we again recognise it as a country with a civilisation that has probably lasted from the Neolithic period of more than 5,000 years ago, but certainly at least since the time of Confucius (531 BCE), that is, at least for more than 2,000 years. It is a tradition that was intimidated during the last one and a half centuries. Now, after that period of intimidation has ended, will China in its re-emergence be able to rise above its feelings of anger, frustration and therefore retaliation, towards a view of sharing power and to a pluralism that nourishes human flourishing?

There are two principles from the Confucian tradition that ought to be applied in this process. One is not to do to others what you don't want others to do to you – the principle of reciprocity. The other one is the principle of humanity – in order to develop myself, I have to help others to develop themselves; in order to enlarge myself, I have to help others to enlarge themselves. The self is always a part of this relationship. The nation ought to have interests that rise above narrow national interests.

PRACHA: You say China paid a high price for this experiment. Can you elaborate a bit more on that?

TU WEIMING: The people really suffered, you know. According to one account, in the period of the three years after the Great Leap Forward in the late 1950s and early 1960s, China experienced perhaps its largest-ever famine. Many people starved to death. I think that according to official records it was 20 million people, but unofficial records are higher and claim about 40 million people died of starvation. There was also the radical destruction of cultural resources in the country during the Cultural Revolution in the mid-1960s. The destruction that took place was not simply because of the actions of the Red Guards, but because they feared that the Red Guards might destroy their heirlooms, the people destroyed their own personal relics. It was irreversible, and of course we cannot bring back those destroyed treasures. This major loss may be unprecedented in human history. Normally there is a cultural clash between peoples: for example, the Muslims may destroy Christian relics or the Christians may destroy Muslim relics. But in this case it was the Chinese people themselves who destroyed their own major traditions and so many historically valuable material goods, documents and precious symbols of their glorious ancestors. That was an inconceivable loss.

PRACHA: What effect did it have on the mentality of the Chinese people?

TU WEIMING: China is still in the process of struggling to rise above that particular kind of mentality. It is hard. The first generation of Chinese students whose education was not interrupted from primary school is now entering college. We are talking about a new generation. Many of the top leadership from the 1950s, 1960s and 1970s still have major scars from the Cultural Revolution. The kind of burden they have to bear is not easily transcended or overcome.

PRACHA: Were there any positive effects from the Cultural Revolution?

TU WEIMING: The Cultural Revolution for a while demonstrated a spirit of selflessness, of sacrifice and of helping others. All these, on the surface, required the very positive values of courage, sacrifice and devotion to selflessness. From the Confucian point of view, one needs to work with the feeling that we each have a family and then to gradually extend outward to broader realms of sound Confucian values. But in the Cultural Revolution feelings for one's family members got eroded substantially when people instead said, 'I have a feeling for the people', yet 'the people' was an abstract idea. It could easily be manipulated into a cult of personality. Later this mentality become counterproductive. In the first phase of the Cultural Revolution there was a certain kind of idealism. Workable or non-workable, it was idealism nevertheless and it was pervasive. In China some people still lament the fact that because of capitalism and selfishness the age of idealism is gone forever.

PRACHA: In this regard, when looking at the countries with newly industrialised economies, we see that most of them come from a Confucian background. How do you relate Confucianism to capitalism and democracy, because these countries are also authoritarian as well?

TU WEIMING: You have heard of my colleague in Harvard, Sam Huntington's view on the clash of civilisations. He noted that the two major challenges to the Western or American way of life are Islam and Confucianism. Confucianism is authoritarian. Sometimes, he also talked about soft authoritarianism as a very important part of economic development, as in Korea, Singapore and Taiwan, and to some extent even in China and Japan. Of course Max Weber talked a lot about the relationship between the protestant ethic and the spirit of capitalism in the Christian tradition. The axial-age civilisations or the spiritual traditions that address the fullness of human flourishing do not simply focus on economic development. Actually the relationship of any one of them to economic development is ambiguous.

The protestant ethic is really not very Christian. The Christian idea is that you do not get into the Kingdom of God by wealth, but the protestant ethic, which is about the accumulation of wealth, is a kind of distorted or transformed version of Christianity.

Confucianism puts a lot of emphasis on righteousness rather than simply on profit. Confucian views strive for a broad humanistic sense rather than seeing human flourishing defined exclusively in terms of wealth and power. Thus there is conflict between these views. On the other hand, by following the Confucian ethic people are mobilised to work hard, they are encouraged to network with other people and to engage in some joint effort with feelings of trust. That approach may be a congenial way to encourage some form of economic development. I always feel uncomfortable in using the term Confucian capitalism. However, the kind of industrial capitalism needed in order to bring about a massive transformation of China's economy would inevitably be intertwined with various other traditions. In thinking about how an economic transformation in China might take place, it is possible to imagine not just a Confucian contribution but also a Buddhist contribution, an Islamic contribution or a Christian contribution to various kinds of economic activities. Because economic culture is all-pervasive, penetrating into all domains, one cannot say that the economic arena has nothing to do with culture.

PRACHA: What about authoritarianism?

TU WEIMING: The word authority need not carry a negative connotation. When someone in Shakespeare's plays has authority, it is taken to mean that he has legitimate power. It could be argued that people who have more power and influence have more access to information and hence they ought to be more obliged to take responsibility for the well-being of the society as a whole. One very important feature of Confucianism is to argue for the responsibilities of the elite. The elite ought to be responsible. Singapore, in a way, follows that principle. The government in Singapore is basically uncorrupted, or at least corruption is very limited. That provides a certain positive kind of leadership and example for Singapore's society. But this concept could be politicised in a wrong way, for example, by saying that people who have power can enjoy coercive power to dictate from the top down.

That's quite against Confucian principles. The Confucian process is always from the bottom up. The elite must take responsibility for the well-being of the people. The success of the elite, their prominence, is predicated not on their own strength but on the support of the people. If the elite fail to live up to their responsibility, the people can replace the elite. So there is an inherent predisposition in the Confucian tradition that the people are the most important, the state comes second, and finally the emperor or the government is in third place. The legitimacy of the government is based on the support of the people.

Therefore the obligation of the elite to society is immense. If the leadership has earned the right to lead, in other words they have gained the legitimate authority to lead, that is a good thing. Leadership is a gentle persuasion. It should not be coercive. However, if the leadership has some kind of political power that is coercive, that goes against the principles of Confucianism.

There is, however, a separation between politics and morality. If there were no separation, authority would turn out to be non-detrimental, it would always be viewed as positive (might makes right). But because they are separate, it turns out that improperly used authority becomes merely an authoritarian mechanism for controlling the people.

PRACHA: Am I wrong in assuming that the goal of the Cultural Revolution was to destroy the authoritarian mentality of the Chinese people?

TU WEIMING: Its goal was to destroy the party structure, to destroy the hierarchical control mechanisms of the Chinese Communist Party. Such hierarchical control mechanisms all too easily fall into popular use. For example, Confucianism has long been criticised for the male domination it seemed to endorse, for the strict authority of the father over the son, and of the ruler over the ministers. But even that version of Confucianism was a highly politicised version and was not part of the classical tradition. It developed during the Han dynasty. Moreover, Confucianism should always function in terms of reciprocity. The father should be loving and the son should be obedient. The ruler should be benevolent so that the minister will be loyal. Even the relationship between husband and wife should be based on a division of labour. The traditional view of the division of labour may be outdated because it meant that women do the domestic work and men do work outside the home. The specific allocation of tasks may be subject to change, but the division itself should be considered as a significant principle.

We need to have a division of labour before we can have any real collaboration between workers. Authority is important, a division of labour is important, leadership is important and none of these key principles justifies coercive power at the expense of voluntary participation.

PRACHA: Does the Confucian concept of authority and governance go along with the idea of a single nation-state that is dominating the world right now?

TU WEIMING: The Confucian concept of governance that is part of its great tradition is the idea that you cultivate in yourself a basis for the regulation of the family. When families are well regulated, the state will be well governed; when the state is well governed, there is peace. Thus the governance of the state is predicated on the quality of the people. The quality of the people is developed by the ability of the family members to cultivate themselves. There is a progression, first from self-cultivation, to regulation of the family, to governance of the state. Actually, the governance of the state is considered a precondition for universal peace. In this sense the notion of governance is fully compatible with the idea of the nation-state, though it also has very different connotations in terms of the state itself. For example, the state ought to be able to provide security for the people. At the same time, the state is also obligated to educate the people. That is one of the reasons why all over the Confucian world the major universities and high schools are government-sponsored. This situation is very different from that in the United States.

PRACHA: Does Confucianism make a strong point about how a government should be formed?

TU WEIMING: Absolutely. Traditionally there was a lot of pressure exerted upon the leadership and the future leadership to prepare well to become a leader. Even the nationwide examination system was geared toward that end. How one became culturally sophisticated was rather specifically defined. Equally, the manner of dealing with policy questions in a concrete situation, or what was the quality of one's personality, those sorts of subjects were discussed in some detail.

The selection of leaders was a two-step process, and it included both recommendation and selection. In one book of Mencius there is a statement saying that when the top leader, such as the emperor, chooses someone to be promoted, he should ask for the opinions of his ministers and other officials. If they also feel that the person can be promoted, they have to then ask the people concerned, and only if they also recommend the promotion can the official finally be advanced. Promotion depended upon actual performance. Only if the people concerned considered the performance of the official up to standard was the recommendation made. In other words, there was a lot of discussion about public accountability and about transparency in the process of career advancement.

PRACHA: In Confucianism was there moral support against a corrupt government?

TU WEIMING: That concept was extremely strong. China had what scholars call a censorial system. Some officials with very low titles were appointed as censors, but they could move beyond their rank and censure anyone, including the prime minister or the emperor, in the open court. That censorial system, which functioned continuously in China for centuries, became dysfunctional in an institutionalised way in the People's Republic of China, which was a most unfortunate development. That is one reason why Mao became so uncontrollably powerful. There was no one to criticise him. A related point made in traditional China was that it was obligatory when dealing with corrupt officials to demonstrate a critical understanding of the situation by becoming a feed-back mechanism within the bureaucracy. Tied in with that idea is the issue of the loyal opposition: one can totally oppose the government but still be loyal. Loyal opposition, though, is an idea that still could be further developed in China. Would it become possible for dissidents who do not accept national policies to still be considered worthwhile citizens of the larger community? That is a much more difficult issue within the Confucian tradition.

PRACHA: But hasn't Confucianism developed in a quite elaborate way?

TU WEIMING: The degree to which it developed in the past is perhaps less important than the larger idea that Confucianism needs to develop the concept of reciprocal community. That is, a community based on trust where everyone is an individual part of the larger community. The issue is whether Confucianism can allow someone who is a total outsider to the community to be critical of the community and yet be accepted by the community as a worthwhile citizen. In the West, this idea is widely accepted. But in traditional Chinese culture the concept was not strongly thought about or debated or developed.

Within Chinese tradition there were people like hermits, people who wanted to get out of the system. They were still respected. Their views were taken seriously, but whether they constituted what we in the modern political culture call a loyal opposition is still an open question.

PRACHA: In the Confucian political culture what is the view about modern parliamentary democracy?

TU WEIMING: Parliamentary democracy has been predicated on an adversarial system, where people represent different interests. Each person has their own constituency and presents arguments based on their own interests. Through conflict resolution among the contending parties, the system tells us, the broader interests of the country will be served. The Confucian approach, in contrast, emphasises consensus and agreement. Of course in a crisis, for example in countries like the United States when the government was considering a possible war with Iraq, consensus formation became much more important than the local interests of the various contending parties. The Confucian model is much more congenial to the idea of consensus formation than is the adversarial system, and that is something that requires an adjustment in Confucian thinking. Look, for example, at how democracy is being practised in Taiwan. In Taiwan there is a pervasive sense that democracy may collapse if local interests are the only concern of those who represent the people. Money and underground elements have become very powerful in shaping the democratic process. Money of course is of major importance. So it is called a negative factor in the democratic process, but actually democracy has never been about efficiency.

If democracy is hijacked by interest groups with more resources to manipulate public opinion, the situation can become unmanageable. So there is a pervasive sense that democracy will not work as a system unless the people who engage in the democratic process are also cultured in a sophisticated way and understand not only their own interests but the interests of the larger community as well.

PRACHA: Could we say your last statement is also true for the Confucian tradition?

TU WEIMING: Yes. Confucians put more emphasis on education and on responsible citizenship as a precondition for participation than do those espousing democracy, because Confucianism never had total faith in the workability of the system itself. They always had a strong sense that the system could work only when people who were a part of it were cultivated enough to make it work.

PRACHA: Could this be a major difference from Western culture, which seems to rely so strongly on institutions?

TU WEIMING: We could say that, but increasingly in the West, too, there is a major emphasis being put on the quality of the people.

PRACHA: Would you like to make a comment on the emergence and dominance of multinational corporations (MNCs) from the Confucian point of view?

TU WEIMING: I have been a member of the World Economic Forum for quite a few years, and I was surprised to learn that these MNCs sometimes can even undercut the authority of many of the major nation states because they are so very powerful. There are in fact many statesmen who worry that the political process in their countries or among nations may be deeply eroded by these MNCs and their power. Many of these corporations sanction absolute managerial control, where the CEO of the corporation has incredible power to do things that would be unimaginable in the normal political process. MNCs are based upon a neo-classical economic view of the free market, which is to say upon the idea of marketisation in its highest form. All boats are lifted by the rising tide.

While the Confucian tradition put a lot of emphasis on good governance, Western economic thinkers often felt that totally unregulated market forces would regulate themselves. It is something that Confucian thinking would never accept. Confucians never believed in market fundamentalism. Confucians always believed in terms similar to those of the liberal traditions of the

United States; more like the Harvard school of thought rather than the Chicago school, which endorsed the idea of a more free and unrestrained market. The Harvard school of thinking was always more concerned with governance, and on the responsibilities of government or parliament, rather than just emphasising regulation. For instance, many of the great initiatives in the United States, like the civil rights movement, were supported by the federal government. Without the support of the courts and other government machinery, the civil rights movement could not have come this far. We could also cite the example of the welfare state. The New Deal instituted by President Roosevelt was based on the idea of the reciprocal role of government. Government was very pervasive under the New Deal, much as Confucianism always postulated a very pervasive existence for the government.

PRACHA: I'd like to move on to another group of issues. Could you discuss the present world-view that seems to dominate us? East and West, North and South, these divisions all seem to be products of the Enlightenment. This is especially true for the main conceptual ideas of, for example, the idea of progress, the idea of scientific knowledge, the idea of human domination over nature, ideas of competition and individualism. How, from the Confucian point of view, should we look at the basic ideas of the European Enlightenment?

TU WEIMING: In a sense the Confucian tradition in China has been deconstructed by the enlightened values of the modern West. Some of the most brilliant minds in China from the 4 May period of 1919 onward were so much children of the Enlightenment that they abandoned their own traditions. Confucianism became, as it were, a victim of the Enlightenment, of the mentality of the modern West.

PRACHA: Were those the first generation of modern intellectuals in China?

TU WEIMING: Yes they were. Some of the more sensitive and philosophically sophisticated scholars in later decades also tried to transform the Confucian tradition. This was in such a way that it might be seen as compatible with all the Enlightenment values of liberty, rationality, the process of law, the dignity of the person and human rights. I think maybe for the three generations from 1919 to 1979, and even later, one can see that the Confucian tradition tried hard to adjust to the Enlightenment values of the West. It tried to make itself compatible with the ideas of a market economy, a democratic polity, a vibrant civil society, with the dignity of the person and even with some aspects of individualism. The overwhelming pattern was basically defining how the Confucian tradition could become modern itself. More than, say, Buddhism, Islam or Hinduism ever accommodated themselves to Enlightenment values, the Confucian tradition worked hard to become accommodative. It was quite an exception, in this sense, to the other major philosophical traditions.

In recent decades we can look at the human condition in terms of the Enlightenment mentality and appreciate how deficient that mentality is. We are not talking about liberty, equality or rationality, but about all of the negative factors associated with the Enlightenment mentality. We are talking about exactly what you have pointed out. From the point of view of an ecological consciousness, our strong commitment to anthropocentrism is not good. Also there is the feminist critique. Why should we have more emphasis on liberty at the expense of justice? Why is there too much emphasis on rationality at the expense of compassion and sympathy? Why is there such a strong emphasis on legality rather than on civility? Why is there too much emphasis on individual rights rather than on individual responsibility? Why is there too much emphasis on individualism rather than a stronger emphasis on the communal, or on the idea of a person as a centre of relationships rather than as an island of individualism? These issues must be explored.

The whole Enlightenment mentality grew out of the European medieval spiritual tradition, and, as a process of secularisation, became quite insensitive to spiritual matters. In fact it became very materialistic. Yet what we now desperately need is a set of universal ethics and not the Enlightenment's over-emphasis on the accumulation of wealth and the domination over nature, or on the theme of knowledge as power. These aspects of the Enlightenment are incapable of providing the understanding of what the world really needs to navigate the new century.

We can see in Confucianism the emergence of the retrieval of a very broad humanistic tradition. It is a much more comprehensive version of Confucianism, which looks at not only the person and the community but also at the human species as well as at the human heart, mind, and the way of heaven. This version of Confucianism emerged as a response to the challenge of the West, and also to the ways in which Confucianism first tried to accommodate itself to this challenge. Confucian tradition is now at the stage where it can offer a broader humanistic vision to strengthen and extend the moral and spiritual basis of the Enlightenment. This does not represent a rejection of the Enlightenment, but it is a critical reflection on the Enlightenment without losing sight of a sophisticated understanding of tradition.

PRACHA: What about science and technology?

TU WEIMING: There is a great deal of emphasis on the importance of science and technology as a flourishing form of knowledge and power. But our appreciation of science and technology ought to be guided by a broader humanistic vision. Right now, in terms of genetic engineering and nuclear weapons and such recent areas of inquiry, I cannot say that the unlimited quest for knowledge itself is necessarily good or bad. You have to work out what kind of knowledge is required, how it is applied, and what sense of priorities they used.

PRACHA: When you use the word 'humanism', do I understand correctly that your meaning is different from Western humanism.

TU WEIMING: Yes it is, because Enlightenment humanism is against spirituality on the one hand and it is against nature on the other hand. Then there is also its emphasis on anthropocentrism. Confucian humanism is much more comprehensive and inclusive. Confucian humanism is very much related to nature and in fact it is compatible with spirituality.

PRACHA: Do you feel that the Enlightenment ideas of equality and human rights have a valid position in the Confucian world view?

TU WEIMING: Yes, I do. Absolutely. But these ideas need to be further developed. We know that human rights have gone through a number of phases, an emphasis on political rights in the first generation, then civil and economic rights and then on cultural rights that are all-inclusive. The Chinese have always been criticised for not abiding by Western standards of human rights, but they instead put more emphasis on the second generation of economic rights and do not so much emphasise political rights. So the question as to whether China is willing to discuss political rights is related to the West's willingness in turn to explore the issue of economic rights. Whether there can be a good reciprocal relationship between the West and the Confucian humanistic traditions we are not sure, but at least the terms used by each side need to be further clarified.

PRACHA: What about the idea of equality in Confucianism?

TU WEIMING: Confucius put a lot of emphasis on the division of labour and not in an abstract notion of equality. Of course every human has a right to develop himself/herself according to the conditions in which they find themselves. So equal opportunity to develop one's human potential is an important right, and that opportunity should be available to all. But implementing that does call for levelling everyone down, so that everybody will have to start from the same position in the state of nature. In Locke's thinking, hypothetically everybody is exactly the same, and he tries to figure out a principle that is applicable to all members of the human community, even though we are in fact all in different positions. In this regard, Confucianism begins with concrete human persons, in the here and now, as a point of departure. As a concrete person, each one is unique, and that uniqueness should be recognised. But

I think Confucianism accepts, as a basic principle, that everybody should be offered the same kind of human rights and a chance to flourish, because everybody is born with moral qualities and with an internal predisposition to become a useful member of the community. So everybody should be respected in that way.

PRACHA: What about the idea that there should not be too big a gap between the rich and the poor? Does Confucianism say anything about equality in term of economics?

TU WEIMING: There is a very strong feeling in Confucianism that property should not be seen as a source of inequality. There is a very strong feeling in the tradition that if we are all poor, then we will try to flourish together. This situation, actually, is preferable to having a major gap within the community. There is a statement in Confucian writings that 'we are not too worried about poverty but we are deeply worried about inequality'.

PRACHA: Does that position date from Confucius' time?

TU WEIMING: That is from the *Analects*. The position turns out to be not too compatible with modern economic development. Right now, for example, in China, inequality is tolerated, especially if inequality enhances productivity.

PRACHA: How did Confucius look at the issue of progress? Did he endorse the idea of linear progress as presented in the European Enlightenment?

TU WEIMING: I think Confucianism has a more cyclical notion of historical development and regards the human factor as absolutely important. It says that the human community can reach a level of prosperity if the leadership and the people who are involved have the needed qualities. If at a particular time the ruler is irresponsible and the bureaucrats are not adequately serving the society, that moment will be detrimental. So the human factor is most important, but there are many possibilities within that construct. Maybe economically the society is progressing, for instance, but spiritually is lagging behind, or it may be culturally flourishing but with no stability in terms of the political order. We can see, in Chinese traditional society, that there are different criteria by which to judge a society, depending on the position at which that society finds itself. So the strong Western notion of linear progression as an inevitable process is quite alien to Confucian thinking.

There is also an assumption that human beings are co-creators, that they are an integral part in the scheme of the cosmic process. Thus they can become major factors in determining the development of this process. At the same time, as co-creators, they can become major destroyers as well. So the quality of people, individually and collectively, determines whether a particular period is considered congenial for development or not. This is related to the idea of the sage-king.

PRACHA: So Confucianism is humanistic in the sense that humans have a role in the cosmic process, and in emphasising what humans can do?

TU WEIMING: Correct. For example, if we do not do well with ecology, we are not doing well in terms of human relationships. We may grow rich but at the same time we will create social disintegration, with a lot of people suffering from poverty and famine. Then we would say that this period is not necessarily a good period. Maybe earlier periods were good periods in terms of cultural flourishing, but perhaps they were politically unstable. So in that sense as well, one cannot simply accept the idea of linear progression.

PRACHA: When you use the word 'prosperity' in Chinese what does it mean?

TU WEIMING: Prosperity means abundance in terms of economic well-being, but with aspects of an environmental balance, as well as being rich in culture, and in spiritual matters. Prosperity means conditions that are congenial for human beings to flourish in a broadly defined way. It deals with not just the body, but with the heart, the mind, and the soul as well.

PRACHA: So it's really different from economic prosperity?

TU WEIMING: It is not just economic prosperity.

PRACHA: Do you have the concept of sustainability in Confucianism? And what does it mean?

TU WEIMING: Well, sustainability means that material goods need to be renewed. There is a notion of new and renewal. Things have to be renewable, only then can they be called sustainable. The *Book of Changes* gives one a sense that people are always moving in the direction where creativity, not just cosmic but also human creativity, can be maintained, and that requires adjustment of various human and natural factors. It also requires the optimisation of current resources without unduly wasting any of them, because the notion of renewability is interlinked with the idea of sustainability.

PRACHA: So in this sense Confucianism cannot accept the throwaway society?

TU WEIMING: Any kind of waste is counter-productive.

PRACHA: When we talk about the issue of culture, like other Asian thinkers you see the importance of going back to Asian cultural roots. Why do we have to go back to our cultural roots?

TU WEIMING: So that we do not confuse information with knowledge or knowledge with wisdom. The existence of age-old civilisations is a product of wisdom. The major source of wisdom has been found in the inexhaustible spring of our culture, which we have when we go back to the classics. Or in the Buddhist tradition we would go back to the sutras. To return to the Chinese classics is not simply to return to the past nostalgically, but rather to get in touch with the inexhaustible supply of wisdom from the spring that flows in our cultures. When Whitehead talked about all Western philosophies as just footnotes to Plato, that is comparable to the notion we are talking about.

Of course we can have new visions and new possibilities, especially in science and technology, and many of the things we do. Nowadays, the average person has knowledge about physics and chemistry far beyond what was known by people in pre-modern society, no matter how intelligent and sophisticated they may have been. But cultures show the way of learning how to be human, how to conduct your life and how to grow up with a sense of dignity, how to interact with other human beings, how to manage your own affairs, how to work in a family. Many of these issues require wisdom and a willingness to listen. That is something that cannot be quantified, and is not cumulative in the sense that scientific knowledge is cumulative. They are special issues and problems. To address these irresolvable issues we need to return again and again to our cultural roots in order to enhance our insight and wisdom.

PRACHA: How do you define wisdom and knowledge?

TU WEIMING: Knowledge is a system of thinking based on information, some of which can be quantified. It consists of a vision and an understanding of natural phenomena and of human affairs. It can provide one with certain guidelines and skills of how to do things effectively in the world. Wisdom is something always embodied, not just through experience, but at times it can also be inspirational. Sometimes it turns out to be particularly significant for one's own development. Wisdom has to be embodied and has to be practical. It is not simply the clarity of theoretical principles, but it is related to insight. It has some kind of prophetic power to anticipate, to distinguish deep structure from its surface manifestations, and it is able to probe the roots by observing the branches.

PRACHA: Do you have a tradition of meditation in Confucianism?

TU WEIMING: Actually, yes. We call it 'quiet sitting', but it is not necessarily meditation or *zazen* in a rigorous Buddhist sense, although it may have benefited from the Buddhist tradition. But even before the introduction of Buddhism into China, Confucianism had always put great emphasis on the tranquillity of the mind. Some breathing techniques were used. Mencius talked a lot about them, about how to allow your energy to flow and to be fused with the cosmic forces. Meditation is not to promote a sense of individualism. Confucianism has been characterised as a system of social ethics, so cultivation of the spiritual sense is also seen as being for social ends and is not at all incompatible with the tradition of meditation.

PRACHA: Would you give us your views about Lee Kuan Yew's way of propagating Asian cultural values?

TU WEIMING: In a way, I think Lee responded to the dictatorial power of the West, together with Mahathir, who has tried to find an Asian way for Asian countries. I think Singapore may be the most Westernised country in Asia, and Lee may be the most Westernised among all the Asian leaders. He attended Cambridge and sees things in a Western way very well. He's quite aware how the legal system works, and yet he's very, very unhappy about the imperialist powers of the West that can dictate the agenda for the rest of the world. It is a kind of reaction to the overpowering Westernisation imposed especially by the United States.

The problem with the United States is that it imposes rules on the Asian nations without having any kind of knowledge about the complexity of Asian cultures. Singapore believed that it could develop modern civilisation by incorporating Western science and technology, economic rationality, even bureaucratic efficiency, but not necessarily importing Western ideas of individualism. Lee was, I think, earlier reacting against the hippie culture – the counter-culture of the 1960s and 1970s. Singapore wants to develop an efficient culture with limited freedom for its people, but a culture not associated with drugs, long hair, promiscuity and so forth. That's a choice.

But is Singapore truly following Confucianism? I am not sure that we can say that in Confucianism a nation as a community is always above the individual. I don't think that is Confucianism. The Confucian idea is that you learn to be yourself. A country can be corrupted, the society can also be disintegrated, and the person's dignity should not be dependent just on service to the country. That dignity is something deeper, something more profound. So in that sense Lee Kuan Yew may feel that his approach is Asian Confucianism, but within a Confucian context it is subject to critical revaluation as to whether authoritarian mechanisms and controls can be honestly and accurately justified in Confucian terms.

PRACHA: What would be your suggestion for a general healing of the feeling of Asian inferiority to the West? Because even though we have rich cultures in every part of Asia, we have unfortunately developed an inferiority complex.

TU WEIMING: This feeling of inferiority is quite understandable. For more than a century, the West has been dominating the rest of the world, in terms of not only science and technology, but institutional development, organisation, bureaucracy, government, and also basic values. In addition, often when we talk about universal values such as human rights and so on, they are all of Western origin. I think many Asian countries have learned the lessons of how to become modern in a Western sense. Now the time is ripe for Asian countries to retrieve their cultural sources and to broaden the whole concept of modernisation. I think the meaning of this is not simply to develop a degree of hostility to modernisation. Resistance can be very useful, but when resistance becomes the sole occupation it becomes counter-productive, and you will be defined by your anger against someone and by the rules of the game that you are in fact playing. They will determine who you are.

I think the time is ripe for Asian societies to retrieve their own cultural resources, to understand the West for what it is, to be able to appreciate many of the values of the West and then to broaden those values with universal values that may have their origin in Asia.

We need to remember that all the major religions emerged in the East, even Judaism, Christianity and Islam. So there is a chance for Asia, as a part of the East, to be a mediator. If we look at the conflict between the West and Islam, especially in the Middle East, East Asia in particular and Asia in general may serve as a mediator, trying to reconcile the East and the West. It is not an 'either–or' choice; it is 'both, and', How do we develop 'both, and' options in order to help the world community to become more peaceful?

PRACHA: Let's move to the next subject. If we are going to organise our society according to Confucian values, then what would it be like in terms of basic character and institutions?

TU WEIMING: First of all, society would use the principle of 'do not do to others what you do not want them to do to you', and the principle of 'in order to establish myself, I have to help others to establish themselves'. That is the principle of reciprocity, on the one hand, and of humanity, on the other. Dialogue has to be the method by which global communities interact. Dialogue is a complicated process, and tolerance is the minimal requirement. We have to recognise the other. We have to acknowledge not just the inevitability but even the desirability of co-existence with the other. We need to have mutual respect. Then dialogue can lead to mutual reference, to mutual learning and eventually, hopefully, to the celebration of difference. That process, in terms of leadership, is the kingly way, as defined in classical Chinese Confucian texts that postulate a sage-ruler, rather than a dictatorial power.

The United States ought to be involved in this process because it is a powerful, strong and economically advanced country. We are in a position to develop this particular model. But we have to go beyond our unilateralism. We have to go beyond our outdated notion that national interest is the most important factor that guides our policies. This world of ours is highly diverse. Those who are more powerful ought to feel more obligated to exercise responsibility carefully, and therefore negotiation has to depend on the willingness of the more powerful and influential nations to give rather than simply to dictate to the less powerful nations. China as an emerging powerful country really has to develop a lot of better resources to support the principles of co-existence and negotiation, so that organically and gradually there can arise the possibility of a more peaceful society. On the surface this may make us sound extremely idealistic, but if, for example, we look at Israel in the Middle East and Singapore in South-east Asia, it appears it could be a more realistic probability.

Singapore was established in 1965, and really viewed itself as a tiny island in the sea of Malays. So they sent their military personnel to Israel for training and invited many Israelis to help build up the Singaporean military forces. Fortunately for both Singapore and for South-east Asia, Singapore never really adopted the Israeli model. They decided first of all to cultivate relationships with their neighbours in Asia, and they also had the sense to stay away from the concept of 'an eye for an eye and a tooth for tooth'. Therefore they thought that Singapore should be perceived not as a threat to the region but as a really committed partner in the region. It is one of the most active members of ASEAN. They gave a promise to Indonesia that Singapore would not recognise China before Indonesia did, and they kept the promise for more than 20 years. Another thing Singapore did was to build a good university, a good banking system, a good health-delivery organisation, a good transportation infrastructure and a good airline, so that the whole region could benefit. They enhanced their own competitiveness, and then Singapore sold the idea that if we flourish, our neighbours will benefit from our way of flourishing.

I think the ASEAN model was really predicated on the Indonesian method of consensus-formation and negotiation, and Singapore is very much a part of that model. ASEAN in fact stabilised peace in collaboration with Indonesia. For example, in relation to Spotty Island, which China, Vietnam and many other countries claim as their own, Singapore's position is ASEAN's position, not the Chinese position. Thus in many ways Singapore attempted to cultivate neighbourhood peace. That model in the long run seems to be a much more acceptable method of peaceful negotiation than is the Israeli model, even though the situation is totally different, since Singapore is a small country without complicated political–historical roots.

PRACHA: In terms of reorganising a new society, what sort of institututions or structures are needed?

TU WEIMING: I think the market economy, a democratic polity, a vibrant civil society, and the underlying values such as human rights, these so-called Western ideas ought to be incorporated into the Confucian vision of a good society. For example, liberal democratic societies are more congenial for human development than either traditional imperial societies or modern authoritarian societies. Even though imperial society developed Confucianism, and some modern authoritarian societies could still be considered Confucian societies, nevertheless, for the flourishing of the Confucian ideal of human development, liberal democratic societies are much more congenial. That is something I think most people recognise. And yet, let's face it, democratic society is not ideal for human flourishing if it is based simply on a psychology of greed, if it's not secure, if there is a sense of fear and nervousness. In other words, we should accept modern liberal democracy and improve it.

Accepting some of the basic premises of modern society does not necessarily demean our own cultural sources, nor do we have to be exclusively receiving values and ideas descended from Western roots. We can have a modern version of Confucian society, and I think that is the kind of society that mainland China will develop, and for that matter so will North Korea and Vietnam, not to mention Hong Kong, Taiwan, Japan, South Korea and Singapore.

In my assessment, Hong Kong is modern in some senses, yet the cultural forms developed there are significantly different from the West. Because although modernism is deeply under the influence of the West, it is not necessary that modernism means to be totally Westernised. There always seems to exist powerful government leadership, though a strong government is necessarily a mixed blessing. In Hong Kong the best of the elite are in government service. They all consider the family as the basic unit of society. Family cohesiveness is strong. Their education is a civil religion; their investment in education is a commitment to the future rather than simply based upon a utilitarian principle of social service. For them education truly comes first. Hong Kong is still too much a commercial society. Yet, undeniably, Hong Kong civil servants are more British than Confucians. The life orientations of Confucians are different.

PRACHA: Is it true that education in Hong Kong is very much Western education?

TU WEIMING: But their commitment is to education, especially to education to build character and not just education as the accumulation of knowledge. This may change according to those principles and, as for the present, you are absolutely right. Given that situation, at present in China, to be honest, formal education is also basically Western. It is moving away from the Russian model towards the American model. But I think there is yet another variation.

In Japan, they try to teach Japanese children to be Japanese, and put an emphasis on civility and rituals, not just on law and individual rights. They have an emphasis on responsibility. The Japanese also put greater emphasis on the cultivation of the person through meditation and how to make your body healthy, your mind clear and your spirit sound.

China needs liberal arts colleges like those in the United States. Chinese education is too technical now. The form of liberal education offered in the United States seems to be more compatible with the Confucian idea of how human beings need to be developed. It broadly encompasses humanities, the social sciences and the natural sciences. These are all features that need to be incorporated in a modern Confucian society.

PRACHA: You mentioned the idea of a vibrant civil society. How do you link that with the Confucian tradition?

TU WEIMING: The Confucian tradition is very strong in emphasising the role of the public intellectual. That is, someone who is not just tied to one profession but who could be in government, or in the academic community, in business or in various kinds of religions or civil organisations, or active in social movements. These are the people who are politically and socially engaged. They are culturally sensitive, and want to address national interests and national issues from their different perspectives. They may be members of a professional society, such as the legal or medical professional organisations, but they don't simply focus attention on enhancing the interests of their own groups. Instead they address public issues. This is very congenial to the idea of the Confucian scholar–official. It's very different from the ideal Greek philosopher, from the Jewish idea of a prophet, from the Indian idea of a guru, from the Catholic idea of a priest or the Buddhist idea of a monk. These people are not engaged in the world here and now. The Confucian scholar, in contrast, is this-worldly, rather than being detached from the world. If we were to have in China public intellectuals in the various different social domains, the vibrant civil society which is now emerging in China would not be at all incompatible with the idea of community building at the national level, because public intellectuals have to address national interests as well.

PRACHA: Is this public intellectual the same or similar to the Russian notion of the intelligentsia?

TU WEIMING: It is very different from the Russian intelligentsia of the nineteenth century, which is the origin of the term 'intellectual' in the West. They were members of the aristocracy who were very much against politics, and in fact to be a member of the intelligentsia by definition meant to fight against the establishment. That was not true in France, in the United States, in Germany or in England. But it has become somewhat true in the modern world, with the emergence of a kind of critical consciousness, where intellectuals are considered to be rather independent from the government.

But the notion of the public intellectual in the Confucian tradition covers many people who are actually in the government, who are the publishers of magazines, or editors of major newspapers owned by the government. Many of the intellectuals in China in the protest movements of the past 100 years are people who are in the government. So it is not simply people outside the system trying to change it, but can include people from within the system who try to change the system according to certain ideas.

PRACHA: Do you see these intellectuals emerging in China now?

TU WEIMING: Yes, very much so.

PRACHA: In the field of politics, what would Confucianism say about centralisation and decentralisation?

TU WEIMING: There was always a kind of balance going on in China, either in the feudal system or in the government ministry system that developed later. China is not as centralised as the United States. If you look at China's tax system, the Chinese Government's ability to levy taxes is quite inferior to the American system. There is a lot of negotiation that goes on between the central government and various provincial governments. Certainly it will take a lot of time for the central government successfully to tax their commercial sector and also their successful businesses.

China developed a very elaborate bureaucracy as its administrative system. In fact even some of the traditional features, such as the rule of avoidance (not assigning an official to his home area in order to avoid a conflict of interest), is still relevant but rarely applied. In traditional China, none of the people from a given province would be assigned as an official in their home province but would be assigned somewhere else. They were forced to develop a broader vision about the whole society.

PRACHA: You mentioned earlier that the community is the first priority and then the state.

TU WEIMING: First are the people! Then the community, then the state and then the higher officials. They should be ranked in that order in the Confucian world-view.

PRACHA: What does that imply in terms of political structure?

TU WEIMING: It means that no matter what kind of a structure one wants to develop, there is this kind of democratic dependence on the people at the root of the system. The system is not simply the product of negotiations among various interest groups. In order to develop a viable social and governmental structure we have to make the well-being of the people the first priority. Only after placing the well-being of the people first will we then be able to do other things.

PRACHA: Does this idea of participation at the grass-roots level have some similarity with Mao's experiment with the commune system?

TU WEIMING: Unfortunately, the commune or the collective was part of a programme for economic development. The notion was to get rid of the family structure, to get rid of all the natural loose organisations that had formed in the countryside and to mobilise the people into production units. So the people would all eat together and use the production unit to enhance productivity at the expense of the social roots and cultural resources of the country. In fact many people believe that the major famine of the early 1960s could have been avoided had these underlying traditional structures remained, because normally the cause of famine is not simply the lack of food: usually famine develops because of unworkable transportation and distribution systems.

PRACHA: In Confucian thinking can material wealth and a good life go together?

TU WEIMING: They may or may not go together. For example, we should retain the basic stability of the family unit. Once that is maintained then we can enrich the people in other ways, such as educating them. Wealth in itself is neutral. Wealth can be put to good use, like educating people, or it can be put to poor use, like developing certain habits of greed and exaggerated spending patterns. There is a very strong sense that profit itself is not a negative factor, but only when profit is linked to a selfish desire or to benefit a very small group of people at the expense of the larger society does it then become a detrimental thing.

Negotiations have to go on, and in fact the Confucian tradition is not against the merchant's activities. There are four basic divisions of labour: the scholar, the farmer, the artisan and the merchant. The farmers, the artisans and the merchants each have their respective well-defined functions: the farmer's function is to produce, the artisan's is to manufacture and the merchant's is to trade. The most difficult position to defend is that of the scholar.

Why should we have the scholar or scholar–official? People like us, who are not producing, manufacturing or trading anything, and yet we should be respected by society? What the Confucians try to do is to articulate the position that these people are mediators. They help the rulers to understand the situation of the people. They help the people to develop the sense or meaning of life and then to educate them. This is the root that links the human world to the world of the cosmos and that is why scholars are important. It is a tradition that Confucianism puts a lot of emphasis on agriculture, but not at the expense of merchants. It was only the Legalist school of thinkers who thought that farmers and soldiers were indispensable while the other occupations, like merchants and scholars, were not only dispensable but also detrimental to social solidarity imposed by a strong ruler.

PRACHA: Are these four categories organised in a hierarchical way relating to social status?

TU WEIMING: Well, in a way yes. In ranking order we have the scholars, the farmers, the artisans, and the merchants. Part of the reason for this ranking is that in reality the merchants are most powerful because they have wealth. So in order to regulate society, we do not want the merchants to be powerful to the extent that they dictate the value system of the society. Today we think that a market economy is very vibrant, but a market-based society is no good if the society becomes totally market-oriented, because then family values will be easily eroded.

PRACHA: So you still think that this division of labour may somehow work in modern society?

TU WEIMING: No, I don't think that this ranking system will work in a modern society. But it is necessary to establish a system where due respect is accorded to all participants. For example, why do we put a lot of emphasis on the service sector? Service can be many things. If you are working in a restaurant, that is service, and if you are working in a law firm or in a university that is also service, but they are different types of service. How do we give all these people due respect for their contributions? Sometimes we have prestige but not necessarily economic gain. Sometimes we have a lot of economic gain but not necessarily status. Status, prestige and economic gain have to be balanced in some way. The merchants have abundant wealth, but if they also have status and privilege, as they do in contemporary America, then it becomes overwhelming.

PRACHA: Do Confucians mention violence and non-violence as possible means of social change?

TU WEIMING: Not only are peaceful solutions always preferred, but even civil unofficial negotiations are preferred to legal constraints. So, in that sense, the more we are able to reach consensus through negotiation the better.

The Singapore model, to refer to that again, of harmony between differing linguistic, ethnic and religious groups is very much in the spirit of the Confucian tradition. It is a path leading towards a certain goal that allows the people to co-exist and live peacefully among themselves. Negotiations and achieving a peaceful consensus to all issues is always considered most important.

PRACHA: Who would be the agent of change in the Confucian framework?

TU WEIMING: Society changes according to a lot of unintentional and uncontrollable forces. Public intellectuals, who constantly have on their minds the idea of rising above their own personal interests and the interests of their own group in order to serve the larger society will be agents for social cohesiveness and social change. However, they cannot achieve that without having the opportunity to be in an institution or to be an integral part of a functioning institution, whether it is a legal, ritual or administrative organisation. They need to combine their personal initiatives with those of the institution. They are agents of change because they are critically aware of what is going on.

PRACHA: So do they work inside an organisation or might they have to create a new institution?

TU WEIMING: The necessity for them to go through the process of building communities such as an institution or the fellowship for education is absolutely critical. If they fail to become a part of the larger organisation of society or to be an integral part of the political structure, they can still have alternative structures to work through in education, through mass movements, and through teaching. Especially through education and teaching at the grass roots, they can gradually transform society to a greater extent than those people who have actual power. Of course if they can influence and change the minds of the people who are powerful, that would be even better. But if they try and cannot do that, their failure does not necessarily mean that they will be unable to find alternative ways to achieve their goals.

PRACHA: Can we say that this tradition is very valid today because of what we are doing all over the world with, for example, NGOs (non-governmental organisations)?

TU WEIMING: The idea of NGOs in terms of social movements is very congenial to the Confucian vision.

PRACHA: One last thing: would you please say something about the Muslims, Islam and perhaps even Iran?

TU WEIMING: Not long ago I was in a meeting with Muslims in China, where they are one of the minorities. They are Chinese-speaking Muslims. Of course, there are differences between the Asian Muslims in Indonesia and Malaysia and the Muslims in the Middle East, Iran and Iraq. In China, the Chinese-speaking Muslims have been very deeply integrated into the Chinese social structure. They are very much a part of Chinese culture and they are fully recognised by the Chinese government. Recently I have been working with some colleagues on seventh-century Islamic Confucianism in terms of

Islamic theology, and I have found it very sophisticated and very congenial to my understanding of neo-Confucian premises. They accepted all the major premises of neo-Confucian culture, except that they believe Confucianism falls short of the idea of belief in a monotheist God.

There is a very persuasive argument that some of these people who had a Persian linguistic background came to China, learned Chinese and became part of the Chinese community and consider themselves very much a part of Chinese culture. They have developed an incredibly sophisticated vision of traditional Islamic premises. There is no reason to doubt that the Islamic tradition has been accommodating and has been able to develop successfully in a multi-religious society, according to what we find in the historical record. Without understanding this, how can the West, particularly the United States, understand the dynamics of the Islamic world, and especially in the Middle East? That of course is related to Israel and Palestine. That story looms extremely large in America's consciousness.

How will the United States be able to understand the Islamic world in the context of trying to appreciate both the possibility of a pluralistic universe under Islamic control and the possibility of co-existence with Islam and even of mutual references between the Christian and Islamic worlds? After all, the Islamic world contributed to the Renaissance when they preserved the classical Greek texts, and also contributed to the development of medieval Christian theology.

We can take this as a background for mutual appreciation. To simply consider the Islamic world as an enemy and an area toward which tremendous hostility has been targeted would be counter-productive. I recommend we adopt a dialogical mode of thinking. The dialogical mode is not to convert, to persuade, nor even to find our own alternative statement to present to others, but rather to broaden our intellectual horizons, to deepen our cultural awareness and also to engage in a genuine mode of learning about others.

The United States has, I think, to transform itself from a teaching civilisation into a learning civilisation again. This learning is not for the purpose of strategically trying to manipulate others, but is learning designed to broaden our scope of understanding and also to enhance our flexibility. So if that were the case then not just the Islamic world but also Africa would be considered extremely important for our own understanding and flourishing. We in the United States tend to ignore Africa because it is not a threat to us. We became too sensitive to Islam because it was presented as a threat. In both cases our vision has been very narrowly defined, very much based on the idea of our national interests. The need now is really to have an ecumenical vision that is more accommodating and non-judgemental. We need to learn how to understand others, particularly the radicals, because we are not talking about national security, which is only a part of the story, but we are in reality thinking about human security. If we cannot do that, we are going to suffer not only in terms of our view of the world, but also from some dangerous threats that can seem to come from out of nowhere. Not just people in general but even our top leaders seem to have no understanding of why so many of these things are occurring.

PRACHA: Is that also your message to the American people after September 11?

TU WEIMING: Yes it is, very much so.

PRACHA: From your previous analysis you indicate that we are too occupied with protesting against the perceived enemy, and that has become our identity. Can we apply that to the American collective consciousness? America fought the Cold War for so long, and after the Cold War does America need some enemy as a way of defining itself?

TU WEIMING: It is a very dangerous way of thinking to believe that you need an enemy to rally the people. It is different if there is a perceived conflict between good and evil like the situation during the Second World War. That was more legitimate. Now, if as a superpower we have to create an enemy in order to rally the people, that is most unfortunate. It is actually dangerous. I would hope we could develop the dialogical mode of thinking I mentioned earlier. It is more critical for the United States, more critical than for other countries, that we do so, because what we do can benefit not only ourselves but much of the rest of the world as well. If we fail to do it right, not only will other people suffer but eventually we ourselves will be the real victims.

PRACHA: Thank you so much.

5 | Mahmoud Ayoub

A graduate of the American University of Beirut, with an MA from the University of Pennsylvania, Dr Ayoub earned his Ph.D. in the History of Religion at Harvard University. He has been Professor of Islamic Studies in the Department of Religion at Temple University and Research Fellow at the Middle East Centre of the University of Pennsylvania since 1988. He was previously Lecturer in Religious Studies at the University of Alberta; Assistant Professor of Religious Studies at San Diego State University; Visiting Professor of the Institute for Islamic Studies at McGill University; Visiting Professor at Belamont Greek Orthodox Seminary in Koura, Lebanon; Research Associate at the Centre for Religious Studies at the University of Toronto; and Adjunct Professor of Islam of the D. B. Macdonald Centre of Islamic Studies and Muslim–Christian Relations at Hartford Seminary, Hartford, Conn. Dr Ayoub is an editorial consultant of the *Muslim World Journal*; chief editor of *Qur'an Commentary al-Mizan* of Muhammed Husayn Tabataba'i, under the aegis of the Alawi Foundation; and a member of the editorial board of the journal *Islam and Christian–Muslim Relations*.

The Interview

PRACHA HUTANUWATR: From a spiritual point of view, why do we need a government?

MAHMOUD AYOUB: We need a government from the point of view of Islamic tradition. Islam is concerned with the affairs of society, and the government is the servant of society. Islam is about how to rule and how to govern. Justice is central to the ruler or the government in their relationship towards the subjects. In order to maintain justice in a society and manage the affairs of society we need to ask, whom do you obey? In Islam you need to submit to God. Muslims believe that it is necessary to have leadership, and the first rebellion in Islam, which happened 25 years or so after the Prophet's death, came when people wanted to say that they did not accept the judgement of men and would only accept the judgement of God.

Some argue that they do not need leadership. But the law of God that is important in Islam does not operate by itself or in a vacuum. It must operate through authority, and that authority has to be exercised by rulers. This is why I feel that Muslims are wrong if they insist that Islam equals democracy.

Although Islam does not clash with democracy, it does not equal democracy. Islam is based on two important principles: they are obedience and justice. As long as the ruler rules with justice then the people owe him obedience, and in that case it is not ideal to change the ruler after four or five years. We need to change our ruler only when the ruler no longer obeys God and refrains from attending to his duties towards the people. People will and should obey the ruler only if he obeys God in managing their affairs and delivers justice to the people.

PRACHA: This way of reasoning seems to give justification to authoritarian rulers.

MAHMOUD: Just rulers, from the Islamic point of view, are never authoritarian. A true ruler is one who does not see himself to be above the law, and legitimate government has to be just government. In my view, Islam can never be an authoritarian religion or a system based on authoritarianism. The problem is, I think, that the Islamic principle presupposes an ideal situation. Because the fact is that authority or power corrupts, and the more power you have then the greater the chances of corruption. This is the reality – and that has been the reality of the Muslim world. But Islam is based on the notion of the possible perfectibility of human beings. Islam does not begin with the idea that all humans are sinful. It begins with the ideal that all humans are good and then they become sinful – or, they could even become better. Therefore human perfection is possible. This is why Islam is like Judaism in its insistence on law. People ideally must live in accordance with the laws of God. I do not mean by this to condone those people who want to use religion to exercise their own political power, with their calls for the application of laws that involve cutting off the hands of thieves, and so on. I mean that, with regard to the rights of individuals and the rights of society, the law of God must be supreme, and the structure of governance of state and society should be based on a set of moral principles. The Sharia as we have it in the Koran and the Sunna of the Prophet are not laws as such. In fact, it would make very poor law if we looked at it as we look at the Roman law, for instance. It is much closer to the Jewish Law – it is a law to live by in order to live a moral life.

PRACHA: It seems to me, from what you have said, that in Islam the main concern is with how to rule with justice, rather than with how to become a ruler.

MAHMOUD: Ideally a ruler in Islam should be chosen through consultation. Either a universal consultation, or at least with people who have status or authority in society. In ideal terms, a ruler in Islam should be instated not through imposition or any coercive power, but through consultation. This was imperative in traditional Islam, and it is still a kind of principle practised in some places, even today: where there are monarchies, for example, as in Saudi Arabia and in North Africa. The people consulted are the chiefs of tribes or representatives of the people, who come to offer vows of allegiance to the new king. These vows of allegiance have often been extracted with extreme oppression. That, from an Islamic point of view, is not valid. Governance has to be assumed through consultation and the expression of the free will of the people.

PRACHA: Could you please compare this consultation process with Western or parliamentary democracy?

MAHMOUD: It does not compare with the Western system of democracy. It is not democracy, as it is understood in the West. Say a ruler needs to do something in the affairs of the state. In Islam the ruler must consult the people and take their advice, but ultimately *he* has to make a decision as required. It is necessary to consult with others regarding the affairs of society, and after that you need to make up your mind. Once you make up your mind then you proceed and trust in God.

I said earlier that Islam is not necessarily democratic, but that it does not clash with democracy. But I must qualify my statement. Any Islamic form of democracy will be quite different from American-style democracy because of the fundamental difference regarding the economic doctrine of *laissez-faire*, as practised by American-style democracies. Islam does not accept *laissez-faire* economics. Islam is much closer to the parliamentary democracy of Europe than to American democracy. The nature and practices of the market that America is imposing on the world fly in the face of Islam. For instance, interest charges, speculation, hoarding, and buying things without actually having whatever is for sale in front of you. All these things Islam does not accept; Islam neither shares nor accepts these values. But they are basic to the international economics of today's world. In Islam, you cannot go to market and buy all the sugar very cheaply and then sell the same sugar for a higher price. You cannot do that. This is what Islam considers to be unlawful profit.

PRACHA: What is the main difference between the European model and the American model?

MAHMOUD: When I refer to the European model of political democracy I am actually speaking about the parliaments chosen by the people. All the Muslim countries, interestingly enough, consider themselves to be political democracies. This includes Iran, for instance, which is known as the Islamic Republic of Iran. Iran has a parliament and it has a president who is elected through an electoral process that is democratic. The last two elections in Iran were better than the American elections – they were cleaner.

However, Iran has another problem. The President of Iran has very limited authority, and the final authority is in the hands of the clerics. I think this is wrong and I do not agree with this situation. From my perspective, as a scholar and an historian of Islam and of religions, two kinds of people should never rule. These are the clerics and the army. They should not rule. I think the Iranian Islamic Republic is doing well, but it has many, many problems. The dignity of the religious leaders has been undermined.

There is a very important saying attributed to the sixth Imam of the Shia, Jaffer Saddique. He said that religious scholars (in the case of Islam these will be the jurists) are God's trustees of the revelation until they come knocking at the door of the monarch – the sultans who are the rulers. Once they do that, then suspect them. I once asked the Iranians: 'Do you mind if I remind you of Imam Jaffer's words and ask you one question: how come the scholars themselves have now become the sultans?'

You see, in traditional Shia society, Iranian or non-Iranian, the scholars always led a very humble life. They had simple demands. I used to visit them before the revolution. I visited a very famous scholar who used to live in a house of three rooms. In one room he received visitors and it was his library as well, his children occupied the next room, and the third room was meant for him and his wife. That was it.

Now, of course, the clerics of Iran have to live in big houses with metal detectors, and travel around in bullet-proof cars, and require more comforts. It is not dignified. All these developments have undermined the dignity of the religious scholar. This is why I consider that two kinds of people should not rule, clerics and people from the armed forces.

PRACHA: But you said earlier on that the main point of Islam is justice. Why can't the clergy support justice?

MAHMOUD: The clergy should be the *guardians* of justice, not the *executors* of justice. It is also assumed in Islam that absolute justice is God's prerogative alone. Only God can wield an absolute power of justice. We humans can do justice only as far as we can. In Islam, there is an important principle: namely, that God will not burden the soul beyond its capacity. God will not, for instance, ask Muslims to fast for three days continuously, or pray ten times a day, because these would be beyond their capacity. Thus justice in Islam means to be balanced. This is very important. To carry out justice essentially means to be fair in weighing things. You must practise justice even towards yourself. If you deprive yourself of food and sex, you are being unjust to yourself.

PRACHA: If it is better for the clergy to be the guardians, to balance state power, rather than use their power directly, can we say that the role of the clergy in Islamic societies is similar to that of civil society in present day secular societies?

MAHMOUD: Yes, in some ways. Islam also accepts that power can potentially corrupt, and you must always have somebody who can speak against the corruption of the rulers. This is the responsibility first of the clergy and then of every good Muslim. The Hadith (the body of traditions concerning the sayings and doings of the Prophet Muhammad) is very important in guiding us here. The Prophet said that any one of us who sees something wrong and indecent must try and change it with our hands if we can. If we cannot do this, then we must try with our tongue, by speaking against it. If we cannot do that, then we must try with our heart. This means to pray and wish that it does not happen again. One can also disassociate oneself from it. The Prophet says that this is the weakest of all actions, and that it is the least that a person should be prepared to do. He also asks us to become more involved in the reform of society and in safeguarding justice and equality in society.

PRACHA: Do you consider that the nation-state system is a good form of governance for the Islamic world?

MAHMOUD: We have to speak from two points of view, from the point of view of the ideal and from the point of view of reality. Ideally the Muslim world is one Ummah (Muslim community), what is known as the sphere of Islam, Dharal Islam. In a way this remains as it was when Muhammad founded the Ummah, with me and the Muslim from black Africa or the Muslim from white America or Turkey or Iran, or any Muslim from anywhere in the world being my sister or my brother. We are all members of the Ummah of Islam. But in reality the Ummah of Islam has been fragmented into the nation-states. The nation-state is a modern concept that does not agree well with the concept of Islamic government. But it is a form of state that all the Muslim countries, except Saudi Arabia, have accepted. (Saudi Arabia claims to use the traditional consultation process.) Now, with the nation-state, what do we do? Do we then forget that there is a Muslim Ummah, or try and look at the Ummah of Islam as being made up of the nation states? In that way each Muslim state will be sovereign within its own border, but it will also be a part of the worldwide Islamic Ummah.

The Iranians – and here again I give them credit – some years ago started trying to establish what they called the Islamic Common Market. They wanted this initially to be made up of Iran, Turkey, Pakistan and the countries of central Asia, such as Uzbekistan, Azerbaijan and so on. Now, altogether these states contain over 400 million people, and they would actually have many more resources, especially natural resources, than Europe. Europe does not have much. But of course the West would not allow it, especially when Turkey is trying desperately to become part of the European Union. I think it is unfortunate that Muslims are not allowed or encouraged to form an important economic power bloc, like the EU. My question is: why not the Muslims?

PRACHA: What are the pros and cons for Muslim countries in adapting the modern form of nation-state?

MAHMOUD: The Muslims led the West in science, technology and philosophy until about the sixteenth century. Then the Muslim world began to decline, and many reasons are given for this. I have my own. My reason for the decline is the fragmentation of the Muslim Ummah into sometimes warring states. There were three Muslim empires that grew up at that time: the Mughals of India, the Sufists of Iran and the Ottomans of Turkey, Europe and the Middle East. In Iran and Turkey, and also in Mughal India, there was a brief flowering of culture and creativity and so on. In the end this did not last, whereas within the non-imperialist Muslim Ummah, even in times of political unrest, there was a great deal of intellectual activity. For example, in twelfth-century Spain there was a lot of unrest, but during that time of unrest the three most important philosophers of Islam for that part of the world were at work. It's very important for the Muslim Ummah to be open, so that there is a free flow of ideas, of trade, of interaction, and so on.

I no longer believe in the notion that the West is technologised and the rest of the world is not. Now technology is a commodity. If you have the money to pay for it, you can acquire it. It is no longer the West's secret. Japan is not a Western country; it's very Eastern. Thailand is not technologically backward; nor is Malaysia. The real problem is who has the economic power.

PRACHA: The Iranian efforts to build an Islamic Common Market are interesting to hear about. How would it contribute to the building and preservation of world peace if the efforts were successful?

MAHMOUD: I believe the greatest contributions towards world peace are security and prosperity. It is not my view that the Japanese of today are better people than the Japanese of the Second World War era. Nor are the Germans today better than the Nazis; they are not. It is just that they don't have to be Nazis anymore. The Japanese don't have to be Samurais and Kamikazis, because they have security, they have economic prosperity.

So I am convinced that the American approach towards the world's problems is very short-sighted, it's very stupid, it's very costly, and it will lead nowhere. Encourage security and prosperity in an area and you will have a different outcome. Look at what is happening now in Palestine, in the heart of Tel Aviv. The cases of suicide bombing are on the rise, in spite of the fact that Israelis are killing Palestinians with their 'defence' forces every day. You cannot deal with world unrest by creating more unrest. You cannot stop killing by more killing; you have to stop killing by working on removing its root causes. The root causes of violence and the lack of peace in the world today are poverty, neo-imperialism, and depriving many human beings in the world of their basic human dignity.

PRACHA: Is it an Islamic teaching, not to return killing with killing?

MAHMOUD: Yes, Islam teaches exactly that. The Koran clearly commands us to repel evil with good, so that the person with whom you have an enmity becomes an intimate friend.

PRACHA: So it is a popular misunderstanding when we say that Islam promotes the way of the sword?

MAHMOUD: Actually, historically, the bloodiest people in the world have been Europeans and not Muslims. I am not going to say that Islam is like Christianity, as in turning the other cheek. But Islam is not a religion of violence by any means. Islam is a religion of power. You must have power in order to prevent violence.

PRACHA: With regard to ensuring economic security as a basis for peace, can you elaborate a little bit more and assess the so-called success story of Asian development in the case of the newly industrial countries, Japan, Korea, Taiwan, Singapore and Malaysia in particular? What is your analysis, from a Muslim point of view?

MAHMOUD: According to Islamic teaching, whatever happens happens by the will of God. The Koran says we should always compete with one another in the performance of righteous deeds. So, by Islamic standards, the prosperity of Asia is good. Islam does not deny the West its right to prosperity, it merely denies the West a right to achieve prosperity at the expense of other people by exploitation and domination.

PRACHA: So you see Korea, Taiwan, and Singapore as good examples?.

MAHMOUD: Yes, examples we should emulate. But I wouldn't want to live in Singapore: it's too over-disciplined. I like countries that are a little crazy. Singapore is like an anthill; everything is in place. Japan is almost like that, but Singapore is worse.

PRACHA: You don't like those countries in that respect?

MAHMOUD: No. I mean, this is my own personal preference. I like countries like Indonesia, like the Middle East, like India. There is a bit of craziness in them.

PRACHA: I would like you to make an assessment of the successes and failures of the Asian experiments with communism and Marxism.

MAHMOUD: I am not dogmatic. I think that Marxism has some positive things. What I disagree with is totalitarianism, in the name of anything, whether it is Marxism or democracy or whatever. I think communism has been least successful where a country was unable to internalise it and make its own version of Marxism. The Russians were too totalitarian, and actually, in the end, they practised what may be called state capitalism. I think the Chinese are better. We don't think much of China, but I really admire China very much, because in my view the Chinese are changing, but they are changing slowly. Look at the price we paid for the change in Europe: the millions that were killed and raped and displaced, the misery that was created. Was it really worth it? We got rid of communism in the Balkans, but I think Yugoslavia was better than what we got. I am not dogmatic, I think any ideology has some good, some bad. I just don't think we should impose any ideology on the world.

I told the American ambassador the other day in Jakarta, I said, 'you must realise that American democracy will not work here because people here are polite, they don't know how to insult their leaders'. A colleague of mine said, 'I want freedom so that I can call Bush the father a farce'. I said, 'that's fine. But what happens after you call him a farce? Nothing.' But the Americans value this freedom – that you can be critical of your elders or leaders. One of the things I found very shocking when I first came to the West was when a child wants to speak and the father wants to speak, and the child will say, 'Daddy, shut up.' I couldn't say that to my father. So that's very important for people in Asia, particularly in Indonesia, with its Hindu and Muslim cultures. A democracy there has to be a democracy of respect, reverence and so on. When we hear about all the problems in Indonesia, they were only in Jakarta, not everywhere. I think we must allow each nation to develop the system that's best for them.

PRACHA: You mentioned Iran. Do you think that Iran could be a model for alternative politics among Muslim countries?

MAHMOUD: I am not sure that the Iranian case could be duplicated by other Muslims, because it comes out of a peculiar Shia Iranian world-view that is not shared by the majority Sunni community. But it has some positive aspects. Iran is now the most stable country in the region. Iran has a rich culture, a rich tradition, and a solid infrastructure. They also have their ways of dealing with things, an Iranian way. They may riot and want things, but they don't go on a rampage of destruction, as we do in the Arab world of the Middle East. In the Arab world, the first thing you do is go out and burn cars and loot shops, and the Iranians don't do that. The way that the students operate in Iranian politics is very useful; people could learn from that also. The students played a crucial role in the downfall of the Shah, who was not just or moral. The students are now playing a very important role in the democratisation of clerical rule, and there are many right-wing clerics who don't want that to happen. Again, it's about power. There are power-mongers in Iran. I don't say that the Iranian regime is perfect, but I think it's working. It is definitely *not* an axis of evil. The funny thing is, none of these countries that Bush is calling the axis of evil has ever done anything to America.

PRACHA: You mentioned that Saudi Arabia is still using traditional Islamic consultation in their political process – what did you mean?

MAHMOUD: I meant that it is happening only in principle. In practice, the Saudi regime is the worst regime in the Muslim world, in my view, because it's an absolutely totalitarian regime ruled by one family. All the government positions are distributed among this family. They are the ministers, they are the kings, they are everything. So this Saudi regime doesn't work anywhere else – and it shouldn't work in Saudi Arabia either – but the Americans don't see it as a bad regime and regard only Iraq as bad.

PRACHA: What about the countries that use parliamentary systems, like Pakistan, Indonesia, and so on?

MAHMOUD: Indonesia is good. In Bangladesh they are trying very hard, and I think it is good. Pakistan is problematic. I think one of the tragic mistakes of the twentieth century was the partition of India. It shouldn't have happened. I think that Muslims in a united India would have had a far better chance. There would have been a big minority of them. They would have had a better fighting chance. Pakistan started as a fortress of Islam, and it has never achieved anything really important. Now it is a nuclear country, which is a great paradox. Both India and Pakistan have nuclear weapons, but there are lots of hungry people, so what's the use?

PRACHA: What about Malaysia?

MAHMOUD: Malaysia is actually good. I don't think their system would work anywhere else, because it is so peculiarly Malaysian: this imposing of Islamic rule over the whole country, when the Muslims are not the majority, really. They are making them the majority by encouraging them to have more kids, and all that. The way that power works in Malaysia is not really democracy. It's a kind of a directed democracy. I think now in the region (apart from Singapore, which again is too small, just a city state), the most interesting experiment is what's happening in Indonesia. Where will it go? That will be very interesting to see. What will happen in 2004? Who will become the next president? They have passed a law in the national assembly to have the president elected by direct vote. They have actually gone ahead very well in this process of democratisation, and I wish them all the best. I am a Muslim, and it is the largest Muslim country, and that's why I didn't like Abdurraman Wahid's politics. I told him he should not have called for the recognition of Israel or become too close to the state of Israel. Indonesia can play an important role as a Muslim country that has credibility with Muslims. But Mr Abdurraman Wahid liked to be in the limelight, liked to travel, liked to be invited as a guest of honour, and so on.

PRACHA: At the moment, multinational corporations have an important role in the world. How do you see multinational corporations?

MAHMOUD: We talked a little bit about the world problem of international economics. Basically, the problem with multinational corporations is that they are economic giants. This is not acceptable from an Islamic perspective, but right now Muslims don't have the power, so what we say and do does not count for very much.

PRACHA: So how can we resist American domination?

MAHMOUD: That is a different issue. I tell many of my Muslim friends that opposing America openly is really courting suicide. At this point we have to accept the reality. America is a big power, and it's a ruthless power sometimes, so it's very important for countries, especially small countries like Libya, Lebanon, Syria and countries in South-east Asia, to maintain good relations with America. The multinationals are largely American concerns, and the current American administration has no qualms about favouring them. They actually want to pick and choose, they want free trade only in so far as it benefits America. But they are not willing to face the burden they place on the environment; rather, they maintain that anything that benefits the American economy is good. Otherwise it's no go. I think we are living in a time when it is necessary to maintain good relations with America, within limits.

I mean to say, America has a lot of good and positive qualities. The civic spirit of the American people, the vibrancy of American society, and their initiative in inventing things and in making things and so on are good. I also really believe in the resilience of the American system. Right now Americans are going through a crisis, and it is still my hope that, as with previous crises, the American system will be able to correct itself. How it will do so after the Bush era is an interesting question.

PRACHA: What sort of crisis are you talking about?

MAHMOUD: I am talking about the crisis of the constitution. This includes the constitutional rights of citizens, regardless of who they are, whatever origin they are; the crisis of freedom of expression; the crisis of the equality of all citizens; the crisis of America being a leader for good things in the world. All these things are now overshadowed by America's 'war on terrorism', and, if anything, this war will create more terrorism rather than help to resolve the problem of terrorism. So I don't know what is going to happen. Saddam Hussein was tyrannical and hated by his people, but it was his people who should take care of him, not us. That is why I say we must be on good terms with America, because America sees itself to be above the law. You know that the Bush administration refused to endorse the international court of justice, because they don't want this court to have jurisdiction over Americans. If every state did what America does, there would be no international law anywhere. So all this is part of what I call the American crisis today.

PRACHA: You talk about civic spirit in American society. Does Islamic society have any place for civic spirit?

MAHMOUD: Actually civic spirit in Islam is built into the system itself, and is part of our worship. In the golden age of Islam, every mosque had, as part of its complex, a hospital, a bath-house, and a place for the rehabilitation and care of the poor. That was done through the Islamic system of endowments, what we call '*waqt*', where somebody says that he will buy, for instance, this spring of water and dedicate it to the service of the community for the repose of the soul of his parents. It's done like that. The Islamic form of worship, according to the Koran, always couples the performing of prayers with the giving of alms. They go together. So civic spirit *is* a part of Islam, and it still operates a great deal at the social and the individual level. The problem is that Muslim regimes are not very good and just. I believe that the problem in the Muslim world now is the lack of accountability. The ruler is not accountable to anyone.

PRACHA: Can the combination of civic spirit and praying that is found in Islam be of relevance to the modern NGO movement?

MAHMOUD: Yes it can, and there are Islamic NGOs, within limits, because often Muslim countries are either the rich poor or the poor rich. Indonesia, we say, is a poor country but is potentially quite rich, because it has a lot of natural resources. The rich poor are countries like Saudi Arabia, which have money, but no infrastructure. I mean, they are trying to build the infrastructure. I think a lot of the good of religious tradition in every

Mahmoud Ayoub

society comes out when the society has security and prosperity, and human dignity is safeguarded.

The Koran begins from this; the Koran says that human dignity is so crucial. It says that we have God speaking in honour of the children of Adam – that is every human being. God gave every human being the power to travel and do things. They are preferred over other creatures. It is sad if we look at many Islamic countries and see what happened to the human dignity that God gave us, as a special favour to all of humanity. It's not there. Saddam could kill anybody – he was not responsible to anyone. All good Arab Muslim rulers should be responsible. This situation is not good or healthy.

PRACHA: Now many people look at the NGO movement, the grass-roots movement, as the balancing power to the state. Could that happen in Islam? Do you think it is healthy?

MAHMOUD: It is a very healthy phenomenon. I wish there were more of it in Islam. I think Muslims were more successful when they were open to learn from anybody. We become far less successful when we think we are self-sufficient. I think the West has developed the whole idea of NGOs far better than other parts of the world, and we all, including Muslim countries, can learn from the West. The NGOs could be the conscience, as they really are of the nations of the United Nations. Like Médecins Sans Frontières/Doctors Without Borders – all these international NGOs are wonderful, and they are doing great work. They should be encouraged everywhere, and in this kind of international way, similar to the American initiative with their Peace Corps. There is a lot of good in America. One can see the good in America – I can be an American and be very critical of America.

PRACHA: We have missed one country that many people look at quite positively, and that is Libya. Do you see it as an alternative model?

MAHMOUD: Libya is a problem. I wrote a book on Qadhafi's religious ideas, and published it in Britain some years ago. Libya was founded on a positive note during the regime of King Cenusee. Although he himself was a decent man, a simple Sufi, his regime was a problematic regime, and there was a lot of poverty. Tripoli was the casino and brothel of the West. All that was changed. But Qadhafi's ideas are too far out, they can't work as a political alternative, even though he does have some good ideas.

So far, if you have noticed, I have not accepted any alternative. Every one you have asked me about, I have rejected. You know why? Because I don't believe there is any political alternative that we can all adopt. There is no such thing. There are many alternatives. They all have some good and some bad, and they all have to serve the needs of different countries. But there is no such a thing as a viable political alternative for every country in the world.

PRACHA: But do you see anything positive that we can learn from Libya?

MAHMOUD: We can learn from what a Libyan once said to me: 'I like the revolution and the regime because before the revolution I lived in a tin shack. Now I have a house.' In that way Qadhafi did some good. He gave the people dignity, a home. John Cooley, who wrote on Libya, commented on the fact that he came to Libya once and wanted to give a few pennies to a soldier in the airport to jump the queue. The soldier would not accept it. He said, 'you stand and wait your turn'. So the Libyans have a kind of self-confidence that is good. I like the fact, for instance, that whereas the other North African countries remain French colonies in some ways, Libya did not remain an Italian colony. They value their culture, their language, and their tradition. I like that very much. I like Libya actually. Their basic ideas are good, but the *Green Book* is too imaginative and unrealistic.

PRACHA: As you said, it is too authoritarian.

MAHMOUD: In the end, yes. Qadhafi is like all the others. He says that he's not authoritarian, he says that he has no authority, and that authority is in the hands of the people. Three things have to be in the hands of all the people: authority, wealth and armaments. In fact, none of these are in the hands of the people in Libya.

PRACHA: I asked you about the success of the newly industrialised countries, and you said only positive things. Are you implying that Islam can be successful and grow with capitalism?

MAHMOUD: Islam is not socialism. People try to read into Islam all kinds of things like democracy and socialism. Islam is capitalism in the sense that wealth is a divine gift. You can be wealthy, if you do it by taking lesser profit through lawful business. In fact, if you are wealthy you have a better chance for heaven, because your wealth, if you spend it on God's calls (that is to say, for the poor), will speak for you on the day of the resurrection with God. Islam very much respects private property, without limits. The only limit is on how you acquire it. You cannot steal it; you cannot usurp it; you cannot get it through coercion, or through cheating people by hoarding or speculation. If you carry on trade, putting in, say, 10,000 dollars, and you make 2,000, then you are fine. But if you make 10,000, then it becomes suspicious, because you may have resorted to unlawful practices. I am talking about ideals here, not reality.

PRACHA: We need to find principles to operate from, and how can you be very rich without exploitation, because our wealth came from the labour of others and natural resources?

MAHMOUD: You see? Perfection cannot be achieved. But that fact does not mean that it should not remain a goal. We cannot have a world without exploitation. That does not mean that we should exploit; we should try to avoid it.

PRACHA: Is there any place for equality of wealth in Islam, similar to the Western European model of trying for a more equal distribution of wealth among different sectors in society?

MAHMOUD: To be frank, I am a Muslim, but the best model for me is Fabian socialism – a moderate socialism. I like it very much. It is the best economic system in the world, in my view. Although Islam does not approach Fabian socialism, it once went a long way towards equality of wealth, through the Sarkart (Zakaat – charity – one of the five pillars of Islam). The Sarkart is not now in force because there is no Islamic religio-social authority to do it. The principle, however, is still there – that of all your surplus wealth you must give 2.5–5 per cent for the poor for education and other welfare purposes. Islam thus does go some way towards alleviating poverty via equalisation, but I think it is best done by welfare states. I like Canada; I want to move all my assets to Canada. It is not that I am rich, but I would like to keep little when I retire. In Canada they take a lot of taxes, but you can go to any health clinic with your health card and you get immediate attention. My child and the children of the poor and the rich can go to the same university. I like the welfare state.

PRACHA: Is there any teaching in Islam that supports this kind of Fabian socialism?

MAHMOUD: Not directly. I say it goes a long way towards social equality, but one has to be realistic. Islam started in a culture not of plenty but of scarcity. The Muslims became rich finally through conquests, but that's not the original Islam. The original Islam was born of scarcity, and it is always incumbent on the people to strive to do jihad in the way of God with their wealth and their lives. It always puts wealth before life, because even the little of it that the people had was so precious. If you have a few kilos of dates and you lose them, it means your children can't eat. So it was a culture of poverty.

PRACHA: So the teaching is related to the actual situation of those days?

MAHMOUD: Exactly. There was a man who came to the Prophet and said, 'I have a great deal of wealth, and now I want to repent to God because I did something wrong, and I want to give my wealth to the poor.' So the Prophet asked whether he had children, and the man said, 'yes'. So the Prophet asked him why he wanted to give his wealth to the poor and let his children grow up into beggars at the doors of other people. So the Prophet asked him to give only one-third; one-third is enough. Thus it became a principle in Islam that if you want to give, you cannot give more than a third of what you have.

PRACHA: Now I want to move to another topic: the fashionable concept of 'civilisational dialogue'. The dominance of the Western world-view over other civilisations has been around for some 200 years, if we date it from, say, the Enlightenment period. How is this relevant to Islam?

MAHMOUD: That is a good question. Before the Enlightenment, one could say that Islam was part of this world-view, because Muslims are as much connected to Abraham and Aristotle as are Christians and Jews. Islam was part of what we may call Western or Middle Eastern civilisation. It really covers all of the Mediterranean area, from Alexander of Greece to Muhammad of Arabia. From the Enlightenment on, however, there is a diversion of civilisations, with the emphasis in the West on rationality, materialism and so on, while Muslims insisted on remaining traditional. However, I believe that there are many commonalities between Islamic and Western civilisation, and on the basis of these commonalities we can have a very constructive and useful dialogue.

The calls for a dialogue among civilisations are an answer to Huntington's idea of the clash of civilisations. This is legitimate and good. We have to realise what we are in dialogue with. In its basic orientation and world-view, Western civilisation is Christian, and there are lots of Christian elements in it, but it is now secular, and so we are dialoguing with a Western *secular* civilisation, whether we are Muslims, Hindus or Buddhists.

Here again, there are many good things that secularism has given us. We should not reject it completely. I disagree with Muslims who insist on staying in the seventh century socially. We should learn from secularism. If I may invent a term, I would call for a 'religious secularism'.

The basic meaning of secular is 'temporal'. Secular means 'time', 'century', 'age'. Secular does not mean 'worldly', in the material sense. It means temporal – that we should all live in time, and we *are* all living in time until we die. What happens then – God knows, whatever it is – we can't do very much about it. There is an Islamic principle here that is very, very useful. The Koran tell a story about a very rich man called Karun. He was advised, 'seek with whatever God has given you the abode of the hereafter, but do not forget your portion of this world'. Islam holds that you must learn to live in this temporal life, although no one is going to live forever, and work for your hereafter as though you were going to die tomorrow.

In Islam, every event, every dimension of human life has two aspects: one this-worldly and one other-worldly. That is healthy. I believe that faith in God, or ultimate reality, or *dhamma*, or whatever, is useful. It makes us humble. The problem is that we think we are everything, and to believe that there is a greater thing than my being is a good, humbling thing; psychologically healthier also.

PRACHA: In that case, would you say that the idea that humans should conquer nature, which comes from the Enlightenment period, is not relevant to Islam?

MAHMOUD: It is not, because in Islam, as the Koran puts it, people should walk on the earth gently and should not be arrogant. Within our civilisations we have creation myths. When God wanted to create Adam, according to Islam, God said to the angels, 'I will place my representative as a steward on the earth'. We humans are responsible not for dominating and subduing nature, but for treating it with respect, because it is not ours to exploit. The earth belongs to God. We are only God's stewards on the earth. We have to treat it with gentleness and respect.

PRACHA: In that case, what about the idea of individualism, because this seems to be linked with separation from nature?

MAHMOUD: No, Islam is not individualistic. Islam is of the Ummah, the community. It is very interesting that on the day of the resurrection, God will judge not just individuals – that is you and me, as individuals – according to Islam, but God will also judge communities. The Koran says we shall question those to whom messengers were sent and we shall question the messengers. So Islam is not about the individual in isolation, for then it would be an imperfect Islam. A good Islam is about the individual *and* the society. Individualism is at the root of much of our suffering and the world's suffering.

PRACHA: So this is another point of departure from the Enlightenment era. But with the idea of individualism came also the idea of human rights. What about human rights in Islam?

MAHMOUD: The idea of human rights does not clash with Islam. But Islam speaks of the rights of God and the rights of the people, of the servants of God. Now, the rights of the servants are what God should protect. But humans must also safeguard the rights of God by safeguarding the rights of the people. For instance, if I injure or kill someone intentionally, for a reason, such as to gain wealth or whatever, or for no reason, I am violating not only the rights of the other person, I am violating God's rights, because God forbids this. So much of what we call in the West 'human rights' are in Islam considered as God's rights. God legislates in Islam, and He legislates for human rights. If, for instance, you wrong me and then you repent, God cannot forgive you – He simply cannot – until I forgive you, and that's very important. So there is a lot of emphasis in Islam on repentance. If you feel repentance when you sin against God, then God can forgive you, but when you sin against another human being, then you have to be forgiven by that human being first, before God will forgive you.

PRACHA: What about that other idea from the Enlightenment that goes together with individualism, namely competition? What about competition in Islam?

MAHMOUD: There is a basic ideal of non-material competition, which is for people to compete in the doing of righteous works. The Koran repeatedly says, 'compete with one another as if in a race in the performance of righteous works'. But competition in other ways is not commendable in Islam. Often it comes out of envy, or lack of contentment with what God has given, with wanting to be better than the other person. So it is not considered good in Islam. Again, Islam is not individualistic in this sense.

PRACHA: What about the Enlightenment dream of pursuing unlimited scientific knowledge, regardless of its ethical implications?

MAHMOUD: Islam has classified knowledge into various categories. Useful knowledge is knowledge that can benefit human beings, both in this world and the next. This includes religious knowledge, and scientific knowledge that would better the life of humanity. But Islam does not accept the principle of knowledge for its own sake. In the West, one of the most interesting things is the Faustian idea. You know Faust – this personality may have actually been an Islamic personality because Faust was an alchemist, and alchemy was an Islamic science. But Faust is totally unacceptable to Islam, because he wanted knowledge only for the sake of power, and in Islam that is not right. You must have knowledge in order to benefit yourself and others, in this life and the life to come. So knowledge falls into different categories: knowledge that is beneficial; knowledge that is harmful; knowledge that is neutral. You cannot ideally say, 'OK, I want to see how I can make a bomb that will destroy the world' – the hydrogen bomb – you cannot do that. But now Muslims are doing it. Your knowledge should be put to the task of improving humanity, not destroying it. This emphasis on unlimited knowledge again comes from individualism.

PRACHA: Any other examples of unacceptable knowledge?

MAHMOUD: You should not learn magic, even though you can learn magic. I am talking about the traditional 'science' of magic. You may learn it to avoid it harming you, but you must not learn it to harm others.

PRACHA: Can we bring this way of thinking to bear on issues like genetic engineering?

MAHMOUD: An example of where we can bring it to bear is in the case of somebody who discovered a bug that lives safely in the human host – that is, in the intestine – but if it is taken out and mixed with some other microbes, it becomes totally destructive. Now this could be potentially used for chemical or biological warfare. The man was prevented from carrying on the research on the grounds that it was dangerous. But he said, 'no, I have the right to research because I have the right to knowledge'. This is a good example of where Islam would not allow further research. The whole issue of cloning presents a similar problem. Muslims have gone as far as most in allowing organ transplants, but they will not allow cloning, because that is interfering with God's creation.

PRACHA: Another related concept that came from the Enlightenment is that of 'progress', meaning unlimited material growth. How is that regarded in Islam?

MAHMOUD: We have talked about that already. Islam does not put limits on the knowledge of how to create economic growth. What it puts limits on is how you acquire your wealth and how you use your knowledge. You can be very rich, and if you are rich and you are mindful of others, that's fine. There is then no limit to how much you can have and how you spend it.

PRACHA: But what if we are not talking in terms of individuals but in terms of countries, where the aim of the country is always more and more growth?

MAHMOUD: I don't know that Muslims have yet to face this, because when Muslims were prosperous, they were not alone in being prosperous in the world. Right now this is not a problem, because most Muslim countries are poor.

PRACHA: In Islam, what is the relationship between politics and religion?

MAHMOUD: Islam started as a religion, although Muhammad, in the second half of his career, became a political leader and the head of a state. Yet he did not see himself as an empire-builder, as a politician. His aim remained the spread of Islam in Arabia, and as much as possible in the world. But Muslims very quickly had to face the issue of authority, and who was to succeed the Prophet, so they invented the institution of the Caliphate. But, in fact, neither the Koran nor the prophetic tradition gives us the political system. When Muslims finally began to develop political theory and so on, they did so at least 300 years after the Prophet. So politics always lagged behind religion in Islam. It came to be part of Islamic jurisprudence and law. So there was not a distinctive kind of Islamic politics, until we get to the introduction of Greek philosophy into Islam, when some Muslims began to model some political theories after Aristotle or Plato, and fit them into an Islamic framework.

Muslims today say, without much knowledge, that religion and politics are intertwined in Islam.This is a problem, in that most of the activists are not very well informed. While, to some extent, it is true that politics and religion are intertwined, and that politics is subordinate to religion, in reality politics and religion were always at loggerheads. There was always a tension between the religious establishment and the political establishment. Shi'ite politics has followed a theocratic model, but these are ideal politics, not reality. In the Shi'ite politics of Iran and Iraq, the ideal ruler, the Imam, is believed to be in the world but hidden from view. He is in hiding, in occultation. Now, until the Imam returns, the people will do politics as best they can, but only under the Imam, they believe, can you have a truly just politics. This is why I said earlier that the Iranian model will not serve for all Muslims, because it is based very narrowly on a Shi'ite ideal that is not capable of being realised.

In some ways, the idea of politics in Islam is relatively recent, at least in theory, because even when people wrote books on politics, they really relied on what I call 'precedence', which is what people supposedly did in the early days, the good old days. This was good politics; they did not do bad politics, but much of that train of political thought is an idealisation of things that weren't so ideal. Normality and reality, even in the early times, did not always coincide with the ideal.

PRACHA: What about the idea of decentralisation? Is there support for this in Islamic political thinking?

MAHMOUD: In Islam there is a kind of decentralisation in everything, even in religion. There is no one central authority. That's why Muslims need a voice, an international voice, and that's why I am advocating in my book on Islam that probably Muslims should empower the Organisation of The Islamic Conference (OIC), to speak on behalf of Muslims. We have no Vatican in Islam; we have no central authority. Everything is decentralised.

PRACHA: Is decentralisation also relevant in governing a country?

MAHMOUD: There are many people who still think, with some justification, that the ideal form of Islamic rule is the Caliphate. For even when he did not have much power, the Caliph had a kind of moral authority that was important. Now that we don't have that, Muslims have fallen back on the nation-state model. The feudal Islamic political model is no longer feasible.

PRACHA: How do you analyse the cause of Islamic fundamentalism that is mushrooming in the world right now?

MAHMOUD: There is fundamentalism everywhere. There is Christian fundamentalism, Christian terrorism, Islamic fundamentalism, Islamic terrorism and Buddhist fundamentalism. Fundamentalism is not just an Islamic phenomenon. In many Muslim countries you have a large number of educated men and women who have no purpose in life and no voice. So they turn to religion for that voice and purpose. I believe there is a very close correlation between Islamic revivalism and the corruption of power in the Muslim world. The Egyptian government still refuses to give Muslims a voice, not because they think Muslims are dangerous but because they want power only for themselves. Now Hosni Mubarak is preparing his son, Jamal, to succeed him. Thus Egyptian human rights activists have coined a new Arabic word, which means 'republican monarchism'. Again the Americans are looking in the wrong places for Islamic fundamentalism and terrorism. These are the results of insecurity, frustration, and lack of purpose among young people. If you look carefully, these movements, whether they are in Egypt, Turkey, Algeria, in any Muslim country, they are largely among young people.

PRACHA: If you want to change society, from the Muslim point of view what is the best *means* for doing so?

MAHMOUD: The ideal society in Islam is a society that enjoins the good and forbids evil. Islam is realistic; the Koran says that God will not change what is in the people until they change what is in themselves. Muslims must work to change society; we need rulers who view themselves as servants rather than masters of society. We need to improve the level of education among Muslims, and also we need international help, frankly, to allow Muslims to develop viable societies. At this point, Muslim societies are largely consumer societies of Western goods based on natural resources. In large measure, these are the resources of the Islamic world, not only natural but human resources. Now America builds factories in Asia because of cheap labour. In some ways it benefits the Asians, but it also keeps the Asians poor.

As a visiting professor in Indonesia, I raised objections with an American colleague over the idea that because we are Americans, and we have some money, we can go and buy the cream of the people in Indonesian universities and get them to come and teach for us. I said, 'why do you want to disrupt other programmes, simply because we have a few dollars more?' I can't accept that. We go back again to the issue of justice: we need to create a just world. Right now we live in a world where no society can change itself without doing so within an international framework. If the Americans really opposed the creation of the European Union, it would not have come into being. Unless the West not only allows but *encourages* Muslim societies to become viable, then we are going to continue in this misery of killing people on the suspicion that they might kill us in the future. It's very sad. I think the world we live in is not a good world, a clean world. It's an ugly world. We have to do the best we can as individuals to make it a little better.

PRACHA: Is violence an acceptable means of effecting social change, according to Islam?

MAHMOUD: One should use violence only to defend oneself or to defend one's space, one's family, one's livelihood and the Muslim Ummah. The Koran very clearly says that jihad is for the defence of the oppressed among men, women and young children. So Islam does not say that you cannot use violence, but it does say that you cannot use violence indiscriminately; and violence must have a purpose.

PRACHA: So if you use violence in a revolution to help change the society, this is justified in Islam?

MAHMOUD: Violence must be used very carefully and as a last resort, that's the unfortunate thing. I am convinced as a Muslim that the original message of Islam is very humanistic. But we have lost the message, the humanism of Islam, because of the bad times in which we live. More warfare is not Islamic. In Islam you fight only against those who fight against you. You cannot go and kill indiscriminately. Thus I would have to say, in conclusion: Islam does not justify that what Osama bin Laden and others are doing. You are not supposed to go and kill innocent people. They try to justify it on the grounds that all of America is an army and we are justified in killing anybody because they are part of the whole system. This does not make sense to me.

6 | Bishop Julio Xavier Labayen

Bishop Labayen was born in 1926 in Talisay, Negros Occidental, Philippines. He was educated as an Associate in Arts at San Agustin University, Iloilo, Philippines; then, during the 1950s, went to Rome, where he gained Licentiates in Theology and Canon Law. He has been awarded honorary doctoral degrees in sociology and in education. Bishop Labayen is a courageous and prophetic advocate of a renewed spirituality based on social justice, respect for indigenous cultural values and the preservation of the environment. He has a deep concern for land and human rights, particularly for indigenous peoples. His refreshing approach is of being 'evangelised by the sense of humanity and sacredness of the earth of the indigenous people', rather than the other way around – a more usual practice of the Christian church. He is deeply committed to inter-religious dialogue. Under the dictatorial Marcos regime in the Philippines, Bishop Labayen and religious friends formed the Socio-Pastoral Institute, to discover their role relating to gross human rights violations under martial law. The Institute had an influential role in radicalising the Christian community, leading to its taking non-violent action against injustice; advocating democracy, and playing an important and dangerous role in dismantling the Marcos regime. This placed Bishop Labayen and his colleagues on a military hit-list. Some conservative bishops regarded him as 'not toeing the line of the Catholic Church'. This was a painful, dark period of his life, as he had always identified himself as a good Catholic. He was instrumental in forming the Federation of Asian Bishops Conference, where he served as executive chairperson of the Office for Human Development. This has a progressive influence on Catholic communities in other Asian countries.

He is currently Chairperson of the Socio-Pastoral Institute, Philippines; co-chairperson of the Task Force Detainees of the Philippines; chairperson of the executive committee of the Asian Cultural Forum on Development (AC-FOD), Bangkok; co-director of Asian Rainbow and co-chairperson of 'TIPAN' (Covenant), Alternative People's Politics. He has held positions in the ACFOD co-ordinating team, Bangkok; as co-chair of the Bishops' Businessmen's Conference on Human Development; as National Director of the National Secretariat of Social Action, Justice and Peace, Philippines; as executive chairperson of the Office for Human Development (FABC) Philippines; and as director of the Summer Institute of Spirituality, Manila, Philippines.

Among his major publications are: *Revolution and the Church of the Poor* (1995); *Wisdom and Compassion: Message of Buddhism and Christianity for our times* (1989); *Incarnational Spirituality* (booklet).

The Interview

PRACHA HUTANUWATR: First of all, would you like to give an overview and a critical assessment of the present social and economic system.

BISHOP LABAYEN: Actually, the present system has a long story. Like all stories of men and women, the long story that led to the present system started with a beautiful dream. In my book *Revolution and the Church of the Poor* I hold that all revolutions have started with a beautiful dream. In fact, they started with a noble intention.

Let me just dwell for a moment on the basic point of reference of this noble intention. The noble intention stems from the rightful value given to the human being and to human relationships. The revolutions intended to uphold, vindicate and promote the human being and human relationships. In concrete terms, this noble intention translates into liberation of workers from their oppressive condition of exploitation, deliverance of peasant farmers from their bondage to landlords, ending the massive impoverishment of the poor, and narrowing, if not eliminating, the gap between the haves and the have-nots. Here lies the noble intention at the start of all revolutions. In the process of revolutionary change for a better world, however, something happened. The noble intention gradually shifted from the value given to the human person and human relationships, and we drifted away from it. For this reason, so far, revolutions have not delivered the goods they promised at the start.

The revolutionary process of change shifted the point of reference from the human person and human relationships to the material. Gradually the material usurped the rightful place of the human. The mass media of social communication played a decisive role in this shift. The mass media created a new culture – world-view, values and meanings – which made people accept, participate in, and promote the shift. This new culture is consumerism.

Consumerism dominates the present system today. It stimulates the acquisition of consumable goods. In other words, the culture of consumerism stimulates people to desire even those goods that they do not really need. Consumerism instils in people the wish to acquire and to accumulate even superfluous goods. As such a culture develops, it eventually generates addiction. People cannot distinguish any more between the goods they 'desire' and the goods they really need.

The culture of consumerism shifts the point of reference effectively and systematically away from the human person and human relationships, and towards money. In the present system, money symbolises the capacity to acquire goods. Money also symbolises business profit. Money is also power. It can buy votes at election time. It can make people do things that they would not usually do. Money projects prestige. Money becomes the central focus of the system. Hence the accumulation of wealth becomes the overriding concern of the people, whose attitude has been formed by the culture of consumerism. Such obsession to get rich makes people disregard the social order set by law: take, for instance, illegal drug-trafficking. For the owners of the means of production, the accumulation of wealth translates into profit-making. Profit becomes the key motive of the system.

Consumerism creates its own family. The first member of its family is materialism. Materialism sacrifices the transcendental dimension of the human person and human relationships by reducing it to the material and the temporal. The human person becomes simply a thing to be used and exploited. The sister of materialism is hedonism (the desire for pleasure for pleasure's sake). Hedonism produces addictive consumption. One of its pernicious effects is to place women among market commodities, with a price tag. I refer here to the commercial trade that we call prostitution. The human subject becomes merely an object. This attitude is also true for workers in a factory. The machine is indispensable for production. Individual workers are dispensable. They are hired and fired practically at will. The system takes away from them their job security. A third member of the consumerist family is individualism. The individual self becomes the centre. Individualism erodes human relationships. We are back to the jungle. The law of the system takes after the law of the jungle: survival of the fittest.

Morality has become an empty word because of the erosion of the value of the human person and human relationships. Though justice is founded on the human person and has to do with human relationships, it has no place in the system. Human rights, particularly, get in the way of the present system. This was the reason why former President Ramos banned the Nobel Peace Prize winner, José Ramos-Horta, from entering the Philippines during the Asia–Pacific Economic Co-operation (APEC) summit in November 1996. Ramos-Horta, as we know, got the prize because of his fight for human rights. What, then, is the basis of right and wrong, good and evil, in the present system, given the fact that morality based on human rights has been subverted?

Democracy is government of the people, by the people, for the people. It is a farce under the present system. If the present system regards human persons as mere objects, how can we speak of people? In which case, where are the people from whom the government emanates, with whom the government relates, and for whom the government operates? Governments have continually marginalised the people. The government often does not represent the people. The promotion of globalisation is a fine example of this reality. The globalisation of our economy and the market has been taking place at the expense of the Filipino masses.

Some time ago I had a friendly conversation with an American. I drew something to his attention: 'You Americans came to the Philippines under the pretext of installing democracy in our country. That was almost 100 years ago! I must tell you that today we still do not have democracy!' Spontaneously he retorted: 'I have news for you! Even here in the United States we do not have democracy!' The USA leads the pack that promotes the globalisation of the present neoliberal capitalist system.

Our government initially installed the paraphernalia of the present system during the martial law regime declared by the late President Marcos on 21 September 1972. The government then began consorting with the transnational corporations by giving them incentives such as cheap labour that was not adequately protected by law. Simultaneously, the government subjected itself to the conditions of the International Monetary Fund as a precondition for a loan from the World Bank. These conditions mobilised the whole Philippine economy towards the capitalist open and free world market.

Our government signed economic pacts and treaties with other nations and groups of nations (such as ASEAN – Association of South-east Asian Nations). At the last APEC summit in Manila, Ramos signed the Philippines into the World Trade Organisation (WTO), which replaced the General Agreements on Tariffs and Trade (GATT). The WTO aims at absolute global free trade. Eventually, by the year 2020, all tariff barriers must be removed. We know that tariff barriers are meant to protect local products.

What really struck us most during Marcos's martial law was the build-up, in a short time, of the military and intelligence, from 60,000 to 300,000 people. Obviously, the budget for this build-up was enormous. In fact, the military acquired the maximum allocation of resources from the governments annual budget. The budget for education slid to a poor third, after public works infrastructure. In the wake of this military build-up, perceptibly the role of the military shifted drastically. In earlier times, the role of the military was to defend national constituencies from foreign invasion. Now, in the present system, the transnational corporations have invaded us in the Philippines. Whenever we Filipinos –workers or peasant farmers – protest to defend and uphold our rights against these foreigners, the military breaks up our picket lines. Worse, the leaders are 'salvaged' (summarily killed) by the military to break up and do away with the organised militant protesting groups. This paraphernalia is now called the tripod of stability of the system: the first leg of the tripod is business (TNCs) and finance (IMF/World Bank); the second leg is pacts and treaties among nations, and the third leg is the military and intelligence.

During the angry 1970s, people of different nations rose in protest against the dehumanising effects of the present system. They were met with military violence and suppression. Martial law was declared in Korea in 1972, the same year as in the Philippines. India passed its Maintenance of Internal Security Act (MISA) in 1975. In 1971 the Sri Lankan military massacred the protesting organised youth. This was to be repeated in 1989. All these violations of human rights and the use of violence are a logical outcome of the present system. As I said, and I repeat, what else can we expect in a system where money usurps the centrality of the human person and human relationships, and where the human person is considered merely as a thing, an object not a subject?

PRACHA: What is your analysis of liberal capitalism, which is being globalised today?

BISHOP LABAYEN: Liberal capitalism, as a system, has in itself the seed of globalisation. Schumacher's axiom, 'small is beautiful', is a heresy to capitalism. For capitalism, 'big is beautiful'. The capitalist system aims at unlimited profit. Profit depends upon the market. The size of the profit, therefore, depends upon the size of the market. Globalisation of the liberal capitalist system aims at making the whole globe a free market for the system. If there is a possibility of a market in other planets, the system will move beyond globalisation into planetisation.

The Encyclical of Pope Paul VI, *Populorum Progressio* (on the Development of Peoples, 1967), summarises the characteristics of the liberal capitalist system as follows:

- Its key motive is profit: profit for profit's sake.
- Its supreme law is competition: survival of the fittest. The big fish gobble up the small fish.
- The right to the means of production is absolute, not relative. It has no limits (for making a profit). It has no social obligation.

PRACHA: When you say that liberal capitalism started with good intentions, don't you think this good intention was based on the wrong hypothesis; that is, since the enlightenment period we have given so much importance to the human being? Is that also part of the problem we are facing now?

BISHOP LABAYEN: To respond to your query, I shall present an analysis of the revolutionary process to find out where the whole process went wrong or fell short in delivering the goods it promised in its initial beautiful dream.

Did the whole process go wrong because of the social analysis that preceded it? Or was it because of the strategy that flowed from such analysis? Or maybe it was because of the tactic used in the strategy of adjustment? All these elements – social analysis, strategy and tactic – can hardly be faulted. They do not have any inherent capacity for giving direction for making an evaluation. It is quite plain and simple: they neither have a mind nor a will. In that case, only the human factor can be faulted. The human factor came up with the tools for analysis and applied them accordingly. The human factor implemented the corresponding strategy and also considered the tactic for strategy adjustment. Behind all these, it was only the human factor that made up the initial beautiful dream. The responsibility for the whole process lies with the human factor. The human factor also directed the shift in the whole process. We now ask ourselves, where lies the vulnerability of the human factor?

Once, I was talking to an American friend who is an economist, and I asked him, 'you are an economist. Tell me about economics.' Knowing my social orientation, he replied: 'Bishop, let us not waste time! Let us face it. The long story of the two competing economic systems – capitalism and socialism – terminated in the 1989 European event. History then pronounced its verdict: only the capitalist economic system has weathered all the vicissitudes of the long, hard-fought process. I will tell you the secret of the survival and prosperity of the capitalist system. It feeds on the fuel of greed. No man or woman would invest unless he or she can get something out of the investment. 'The more returns, the more incentive.' I told my friend: 'OK, I think you are right. Let me tell you, as friendly advice: just keep your greed in check!'

Where am I leading to? We have to be honest and accept the truth that in each and every one of us there is a streak of greed. The capitalist system built itself on this innate greed in each and every human being. Its underlying culture of consumerism cultivated and nurtured this greed. It made people avaricious, self-centred, and unmindful of human rights and human relationships.

The initial beautiful dream turned into a nightmare!

PRACHA: Do you really think this weakness can apply to any ideology that does not give serious consideration to the nature of the human being? Maybe you can relate that also to socialism.

BISHOP LABAYEN: Right! At the dawn of the industrial revolution there arose a demand for organising the market, where the goods produced by the discovered machine could be made available to the general public, the consumers. The name Adam Smith is very much associated with the organisation of the market. The organisation and establishment of the market contributed to producers' profit. In the process, the original purpose of providing goods to consumers was compromised for the sake of more profit. Eventually we know that profit-making eclipsed the availability of goods in the market for the consuming public. Profit-making became the key motive of the economic system.

This obsession for profit lay behind the exploitation of the workers in terms of unjust wages and unfavourable working conditions. This situation attracted the attention of a man named Karl Marx. Karl Marx's compassion for the oppressed and exploited workers made him explore the system for the root cause of their miserable plight. He concluded that the root cause was the ownership of the means of production in private hands. Marx sounded the clarion call of his revolution to liberate the workers from their bondage: 'Workers, unite! You have nothing to lose but your chains!' The strategy was to wrest the means of production from private hands and entrust them to a central governing body. The socialist revolution, we know, triumphed in the Union of Soviet Socialist Republics (USSR) and in Mao's China. But eventually the Communist Party fell to the same weaknesses as its counterpart in capitalist society. Clear evidence of this was the cry of the students in Tiananmen Square in Beijing in 1989: 'Clean the [Communist] party of graft and corruption!' The same guns that liberated these voices from below snuffed them out.

Once I had the opportunity to converse with a catholic bishop from Milan: 'I hear that Milan is the bulwark of the Communist Party of Italy. What can you say of the party?' 'The Communist Party?' he exclaimed, 'their top leaders are among the filthy rich of Milan.'

Karl Marx, in his realism, pointed to the economic system as fundamental to any and every society. We have seen that capitalism, the only history-proven viable economic system, feeds on greed. Greed, as we know, is incompatible with both religion and ideology.

The socialist and capitalist economies have undergone several adjustments in order to attend to the basic needs of their constituencies. Today, there is no such thing as a pure socialist economy or a pure capitalist economy. We can only talk of mixed economies. Agrarian reform, which is based on the expropriation of private land for distribution to the landless, is socialist in principle. And so is the policy of social welfare.

On the other hand, after the death of Mao Zedong, his successor, Deng Xiao Ping, opened China's economy to capitalism. At the height of the East–West confrontation, the USSR entered into a contract with Great Britain for the installation of the Siberian oil pipeline. The contract also brought World Bank financing.

Ideology and religion promote the common good. The present neoliberal capitalist system, on the other hand, feeds on greed and avarice. Common good and greed are incompatible. Here lies the dilemma of governments today. How would you blend two incompatible values and incentives?

PRACHA: When you talk about this mixed economy, do you have any specific idea of alternatives to experimenting with socialism in state ownership? Would you say that your ideal society, the Christian form of society, is based on a mixed economy? Can you elaborate on that?

BISHOP LABAYEN: What is an ideal society? The very word 'ideal' denotes something desirable. An ideal society sets the vision and the goal of a process that starts from where we are. Our present situation is far from desirable. We dream of a society where everybody will have the opportunity to grow into fuller life and humanity. We dream of a society where there will be an ecological system that will provide in abundance the resources we need to sustain our lives and those of all humanity. We dream of an ideal society where there will be compassion, love, justice and sharing that bears fruit in solidarity and peace. We dream of a society where there will be perfect harmony among peoples and with the ecological environment. In short, we dream of a society where fuller life, fuller humanity and the integrity of creation will be a living reality.

We have been dreaming. The dream still remains afar. It is almost becoming an impossible task to realise our dream. Even the beckoning star seems unreachable. Revolutions have tried reorganising our social structures and systems, but our beautiful dream and noble intentions remain unfulfilled. At this point, we ask: 'Have we missed an essential ingredient to make revolutions deliver the goods they promised in the beginning, with a noble intention?' The historical and empirical data have shown us that human beings possess a bundle of dialectically contradictory tendencies that alternate between what is humanising and what is dehumanising. Perhaps it is time now that we look into this bundle of contradictions within us.

The reviewer of my book *Revolution and the Church of the Poor* summed up the thesis I hold for the success of revolution by saying, 'the heart of revolution is the revolution of the heart'. Revolution, therefore, must look into not only the external structures and systems of our empirical reality but also, and more so, the state and quality of our heart and being.

I would like to respond now to the question. We have to be realistic! We have to live our lives within this concrete reality. The long story of the globalisation of the present neoliberal capitalist system tells us that, despite the flaws and shortcomings of the system, it has weathered the vicissitudes that accompanied its long journey. The concrete reality wherein we find ourselves today is the globalisation of the neoliberal capitalist system. We ask: 'Is there any alternative we can promote within the system? If yes, how do we do it?' In fact, this is not the first time that people have looked into alternatives within the system. For example, some people have thought of co-operatives. The purpose of co-operatives, as we know, is to evoke and promote participation and equitable sharing among the members. Such participation and equitable sharing is missing from the present system. The co-operative, therefore, tries to provide an alternative within a system where participation and equitable sharing do not exist. The failure of co-operatives is attributed to the lack of a programme or mechanism that would not only initiate members into the co-operative spirit but, more importantly, sustain them; sustaining the co-operative spirit is equally important. Otherwise we would be working in an organisation that does not possess the spirit of an alternative.

Secondly, agrarian reform has sought an alternative to the ownership of land. A large tract of land is expropriated to be redistributed among landless peasants. The spirit behind it is to liberate the farmer–tiller from his/her bondage to the landlord. Moreover, agrarian reform is meant to enable the peasant farmer to become self-reliant in his/her livelihood. For want of an initiating and sustaining mechanism to ensure the dynamic spirit of agrarian reform, some peasant farmers have sold their land. In the final analysis, the ownership of land reverts to those who have the money to buy it.

In the above two instances, it is clear that structural reorganisation is not enough without the corresponding spirit to make it operate in an alternative way.

We have an organisation called MODE (Management for Organisation and Development for Empowerment). Our understanding of a viable alternative flows from the learning I have mentioned above, that is, to have an integral approach. By 'integral', we mean that the alternative must be in terms of both alternative structures and alternative spirit. In particular, there must be a sustaining mechanism that will ensure the survival of the alternative spirit.

PRACHA: What about the idea of ownership?

BISHOP LABAYEN: Ownership denotes the right to own an object. Right always connotes duty. Right and duty are correlates. They are inseparable. The right to own an object connotes the duty to use the object in a righteous way. In the way we use the object lies our responsibility. The idea of responsibility makes the owner answerable for the right or wrong uses of the object owned. For example, an owner of a big warehouse full of grain has many options. He can hoard the grain and sell it when prices go up. The owner can also make the grain available for sale at a just price. Or he can even burn the grain to increase demand, and hence the price, by maintaining a low supply. In this manner, the owner can use or abuse his right of ownership. In the light of the abuse of ownership, it can be safely said that such ownership is irresponsible, self-centred, individualistic, materialistic and destructive. In most cases, this is how ownership is looked upon and exercised in the present system. It is much worse when we consider the fact that the process of globalisation of the liberal capitalist system, and its control mechanism, are in the hands of only a few. Peoples and nations are used and manipulated for the sake of profit accruing to those who control to the global capitalist system.

In communal ownership, the right to own is placed on the entire community. The community becomes responsible for the use of the object owned. Such ownership has better possibilities to promote the common good of the community. In a way, the insight and the initiative of Mao Zedong to institutionalise the communes was correct. It only went wrong because the Communist Party controlled the programme, and eventually deprived the masses of their rightful role meaningfully to participate in and enjoy the benefit of their own development. How ownership is looked upon and exercised is crucial in the programme of development. Upon it depends the reality of whether development is an integral part of human existence or not.

PRACHA: When you say that Marxism is very close to Christianity in its analysis, how, as a Christian, can you reconcile your belief with the basic philosophy of dialectical materialism?

BISHOP LABAYEN: Dialectical materialism stems from the philosophy of Hegel. Thesis and its opposite, antithesis, are in dialectical relationship. Such relationship should be promoted in order to draw out the synthesis.

Marx applied this Hegelian dialectical materialism to the dialectical relationship between labour and management. The relationship between the two is dialectical because of their opposite interests. Management seeks unlimited profit. Unfortunately it works for limitless profit at the expense of the workers. On the other hand, the workers seek equitable and fair labour conditions and job security. Marx formulates this dialectical relationship as 'oppressor–oppressed'. This formula defines the classes in society. Marx had further translated this dialectical relationship into a class struggle. The two classes – the oppressor and the oppressed – must continually struggle against each other. The expected outcome is to bring about the common good under the dictatorship of the proletariat. Our Christian faith recognises the reality of the opposing interests of the oppressor and the oppressed. But the same Christian faith does not advocate the triumph of one class at the expense of the other. Instead, Christians work for justice and equity in order to establish the common good. The common good is the sum total of the conditions of society that allow individuals and groups to attain their rightful growth and development. Christians believe that lasting peace is the fruit of justice and equity in society.

Finally, our Christian faith does not subscribe to the materialism of Marx, which reduces the world to the story of the material and the temporal only. In other words, Marx rules out all reality that transcends the material and the temporal. Here lies the atheism of Marx. The atheism of Marx and the God-relationship of Christians are poles apart. On the other hand, this Western philosophy of Hegel is different from the oriental philosophy of integration and harmony. The enlightenment attained by Buddha puts it clearly: everything in creation is interconnected, interrelated, interwoven in harmony for the sake of life. Our Christian faith subscribes to this enlightened vision of Buddha. Christians believe that the hidden plan of God in Christ is to bring together all things in heaven and on earth in Christ Jesus (Ephesians 1: 9–10).

PRACHA: We spent a lot of energy in the socialist movement in Asia. It also meant a lot of time, lives and sacrifice. What else do you think we learnt from socialism?

BISHOP LABAYEN: Marxist materialism insisted on socialist praxis. The Soviet Bolshevik revolution transferred the ownership of the means of production from private hands to the state. The Communist Party of the Soviet Union became synonymous with the Soviet state. At times, the members of the party behaved in the same manner as private owners of capital. What took place was the dictatorship of the party, not the dictatorship of the proletariat.

Mao won his political revolution over Chiang Kai-shek in 1949. The Soviet Union had organised itself according to socialist tenets since 1917. Mao considered the Soviet Union to be another bureaucratic capitalist state. He was extremely keen that the same thing should not be repeated in China, and hence he institutionalised the communes. The communes were meant to promote the participation of the proletariat. Moreover, Mao thought that there was no guarantee of a future for his political revolution unless a cultural revolution underpinned it. I fully agree with this insight of his. Only the ideological control of the Communist Party of China aborted Mao's Cultural Revolution. What happened in Tiananmen Square in Beijing in 1989 revealed the reaction of the Communist Party to Mao's Cultural Revolution.

Again we learn from socialist praxis the reality of the human contradiction which calls for the restructuring of our inner selves. In fact, this was Mao's insight. In the opposite camp, that of capitalism, the same insight surfaced. When US President Truman pulled General Douglas MacArthur out of the Asian theatre of war, the General shared his insight regarding the way the war had to be won. He said, 'this war could only be won by winning the hearts and minds of people'. We have seen the discrepancy between the noble intention that initiated all revolutions and their disappointing outcome. General MacArthur pointed to the conversion of the hearts and minds of people as necessary for the resolution of this discord.

At this juncture of world history, I think that Asia, with its centuries-old religious and cultural heritage, can make a difference. I am referring to the time-tested spirit of Asia – Asian spirituality.

PRACHA: Can you cite specific contributions of Asian spirituality and Asian values?

BISHOP LABAYEN: I think the Buddha's contribution is outstanding. The Buddha recognised the reality of suffering in the world. He set out to find a way out of suffering. He sought to integrate his body and spirit. He did this through a simple way of living, particularly his practice of vegetarianism, vigilance over disordered lust, and the practice of Zen (meditation). In the entire journey, the Buddha focused his awareness on the heart. Gradually, he experienced the purification of his heart and compassion for all. Finally, he contemplated upon the interconnection, the interrelationship and the interwovenness of the whole of creation.

I feel that a fragmented and broken world awaits the integrating power and life of the human spirit, which has been very much alive in Asia. In fact, the tradition of Zen practice antedates the birth of Christ by 500 years – around the time of the prophet Isaiah.

PRACHA: What implication does this have for an individual's relationship with nature and with other people?

BISHOP LABAYEN: In response I would like to relate my experience in the Asian Cultural Forum on Development (ACFOD). When ACFOD was ten years old, we were called to Bangkok, where the ACFOD secretariat is located. Who was called to this meeting? A Buddhist from Bangkok, a Hindu from India, a Muslim from Indonesia, another Muslim from Bangladesh, a Catholic priest from New Zealand, a woman from the Pacific islands, two Marxists – a Japanese man and an Indian woman – and myself. Why were we called to Bangkok? We were asked to evaluate ACFOD. How? It was meant to be done through two questions. First: what was the original inspiration of ACFOD? Second: given this original inspiration, should ACFOD continue to live by it and to continue in the same direction that the inspiration pointed to?

When the first question was tabled, all eyes focused on me. The group addressed me: 'Bishop, you started this forum. Will you answer the first question?' I was glad to reply. But before I did, I wanted to give a brief review of the story of ACFOD. The story started with the request the Society for Development and

Peace (SODEPAX) presented to me when I was the National Director of the National Secretariat of Social Action, Justice and Peace (NASSA). SODEPAX is the joint body of the World Council of Churches and the Pontifical Commission on Justice. NASSA is the arm for social action of the Catholic Bishops' Conference of the Philippines (CBCP). The representative of SODEPAX asked me to launch a movement that would harness the rich religio-cultural heritage of Asia for the programme of development. Without any hesitation I accepted the proposal. Then I found out that joining me was a political scientist from Tokyo University, Professor Mushakoji.

Originally the acronym chosen was ARCFOD (Asian Religio-Cultural Forum). But at the first organisational meeting the 'R' was deleted because of the presence of Marxists. We did not really mind, then. For we knew too well that the cultures of Asia were deeply religious. Asia, as we know, is the cradle of the great world religions, such as Hinduism, Buddhism, Christianity and Islam. From then on the forum came to be known as ACFOD.

Let me come to the first question. The original inspiration of ACFOD was to harness the rich religious and cultural heritage of Asia for the programme of development. Concretely, this inspiration points to harnessing the Asian spirit. I submit that the life of this spirit is what spirituality is all about. Since spirituality has become a rather misunderstood word, let me explain what was meant in the original inspiration.

Spirituality in development means placing the human spirit and its dynamism at the heart of the programme of development. The human spirit is an essential part of each and every human being. It is common to all human beings, regardless of gender, race, colour, creed, ideology and social status. What is the human spirit? I shall not define it. I shall simply describe it, by pointing to manifestations of its dynamism. The human spirit is our capacity to go beyond ourselves. It is our capacity for self-transcendence. In fact, here lies the very essence of spirituality in every religion. It is the very heart of spirituality. This reality inspired the composition of a song, 'The Impossible Dream'. The lyrics of the song speak of a dream that the dreamer admits is impossible to fulfil alone, and of the human capacity to gaze at an unreachable star. This capacity for self-transcendence translates into the dying of our egoistic, selfish human self into the rebirth of our true human self. How well the farmer knows these dynamics of growth. The farmer knows that the seed that falls to the ground must die before it can germinate and bring forth a rich harvest. Unless our imperfect, lower form of life dies, we cannot go beyond it towards a better and higher form of life. We attain our fuller life and humanity at the cost of labour, struggle and sacrifice.

The second manifestation of the dynamism of the human spirit is our search and drive for meaning. All of us are asking the question 'Why?' in an attempt to find meaning in our lives and in the world of events and relationships, both human and ecological, wherein we live. 'I was born to live; why must I die? I was born into this world. However long or short my life here may be, one thing is certain: one day I shall go away from this world. Why was I born into this world?' When people despair of finding meanings, often enough they end their lives by committing suicide.

The third and last manifestation of a dynamic human spirit is our capacity for the giving of self. Nobody wants to die, yet we witness people who gladly lay down their lives for somebody they love or consider worth dying for, or for a noble cause. We are inclined to attribute this quality only to heroes and holy persons. But if we pause for a moment and think of our mothers, then we discover that they have the capacity to give themselves so that we might live. They patiently and lovingly nurtured us in their wombs for nine months with the very life-substance from their blood. When the time came for them to deliver us into this world, their blood flowed first before giving birth to us. For several months they fed us at their breast. They burnt the midnight oil in vigil when we got sick. They were restless when we came home later than the appointed time. Indeed, true mothers are the embodiment of the capacity of the human spirit for self-giving.

This is the life of the human spirit. This is the spirituality that is rooted in each and every human being. This is the spirituality that the great world religions of Asia built themselves on and nurtured through the centuries. This is the spirituality that helped to shape the rich religious and cultural heritage of Asia. The harnessing, therefore, of the rich religious and cultural heritage of Asia in the programme of development means placing the human spirit of Asians and its dynamism at the heart of the programme of development. Guess who picked up immediately the point I was making?

PRACHA: Muto?

BISHOP LABAYEN: Yes, Muto Ichiyo, the Japanese Marxist. 'That's it. Spirituality! And that is what ACFOD should promote in the programme of development!' The Indian woman Marxist, who was seated beside Muto, picked up where Muto had left off. The birds of a feather flock together. 'Historical processes have moved us to a new level of consciousness today,' she began, 'and the new level of consciousness where we find ourselves today is awareness of the role of our ecological environment. Do you realise what depth of meaning this new level of consciousness gives to our feminist movement? No wonder the planet is called 'mother earth'. The earth, like the woman, is the source and sustainer of life. The human spirit has become sensitive today to this role of the ecological system, and its crucial importance for development, in much the same way as the human spirit has become appreciative of the indispensable role of women in development. The dynamic life of the human spirit is what the original inspiration of ACFOD wanted to harness in the programme of development. Spirituality is what ACFOD should continue to promote in the work of development.'

'Kamla', I rejoined, 'I have known you for more than ten years. Before you opened your mouth just now, all I could picture was you as a woman with a clenched fist raised in the air shouting "revolution!" What I hear from you now is a breath of fresh air.' Before we knew it we found ourselves conversing with one another on a deep level. I would even say that we were in deep communion with each other. We forgot our differences. In fact, we went beyond them. Afterwards, I tried to understand what had happened to us then, at that instant. I felt that we must have reached a certain depth, where our minds and hearts met. There we discovered that our minds aspired to the same 'impossible' dream and the same 'unreachable' star. Our hearts beat for the same dream and strive to reach out to the same star.

Lest we think all this is exclusively religious and cultural, let us recall the words of General Douglas MacArthur. His statement became the basis of several military strategies, in particular war propaganda. Later on, it was to be further refined in the strategy of psychological warfare.

What can we say of Mao Zedong? Mao believed that his political victory over Chiang Kai-shek had no guarantee of a future if people could not accept living according to its underlying utopian vision. For this reason Mao launched the Cultural Revolution. It was meant to convert the hearts and minds of the people to the utopia. The failure of the Cultural Revolution lay in its failure to have an effective programme towards cultural change. Cultural change cannot come about through threats, force and violence.

I have had conversations with Marxists along the same lines, understanding that spirituality is the missing element in failed revolutions. I was taken aback by their reaction. They have said, 'Bishop, we have been wondering what was lacking in our revolutionary struggle. We have searched for it all this time. You just said it: the real need is genuine change of heart and mind. Without this qualitative change of heart, structural change will not bring about the utopia we dream of, to which we have committed ourselves. At best, we shall merely go around in circles.' Asia, I feel, has a tremendous responsibility to make a contribution to the programme of global development by placing Asia's rich religious and cultural heritage at its centre.

PRACHA: How does this wisdom apply to our relationship with nature?

BISHOP LABAYEN: Let me bring in here my experience with the indigenous people in our territory, the Agtas. The setting was a gathering of personnel for our formation [training] programme for the whole prelature. Four Agtas were with us then. The resource person spoke about the Old Testament. He spoke about the experience of the Israelites of Yahweh (God) in their own story. How Yahweh drew water from the rock when they were thirsty in the desert. How Yahweh fed them with quails and manna from heaven when they were hungry. Accordingly, they gave a name to Yahweh, such as the Provident One, their Companion in their story, and so on.

After the resource person's input, I asked our Agtas, 'You believe that there is a God, don't you?' 'Yes', they replied. 'Do you have a name for God?' I further inquired. 'Oh yes! We call God "Makidyepat"'. 'And who is Makidyepat to you?' I asked with great interest. Then came a very surprising and, to me, interesting answer. They said, 'to us, Makidyepat is the source of all life. Whenever we are in the forest and we sense signs of life – the green leaves of the trees, the chirping of the birds as they hop from branch to branch, the living waters that flow through our brooks and streams, the animals that roam in the forest like us: whenever we sense these signs of life, we feel the presence and nearness of Makidyepat.'

These indigenous people lived in the forest for a very long time and did not have any ecological problem. When the greedy capitalists came, on the other hand, they ransacked and destroyed our forests for sordid gain. Now, as a result of the destruction of the forest water catchment, we have flash floods during the monsoon and drought during the summer.

PRACHA: The indigenous people extract very little from nature, only what is necessary for their survival. What does this world-view mean to the modern world?

BISHOP LABAYEN: Let me relate to you another experience I learned from the Agtas. Some of them served as guides to some Christians who wanted to see and experience the Agtas' way of life. The Agtas call the lowlanders Christians. After walking up the mountain for some time, the group felt hungry. Fortunately they were passing a grove of guavas. The trees were teeming with ripe guavas. The group helped themselves and relished the fruit. After the Agtas had eaten their fill they stopped picking the fruit. The Christians, on the contrary, continued to pick the fruit, filled their pockets and started filling their bags. They exhorted the Agtas to pick some more of the abundant fruit. The Agtas simply replied, 'we had our fill. We are mindful of other people who will pass this way. If we clean the trees of fruit they may not have anything for themselves. Like us, they also have a right to the abundant fruit of nature.'

PRACHA: Beautiful story!

BISHOP LABAYEN: Another experience I had when I went up to see where the Agtas live. We passed the banana plants on their territory. I asked my guide: 'Are your banana trees heaping fruit now?' 'Oh yes! Plenty,' my guide replied, and pointed to the fruit to prove his point. I asked him again: 'Are you not going to pick them?' He replied, 'We have enough already. We leave the rest of the fruits that are still on the plant for the birds.'

My experiences with indigenous peoples in other countries reveal to me that their world-view is similar, if not identical. I was listening to an American Indian at PP21 (Peoples' Plan for the 21st Century) in Minamata, Japan. This was at a workshop on indigenous spirituality. Eloquently he expounded his impression of the white colonisers of their country, the USA. 'I could never understand the culture of the white man', he began. 'When they came to our territory and discovered that there was a gold mine they almost went crazy! We could not understand this outlook. Where else will you find gold if not in the land? This time it was our land! When they saw the vast territory before them they wanted to possess it for themselves. We had been living in the territory all these centuries, and now they want it for themselves. So they fought us, to claim their 'right' to our land. This culture is beyond our grasp. To us, on the contrary, land is a gift from the Creator to our people. We live by the land. We are grateful to the Great One who bestowed this gift on us.'

I had the same experience with the Maoris in New Zealand. A Maori dock-worker was our resource person at a seminar on justice and peace. The Bishops' Commission on Justice and Peace sponsored the seminar. He said, 'To us the land is a trust given by the Creator to our tribe. Our chief is the responsible administrator of this trust. He assigns the use of the land according to the needs of the members of our tribe. The assignment of the land goes by a certain priority: the most needy use the land first, and so on. No one can exploit the land beyond his or her need. There are others in line who wait for their turn.' Then suddenly, pointing a finger to the white people before him, he exclaimed: 'You, white people, we cannot understand your culture. When you came to our land we had been living here already. This land is ours! God gave it to us. But then you circumvented our right to the land by putting up a legal system. According to that legal system one is entitled to own the land only when one has the legal title to it. And then you wave before us the paper that you call a land-title and grab our God-given land.'

What shall I say of our own indigenous people in the Philippines? To them the land is sacred. It contains the remains of their ancestors. The land is the symbol of their tribal continuity. For this reason they refer to their territory as ancestral domain. To eject them from their ancestral domain is tantamount to breaking the ties they have with their ancestors. Once I paid a visit to a family whose breadwinner had just died. The corpse was laid on a mat. There was no coffin. To slow down the process of decay they smoked the corpse, to evaporate the liquid within the body. After giving them my condolences I asked about the burial. The eldest son pointed out to me a plot in their backyard. He must have noticed my surprised look. To assuage me he pointed to the neighbour's backyard, saying: 'In that place they buried their dead.' At that instant I understood what ancestral domain meant! The capitalist mind considers the land only in terms of the price per square metre.

PRACHA: Very good. From this perspective, how do you evaluate or criticise modern industry?

BISHOP LABAYEN: Modern industry? It is the fruit of human genius. It converts the resources of nature to cater to the current needs of people. For example, you have computers, cars, the means of social communication, and so on. All these have promoted better communication between people all over the world. Modern technology and industry have made possible face-to-face encounters of a great number of people from different cultures and world-views. This has also accelerated the gains made by human genius, such as knowing the vast secrets that nature holds in store. These advances can be considered positive. But there are as many questions again, which need to be addressed, about its role and impact on the society.

PRACHA: Don't you think that industry is solely dependent on money?

BISHOP LABAYEN: Industry in itself is the fruit of human ingenuity. The way it is harnessed and used depends on the human factor. Is it for promoting the common good or is it for the vested interests of a few, depriving the many, even of their basic needs? As industry is organised today, its key motive is profit symbolised by money. Moreover, the culture of consumerism has become the motivating force behind industrial organisation. It is a culture of wastefulness of available resources, both natural and manufactured. Indeed, it promotes a culture (world-view, values and meanings) that dehumanises people. The result is alienation, frustration and the eventual meaninglessness of human existence and human relationships.

PRACHA: In your vision, what would a more humane form of industry look like? At the moment, industry is not only dehumanising but is also destroying nature, just to produce more and more.

BISHOP LABAYEN: You have already given the picture of industry today. We want industry to become more humane and environment-friendly. The question is how you convert the present industrial system towards this goal. I have always believed that responsibility lies with human agents. This responsibility lies with policy-makers, irrespective of their background, whether they represent the government or private enterprise.

The market is a key factor in present industrial organisation. It is in the market where profit is made. Government regulation of the market means that enough goods for local constituencies be made available and affordable. The local market should take precedence over the global market. Unfortunately, governments are moving more and more towards deregulating and placing industry in private hands. The question I ask is: what is the government's role today? Is it to be a subservient peon of the globalisation of the free market? Or is it to be responsible for the common good of its national constituencies? As we move more and more into globalisation, responsibility for the common good must be shared by an international body, such as the United Nations and its many designated offices. Here we speak of the common good no longer on just the national level, but also on the regional and global levels.

As to responsible policies for an environment-friendly industry, governments should enforce effective observance of anti-pollution measures for cars and factories. There is the possibility of harnessing solar energy. There is, I believe, enough technological capability to do so. This would reduce, if not eliminate, the pollution produced by fossil fuel. Furthermore, the conservation of our natural environment would depend on the policies regarding the conservation of our forests, particularly the water catchments.

Finally, a very important change needed for the conversion of the present industrial system towards humanisation and the common good lies in the lifestyle of our people. There must be counter-moves against the culture of consumerism. Cultural promotion for a simple lifestyle, I believe, would be the key to the conversion of the present industry to a humanising and environment-friendly goal. After all, the pattern of consumption and acquisition of people determines, in the final analysis, the behaviour of the market mechanism.

All that I have said sounds like a beautiful dream. We are entitled to dream, are we not? The crux of the realisation of the dream lies in the strategy. In line with the approach from the bottom up, we are trying to consolidate, on the basis of self-reliance and sustainability, the basic political unit of our society, which is the *barangay* (village). We are trying alternative programmes that will minimise the dependency of the *barangay* on the 'higher-ups'. We have, for example, the Grameen Bank for women, an idea pioneered in Bangladesh. Women, to a great extent, are an untapped resource in development. Their participation through the Grameen Bank programme enables them to be self-reliant. They provide the finance for household needs and some small-scale economic enterprise. We have also shifted to organic farming to reduce the market for chemical fertiliser and chemical pesticides. We have an ambitious programme of sustainable forest resource management. Such management will be in the hands of people who subscribe their meaningful participation in the programme of their own development. Similarly, we are tapping government funds for reforestation by the people in the *barangay* instead of by the government agencies. Ongoing formation of basic Christian communities provides the necessary motivation for self-reliance and much-needed cultural transformation.

PRACHA: You know that the present dominant tendency is to push Asian society to be like Japan or Taiwan. What is your vision about the relation between industry and agriculture and the lifestyle of the people?

BISHOP LABAYEN: I shall continue to pursue my thoughts on this subject. The whole process of globalisation is moving forward. Economic prediction points to the Asia–Pacific region as the centrepoint in the third millennium, chiefly because of its market potential. More than three-fifths of the world's population reside in the region. Then there is the accelerating advance of technology in the area. Japan is among the leading nations in technology. Asian economic tigers are emerging one after the other: we have Taiwan, Singapore, South Korea, Malaysia, Indonesia and the Philippines. They are fast catching up.

However, accompanying the development process are the negative results of capitalist globalisation. Outstanding among them is the pollution of water, land and air. Then there is the destruction of the forests, particularly the water catchments, which ensure the water supply and the prevention of flash floods. Moreover, industrial expansion affects agriculture adversely. Land is converted into sites for factories, business, golf courses and commercial complexes. In the Philippines, we have the Land Conversion Act, which legitimises this incursion into agricultural land, even those areas that had been earmarked for agrarian reform. I have already mentioned the need for a simple lifestyle as an alternative to a consumerist lifestyle. We have to recapture our sense of what it means to be human in a human community. At this point I recall my experience among our indigenous people, the Agtas. On the occasion of our formation programme in the prelature some participants who lived for some days among the Agtas experienced their humanising culture. They gave a glowing report of their experience. This report inspired me to tell the Agtas: 'You know, we used to pity you because you were marginalised in our society. The seashore drove you away from your original place of residence to the mountains. We thought you were deprived of the good things that we enjoy. But this glowing report about your humanising culture has changed completely my attitude towards you. I'm happy that you were marginalised. If you were not, perhaps your culture would have been dehumanised, as ours has been.'

PRACHA: So, in your vision of society, what is the relationship between industry and agriculture?

BISHOP LABAYEN: Today, congestion in our cities is a common phenomenon. The consumerist culture has effectively made people look to the city, dreaming of the 'good life' there. Driven by this attraction, people from rural areas move into the city. For want of available housing for them, they swell the shanty towns, and the mushrooming of squatters in the city is another striking phenomenon. This is true of Manila, Calcutta, Bangkok, Jakarta, and more. I think we need to look seriously into the decongestion of the cities. We need to reverse the city attraction in favour of agricultural attraction. The University of the Philippines has moved in the direction of technology transfer. Particularly, it has trained the farmers in the technique of improving their seed variety through cloning. The university technicians have also promoted among the farmers an alternative way of farming: organic farming. Japan has become conscious of its peoples' health, and for this reason has perfected the technique of organic farming. We send some of our farmers there to learn the technique. I have already mentioned reforestation and conservation of our forests. Decongestion of our cities is badly needed! It will improve the health and sanitation of city-dwellers. It will also contribute to lowering the crime rate, as experience tells us. But incentives must be provided to make people not leave the countryside, and to attract others to return to the healthy life in the countryside. People must be motivated towards an alternative way of life that is land-based and forest-based.

PRACHA: When you say we are not going for the economics of greed, what kind of economics do you envisage? This is connected to your statement about consumerism. What would be the lifestyle of people, according to such a vision?

BISHOP LABAYEN: Consumerism is a culture of wastefulness. A counter-culture calls for a lifestyle that consumes what is needed and does not amass superfluous things. Let us bear in mind also the diseases that accompany the consumerist lifestyle: obesity, cancer, hypertension, heart ailments, and so on. A simple way of life is a healthy life. The bonus that accrues to us through this simple lifestyle is the life-nurturing harmony we enjoy with the environment. We take care of the earth. The earth takes care of us. This line of thinking is very much a part of our rich Asian religio-cultural patrimony. We are talking here in our office of the Asian Rainbow network. By means of our Asian patrimony, with its multi-faceted expressions, we would like to harness what is left of this heritage in our Asian people to counter the dehumanising effects of globalisation. We would like to support and promote a growing network in Asia towards this goal. Together with the movement PP21, we would like to make our modest contribution to the Asian peoples' solidarity for a humane, compassionate and just society and for the integrity of creation. We would like to play our role in bringing about cultural transformation, and promote a consciousness among our people about what it means to be human in a human community. This would be our way of countering the culture of consumerism.

JOST WAGNER: I would like to know your opinion of the mass media, especially television. You mention, for example, that people in urban areas have different needs from people in the countryside. One reason might be television, with all its game shows, advertising, and so on. If we want to change that, perhaps we have to restrict television, or at least change the programmes. What is your position on this matter?

BISHOP LABAYEN: First of all, I am a fervent advocate of mass communications media. In fact, we have two radio stations in our diocese: AM and FM. I myself have a weekly radio programme that lasts for an hour. As you said yourself, it is not media as such that are wrong. It is how they are used; for what objective. Unfortunately, the media promote chiefly the culture of consumerism.

We have already talked about consumerism, how such culture stimulates the operation of the neoliberal capitalist economic system. We have also shown how consumerism is a culture of senseless waste. In my radio programme, I, a priest and a lay person (occasionally, a guest) discuss some vital issues of the day, analyse them, and then address them with the social teaching of the church. The latter touches the whole gamut of human existence: economic, political, social, cultural and religious. The human being and the human community are central to this social teaching.

I believe in the power of media, especially for cultural promotion. It is for this reason that the dominant economic system has invested so much in media promotion. The US-based CNN has even gone on air 24 hours a day to harness this power for specific vested interests. We know also, for a fact, how the media are used in war propaganda. They constitute one of the instruments of cultural promotion that the military victor grabs immediately upon taking over a country.

Vaclav Havel, former President of the Czech Republic, warned of the power of media: 'Television, to an unprecedented degree, can disseminate the spirit of understanding humanity, human solidarity and spirituality, or it can stupefy whole nations and continents.' In fact, mass media have gradually pre-empted politics in democracies. 'Mediocracy' has overtaken and replaced democracy. Mass media also usurps the right and role of the family to form its children.

While it is a bulwark against totalitarianism, freedom of the press, like other freedoms, comes with accompanying responsibilities. Just as democracies have safeguards against the tyranny of majorities, so must media safeguard the rights of minority audiences, children and innovative producers to educate and serve the public interest.

Governments must hold media corporations responsible not only to their stockholders, but also to all stakeholders in the broader public. These corporations can begin by disclosing their corporate principles and mission statements, publishing them along with their codes of conduct, while opening their books to environmental and social auditors, as do other socially responsible corporations. They can earmark funds for more public education and coverage of civic events and interactive 'town meetings'.

PRACHA: What about the other aspects of cultural development? We have talked about lifestyle and economics.

BISHOP LABAYEN: We have seen that culture is historically conditioned. Among the factors that condition culture is the structure of society, which serves as the social environment. On the other hand, culture determines the structure of society. Culture and the social structure mutually interact. The question to ask is: who is the agent responsible for the structure of society and the prevailing culture? There is a human agent who has to answer for these things. For this reason, we focus on reforming the human factor. In our diocese, we have singled out youth as a group that has the potential to make a difference in the formation of a new society. We also recognise the privileged role of families in the formation of youth. We design our radio programming for this purpose. We promote politico-cultural education that will enable our people to put pressure on the government to exercise its responsibility for the common good. By 'the common good', we mean societal conditions that will allow individuals or groups of individuals to grow and develop. Finally, we form and organise basic Christian communities that will respectfully dialogue with different faiths and cultures towards solidarity for the formation and realisation of a new society.

PRACHA: What about forms of governance?

BISHOP LABAYEN: In our new local government code, certain executive powers formerly in the hands of the central government have been devolved to the heads of the *barangay*. In my radio programme, and in our basic

Christian community programme, we are calling upon the *barangay* heads to exercise their duly devolved powers. At least in those areas where they enjoy such powers, they should sever the umbilical cord which is attached to the higher political lords in patronage politics. We are also politically educating our people at the base to support every effort of their *barangay* heads in this direction.

Moreover, we offer our people a programme of alternative livelihood that is viable. Herein lies another strategy towards their rightful autonomy and liberation from patronage politics. Our target is to approximate as much as possible to real democracy, which is government of the people, by the people and for the people.

PRACHA: And in this era of globalisation, one fact affecting governance at a national level is that nation states will have less and less power after signing agreements such as NAFTA, GATS, and so on.

BISHOP LABAYEN: Yes, globalised economic policies transcend nation states. We have established partnership relations with other local churches abroad. We have a partner in Austria and another in Japan. Through these partnerships and other solidarity relations with international groups, we hope to be able to lobby at the international level for policies that will hold international bodies responsible and accountable to the global public.

PRACHA: How do you see the future of state power, the nation-state system?

BISHOP LABAYEN: Very, very vague. With the revolution in media and information technology, it is difficult to predict right now what the future will be. Much will depend upon the solidarity among people who are committed to a just, equitable and compassionate global society.

PRACHA: Would a nation state be able to counteract the invasive multinational corporations, and would the *barangay* be strong enough to protect itself against them?

BISHOP LABAYEN: The heads of the *barangays* have always been beholden to the higher-ups: senators, congressmen, governors, mayors. The reason is simple enough: both power and funds are centralised, and trickle down at the whim and caprice of the power-holders. A dependency relationship is fostered and exploited. Now, with the new local government code, some powers have already been devolved, in areas such as health, social welfare, and so on. The objective of building the base is to break the dependency relationship wherever possible. The final objective is, of course, to stabilise the social base according to democratic principles. After all, any society depends, in the long run, on the stability of the social base.

On this point, we try to engage the heads of the *barangays* and their constituencies to take advantage of the powers devolved to them, and slowly break their dependence on the higher officials. In particular, we organise them so that they can stand on their own, not only politically but, especially, economically. Here is where alternative livelihood has its place. The shift from chemical to organic farming is a case in point. So is the community-based health programme, which capitalises on home-grown herbs, acupuncture, acupressure and the like. In the process, we also encourage traditional cures, which have been proven over the years. Then there is a sustainable forest resources management system. The people learn to conserve the forest water. At the same time, they can live by the resources of the forest. Our indigenous people can teach us how they have lived from the forest resources all these years and still conserve the forest water catchment.

Your question alludes to the formidable power that globalisation wields. But we have to start countering somewhere, instead of flowing with systemic globalisation and thereby making it more formidable. Lastly, I believe that the globalisation of sound, humanising ideas and community models are more formidable in the long run. And with the build-up of the dehumanising and polluting effects of the globalisation of the neoliberal capitalist system, I feel that more and more people, all over the world, are coming to their senses and looking for alternatives.

PRACHA: Connected to the question of governance and political structures, would you like to say a bit more about decentralisation in governance?

BISHOP LABAYEN: In my radio programme, I exhort the *barangay* units, heads and constituencies, to reflect on the fact that the higher officials are interested in them primarily for their votes. If they can come up with a viable model – say, of alternative livelihood – for all you know, the politician may take pride in the people of his territory. He can exploit the model by propagandising it for his own prestige. And who knows, he may even support the said project.

But basically, the objective of decentralisation is to promote the participation of people. Let us bear in mind that no development project will ever be sustainable in the long run without people's participation. Our role is to make people see the meaning of their participation. The United Nations has aptly stated that for development to be sustainable, people must meaningfully participate in the process of their own development.

Is it not true that for want of people's participation, democracy has thus far been a farce? Representative democracy approaches real, working democracy. But it has got to be evaluated regularly to make it operate in terms of real democracy. Centralisation is control from the centre. Decentralisation is people's control, from the bottom. The crucial issue is how, in the light of past history, we bring about operative decentralisation.

Let me continue. Without checks and balances operated by the people, the leader can become despotic, gaining absolute control. But such leadership does not go for authentic development of the people. A happy balance should be struck, where the leader checks the people and vice versa.

I am not saying that we should do away with political parties. The plurality of political parties serves as a control mechanism for one another. What I am saying is that party leaders should be conscious and responsible for the right kind of leadership for the growth of a nation. Unfortunately, this is not the case in many countries today. Political parties tend to rule out, if not suppress, people's participation.

At this point I would like to quote a portion from the American declaration of human rights:

> the most important of these rights are Life, Liberty and the pursuit of Happiness: 4) ... the function of government is to protect these rights, 5) ... governments derive their just powers from the consent of the governed and depend, therefore, on a contract between the governors and the governed, in which the governors promise to perform the legitimate functions of government in accord with the desires of the governed, and 6) ... whenever governments cease to perform their proper functions, and governors seek, instead of protecting the peoples' rights and securing their Safety and Happiness, to reduce them under absolute Despotism, the people have the right – indeed, an obligation – to revolt, to throw off such Government, and to provide new Guards for their future security.

This portion is a reminder to any and every political party, including the Communist Party, of their responsibility and duty when they take over the reins of government.

The split in the Communist Party of the Philippines (CPP) in 1986 was over ideology. On the one hand, the Reaffirmist (RA) faction was dreaming of the 1960s and 1970s, when Marxist ideology mobilised the party and the peasantry of central Luzon, and attracted other discontented groups to rise in guerrilla revolt against the Philippines government. On the other hand, the Rejectionist (RJ) faction realised that, since the widely known people's power demonstrations in 1986, which ousted the dictator Marcos, the consciousness of the people about the Philippine situation and their own potential had changed. Moreover, there had been much disenchantment with the party, particularly the election boycott by the party prior to the EDSA event. The party obviously failed to read the pulse of the majority, and human rights violations and abuses were committed by the party, such as the hasty, somewhat panicky, purging of the communist ranks in the countryside.

I was talking once to a peasant farmer from central Luzon. I said: 'Why don't you write a petition or request to the officers of the CPP, that they end their squabble as RA and RJ, for the sake of their avowed service to the proletariat? Instead of uniting forces, they divide forces.' He replied: 'We have already written them a thick dossier, but they don't pay attention to our petition.' So I asked: 'What now? What will you do?' 'Oh' he answered, 'we continue with our issues: the high price of fertiliser, the low price of our harvest, and agrarian reform. We continue our protest.' 'So how do you see the problem with the CPP?' I queried. The spontaneous reply revealed the peasant farmer's perception of the split in the CPP: 'Oh, that is their problem; they struggle for power among themselves.' Ideologies and party actions on the basis of ideologies stand to be judged before the bar of history. The CPP is no exception.

PRACHA: People are not stupid!

BISHOP LABAYEN: Not at all! At least, not the peasant farmer I was talking to. This is why I say that there is a new level of consciousness among our people. We cannot take them for granted. Nobody believed that the EDSA event could oust the strong Marcos. Yet it happened, due to the power of the people. In fact, the CPP miscalculated. They boycotted both the elections of the President and EDSA. They did not have their finger on the people's pulse.

What about the crumbling of the Berlin Wall in 1989? Nobody expected that, either, but it happened. It was preceded by Gorbachev's announcement of his policy of *glasnost* (openness) and *perestroika* (restructuring) just a few years earlier, and because of the raised consciousness of the people in the satellite countries, a critical mass was reached that led to the tearing down of the Berlin Wall. A chain reaction took place, and after only two more years, the Soviet Union fell apart. All our discussion from a rational perspective has failed to take into account the unexpected turns and twists of history, which seem to be guided by a mysterious hand that we are not aware of.

The conviction in Korea of the two past presidents for crimes committed against the Korean people is also unprecedented. I salute Korea for this. Now we realise that nations can try their former rulers for crimes they committed. This is a good reminder, for all rulers, that they cannot go scot-free after their term in office.

PRACHA: That is very good!

BISHOP LABAYEN: And now the youth are clamouring for the trial of Kim Young Sam and of his son. I admire the militancy of the Korean people.

PRACHA: What about the role of NGOs?

BISHOP LABAYEN: First let me tell you my experience of NGOs. There was a time when a windfall of funds came to the central Philippines province of Negros Occidental. The only condition for its disbursement was that it pass through an NGO. Almost overnight, NGOs mushroomed all over the place, and many of them belonged to the *hacenderos*, the sugar barons who own vast tracts of land. The fund was supposed to alleviate the poverty and penury of the *sacadas*, the contract-workers and farmhands who are daily-wage earners. There are NGOs who give priority to their owners' vested interests over the service they are meant to render to the people. There are also NGOs who use their programme for the people in order to get funds to keep the NGOs themselves in existence and operating. There are NGOs galore. We need to analyse them. It is not enough that they are NGOs. On the other hand, I believe there is a role that NGOs can and must play. They can be a very good mechanism for checks and balances. They can check the management of government development programmes.

PRACHA: What about civil society?

BISHOP LABAYEN: The handbook on the programme entitled Philippines Agenda 21 defines and describes civil society as follows: 'Civil society is the key actor in the realm of culture where the central concern and process is the development of the social and spiritual capacities of human beings in order, among others 1) to advance the frontiers of knowledge, 2) to achieve clarity and coherence of values, and 3) to advocate public interest.'

Civil society aims at a culture that is humanly holistic. Its central concern and process is to develop human potential in the social and spiritual dimension. It places high priority on the clarity and coherence of values. It aims at constructing and promoting a well-integrated body of culture (meanings, values and world-view). Hand in hand with this objective is the humanisation of our patterns and network of relationships, both human and ecological. Civil society, therefore, aims at bringing about a community and a society in a sound human and ecological environment. It strives to accomplish this goal through the formation of integrated, responsible, humanised citizens.

This new phenomenon of civil society is born out of the fast-moving pace of dehumanisation, alienation, frustration and brokenness that people the world over experience. On the other hand, it has emerged indicating the invincible capacity of the human spirit, despite overwhelming odds. Civil society presents a model that integrates all that we have said above regarding the central agent of sustainable development – that is, the human subject as a people – and the people's need for a culture that will make them masters of their own destiny, writers of their own story and singers of their own song.

PRACHA: Can you tell us about your work in the province under your supervision?

BISHOP LABAYEN: First of all, I must tell you that I assumed the position and responsibility of a bishop of the diocese of Infanta when I was only 35 years old, with only two years' experience in parish work. Moreover, I took this office of bishop before the great renewal programme of the Catholic Church, which the second ecumenical Vatican Council (1962–65) launched. I was definitely of the old school, which regarded bishops as 'princes of the church'. As such, I sat on a throne. I had the paraphernalia of a prince of the church: a gold ring with precious stones, a pectoral cross to match and flowing princely robes. Just imagine: young as I was, old people came to kneel before me.

Let me just tell you the experience that brought me to a turning point in my life. As a bishop of the old school, I was diligent at sending monthly memos to my priests. At one meeting with my priests, I found out that all my memos ended up in the waste-paper basket. At that instant, I felt like Saul, who was 'knocked off his high horse'. I was tempted to get back on my high horse to assert my episcopal authority. I will be forever grateful to the grace of that moment. I opted to remain on the ground. From that time onward, my relationship with my priests changed radically. I consulted them. I listened to them. I accepted the fact that I had plenty yet to learn from others. This change paved the way for radical change in my relationships also with my people and with the poor.

With this radical change in my person, I saw to it that participation became fundamental to our programme. Pope Paul VI, in his letter *Octogesima Adveniens* (1971), stated the need for participation and equality, which are two forms of human dignity and freedom. I believed him.

We have a continuing formation programme for the whole prelature. All key people – the bishop, the priests, the religious and the laity, the programme heads, the school heads – have to pass through this programme. Their responsibility is to translate the orientation and vision of the programme into their respective areas of responsibility. In this way, we form a church with one vision and one mission in the world. We hold ourselves responsible and accountable to the history where God accompanied us: the Judeo-Christian tradition that led us to Jesus Christ and the church he founded on the rock with Peter together with the Apostles. Here lies our identity. However, our mission orientation is towards all people. Especially to the poor victims of the systemic injustice in the world today. Thus we reach out to people who are not baptised Catholics; we work with organised sectors of our society such as the peasant farmers, the small fishermen, women, youth and indigenous peoples. We respect each other's identity and autonomy, but we co-operate and are in solidarity on issues that concern human dignity, human rights and ecology. We reach out and join hands even with those who are of other nations, denominations and beliefs. For example, we have partners in mission solidarity with Wiener Neustadt in Austria and with the Hiroshima diocese in Japan. Likewise we relate to other dioceses in the Philippines, such as San José in Nueva Ecija and Ilagan in Isabela.

Recently, we had 26 Buddhist monks from Thailand who spent some time living among us. The story behind this visit was the joint retreat that Tan Santikaro Bhikkhu and I gave to the priests of our prelature and to the lay facilitators of our formation programme. One wonders: a joint retreat by a Buddhist monk and a Catholic bishop? And to priests of a diocese and the laity? How come?

The answer is simple. The approach of St John of the Cross to union with God and the Buddha's approach to *nirvana* resemble one another. John says that to arrive at the possession of all one must go by the way of nothing. Buddha advocates void to arrive at *nirvana*. In fact, an English writer by the name of Abbot Chapman writes of St John of the Cross as follows: 'if you strip John of anything and everything that you can possibly label Christian what you have left in him is a Buddhist monk'. I remember the three-hour conversation I had in Hua Hin, Thailand, with three Buddhist scholar-monks. I came away from that long conversation with the impression that they know enough of St John of the Cross. Such was their interest in him and his teaching.

After the retreat, upon leaving, Tan Santikaro Bhikkhu told us that he would like to come back and experience living among us and our basic Christian communities. In February 1997, he fulfilled his promise. He did not come alone. Twenty-five other Buddhist monks from Thailand accompanied him.

On the last day of their stay, Tan Santikaro Bhikkhu asked me to talk to the monks. 'Where', I asked him, 'should I talk to them?' 'In your cathedral church', he quipped. 'What shall I say to them?' 'Simply tell them your life-story. Earlier you were a bishop who sat on a throne. Now you are a pastor who is among your people, especially among the poor', he suggested. So I did. In telling them my story, I had to talk also about the harassment I suffered from the military and the experiences I had with the conservative bishops. After talking to the monks I asked them if they had any questions. Since the questions were long in coming I asked them myself. 'You heard my story. Do you have any similar story in your own life?' One monk raised his hand. 'In our Sangha', he remarked, 'those monks who are open, progressive and articulate are expelled and disrobed.' 'Did you say disrobed?' I asked. 'Yes, disrobed!' quipped the monk who volunteered the story.

At that I pointed to the big mural on the wall facing us. It was Dali's painting of Christ crucified [Christ of St John of the Cross]. 'Do you see that man?' I asked the monks. 'He too was open, progressive and articulate. That is the reason why he was disrobed also by the powers-that-be in the temple and in the Roman Empire!' The eyes of the monks opened widely in disbelief. They could not believe that Jesus Christ was hanged on the cross for his political convictions. 'How about your relation with the state? Do you have any problems?' I inquired. One monk replied. 'First, we have such a long tradition of royalty. We would never go against the king. But whether the king knows it or not, the state and the military try to co-opt the crown. In the process we too get co-opted.' 'There you are!' I exclaimed. 'Your story and my story are very similar. But that does not make us one. You have your saffron robes. I do not have them. You are Thai. I am Filipino. But I know that Buddha desires that your hearts be purified so that you may have compassion for the poor. You have heard what we are trying to do in the prelature to walk the same path. Don't you think we are at one on this point?'

The older monk, who was commissioned to hand me personally their souvenir, remarked as he handed it to me: 'Bishop, you have touched our hearts!' These words touched me deeply. To me they were a validation of what we are trying to discover. That deep within us human beings there is something common to us all that reveals a certain nobility of spirit. In that encounter, we discovered what was deeply rooted in us, beyond nationality and creed. Discovering that, we understood and valued one another. Despite the fact that it was our first meeting, we felt very close to one another. Many people visit us with the same expectation as that of the monks. Invariably, we have got to understand and value one another. Indeed, deep within us human beings, we discover a oneness of heart that resonates with the same noble values and a oneness of mind that searches for what is true, noble, good and beautiful.

PRACHA: Do you have projects with the villagers and things like that?

BISHOP LABAYEN: We have programmes with some organised sectors – peasant farmers and so on, as I mentioned. With the indigenous people, we have a practical basic literacy programme. The programme raises their consciousness towards their own self-determination. They analyse different situations and organise themselves for concerted action. Their burning issue is that of their ancestral domain. It is on a national scale. We help them to join the national movement for the official enactment of the rights of the indigenous people to their ancestral domain. The organisation of the small fishermen enabled them to obtain a ban from the government on encroachments into their fishing area. The combined effort of various organised sectors forced the Secretary of the Department of Environment and Natural Resources (DENR) to check those of the department's personnel who were conniving with illegal loggers. But these personnel were not punished at all. They were simply transferred.

PRACHA: Transfer is the normal practice in my country as well.

BISHOP LABAYEN: How true that is! At least our people have experienced the fact that if they analyse their situation and organise themselves accordingly, they can get what they want from the government.

But we notice that the militancy generated during the time of martial law gets lost progressively with the passing of time. Through our radio programmes, we try to maintain a high level of consciousness regarding current issues, especially those that affect listeners more directly. Concomitantly, we accompany and encourage them to keep their organisation on the alert for mass action.

PRACHA: How do you cope with consumerism in your diocese?

BISHOP LABAYEN: First of all, we are not yet industrialised. Second, our people are poor. Despite this situation, our young priests find meaning in their work among poor people. I admire them for their dedication. Consumerism will come soon. Already we are an economic corridor. The government has opened this corridor by putting in excellent roads from Manila to Infanta. This corridor is known as *Marilaque* (*Ma*nila, *Ri*zal, *La*guna, *Quezo*n), for the different provinces in the corridor. It will be a highway for export–import trade. In fact, the government has a sophisticated plan of five ports in our area: the Pentaport: an international seaport, an international airport, a communications port, a business port and a recreation port.

Already beach resorts are mushrooming along the beaches. More and more excursionists and weekenders come regularly. The price of fish has gone up. This is also true with other commodities. Land speculators come and buy up the available land.

We try to stem this consumerism through our radio programme and pastoral formation programme. We build and capitalise on our programme for strengthening the basic political unit, the *barangay*. Our basic Christian communities consider this consolidation of the *barangay* as part of their pastoral mission today. Sectoral organisation and consciousness-raising are sustained.

We exhort our people not readily to sell their land. Otherwise we shall find ourselves one day among the 'squatters' in our own land of birth.

PRACHA: It's quite a good story!

BISHOP LABAYEN: Yes, indeed! We hope to continue to write our story with responsibility and personal commitment.

7 | Abdurraman Wahid

Abdurraman Wahid was born on 4 August 1940 in Java, Indonesia. His father was Wahid Hashim, and his grandfather Hashim Ashari – a lineage of prominent religious and political leaders. His early education was in the famous Islamic Pesantren indigenous educational institute. His higher education was at the Institute for Islamic and Arabic Studies at Al Azhar University in Cairo, and in the Department of Religion at Baghdad University. Both at home and in the Middle East he read extensively and had a number of spiritual teachers.

He returned to Indonesia in 1971 and taught Islamic studies at Hashim Ashari University, and became secretary of the Pesantren Tebuireng, founded by his grandfather. In the early 1980s he became the leader of Nahdlatul Ulama (Rise of the Islamic Scholars), a religious and political organisation with a membership of more than 30 million. Under pressure from Suharto, he pulled NU out of party politics and turned it into a large socio-religious non-governmental organisation focusing on Islam, education and community development. NU turned into a political party again when Suharto was forced to step down in 1998, and Abdurraman Wahid became the first elected president, serving from 20 October 1999 until 21 July 2001.

Since the early 1970s, Wahid expressed his thinking through his prolific writing, and later become a prominent public intellectual, debating especially what it means to be an Indonesian Muslim, the proper relationship between Islam and the state, and promoting social reform during the Suharto period. He belongs to a school of thought that accepts the inclusiveness of Indonesian Islam, rooted amid a deep and variegated Hindu–Buddhist culture and taking on much of the mysticism associated with the cherished Sufi orders. At the same time he advocates elements in Islam that support freedom of expression, human rights, egalitarianism and promotion of women's status.

The Interview

PRACHA HUTANUWATR: In Asia we are still following the colonial system of governance. This can be witnessed in the nature of our political systems, modes of economic development, model of administration and the nature of our education systems. The majority of third world countries in Africa and Latin America are also part of this colonial legacy. What is your response to this situation?

ABDURRAMAN WAHID: This should have been gradual. There is no harm in following other countries. We may take only the form without the essence. In this regard we should base our education on the school system of the West and then integrate our own philosophy of education into it. There is a need to abandon the positivist approach to life because positivism stresses our activities in life. Those who are assertive would capture the whole thing because success depends on the ability to talk.

We have to develop our own approach to everything. In the case of democracy, the rule of law is very important, but you should apply the law in such a way that it does not disturb the balance of power within society. It is therefore important for us always to remember that not all things violating the law should be punished. This is very important. This may not be acceptable to the West or to Western-educated people. When I said that I would like to pardon former presidents Suharto and Habibi, several intellectuals, especially those educated in the West, were angry. But I think that in order to achieve peace and stability in this country we have to demonstrate that kind of leniency. It should be proven that the person is guilty, and only then can he or she be forgiven. They should also be given the opportunity to repent. South Koreans adopted a similar approach towards Chun Do Hwan. But we have to apply this kind of principle very gingerly.

PRACHA: Do you have any long-term plans for reforming the present system towards the development of an alternative system of governance for Indonesia?

WAHID: Yes! I do. My idea of governance is based on Islamic principles and humanistic values. In Islam the role of a leader is to ensure the welfare of the people. It means the welfare of all. It is not correct to enrich only one part of society. It is necessary to work for all, especially for the weaker sections of society. In the long run we have to develop a policy that will ensure the well-being of the common people and will help them to gain more than rich people gain.

PRACHA: Given your background in the grass-roots movement, could you comment on the strengths and weaknesses of that movement as a political force?

WAHID: The history and origin of the grass-roots movement in Indonesia can be traced back at least 500 years. It begins with the defeat of the King of Panja, in one of our earlier kingdoms, the Panja Kingdom. He was defeated by his son-in-law. The King then went back to his mother, who lived on Madula Island, where he learnt the so-called 40 virtues. Later he went back to the Kingdom of Panja via the Sola River, which is very big. On his way back, while travelling in his boat, he had a dream, in which he saw his teacher coming towards him and heard him say 'you are not entitled to be a king. You should take care of the ordinary people and educate them.' The King simply followed the message of his teacher. He stayed on an island that is now unified with the land Mosque.

After 500 years of colonialism, we witnessed in the twentieth century the emergence of people's struggle for freedom and independence from colonial rule. We also saw the establishment of all those organisations based on people's power, and later the emergence of non-governmental organisations (NGOs), who were not keen on the support of Marxist groups but worked according to Marxist ideals. In my view, their strength lies in the fact that they work for the community and basically for the people. But their weakness is that they follow a Western pattern of activity. They depend on Western NGOs, which in a way, at least sometimes, is detrimental to them. I can give you the example of Indonesian women activists. Our women activists, dressed in shorts and lipstick and with cigarettes in their hands, came to Jakarta to visit the market place in order to speak with the sellers and other ordinary people. These are very expensive and not so common lifestyles. This is why ordinary people do not understand them. We cannot simply follow the West. We have to develop our own ways and means of working with the people.

PRACHA: How do you foresee the interplay of power centres such as the state, mass movements and transnational corporations?

WAHID: First we have to think about what the government can do. In my view, the role of the government has to be reduced. If the government does not limit its role, then it will try to control and dominate mass movements in the country. In order to be able to control the mass movements, the government will not hesitate to depend on transnational corporations. First, I have already said in cabinet that ministers should not try to curtail or challenge the people's ability to be active. Activity, in fact, rightly belongs to the community. The only thing that the government should do is to plan and then co-ordinate with the NGOs in organising activities. With this kind of relationship a society's activities will be those of local communities and people. Secondly, the multi-national companies are part of big business today. It is to be made clear that they will be given 'the opportunity to invest' in so-called big business but not in agriculture. Agricultural programmes and initiatives should be in the hands of the government, in order to serve the people. The people should be involved in the implementation of these programmes and initiatives. We will be in a position to encourage and develop activities in society through these two steps. Without government intervention, small and medium enterprises of the community cannot compete with multinational companies.

PRACHA: Multinational corporations have much more power than people at the community level. MNCs have more resources and often exploit the mass media, such as television, for product campaigns. How can people at community-level cope with this situation?

WAHID: It depends. If government intervenes effectively then we can solve the problem of the community. In the long run we will be able to defend our ground. Some time ago Swami Agnivesh from India came and talked to me about globalisation, which is affecting industrial development in his country. I said to him that we also have the same fear but that I would like to use the technology developed by the multinational companies for the benefit of Indonesian industry. This is the only way our industry can compete with others. In the United States 43 per cent of the economy belongs to small and medium business enterprises. Only 28 per cent belongs to the big companies. The rest are managed through municipalities and other initiatives.

PRACHA: What about consumerism? If you allow radio and television to continue to advertise as they do now, they will only promote consumerism among the people. People will soon overlook their own cultural and traditional identities and buy brand-name products rather than traditional handicrafts. They will prefer multinational products.

WAHID: It depends on several factors. If we actively help NGOs to raise the level of consciousness among the people and support their campaigns to produce culturally valuable goods, we will be able to face the challenge. I would like to repeat what I said earlier: we should not oppose these multinational companies or the present process of globalisation. We should, rather, use them.

SULAK SIVARAKSA: Our concern is that government and NGOs try to work together. The government is on the whole represented by bureaucracy. This is the misery of the system. This is the predicament. In my opinion most governments knowingly or unknowingly represent TNCs, the IMF and the World Bank. In this light we need not see governments as our enemies; rather, we should regard them as good neighbours.

ELIAS AMIDON: There should be a forum for building good neighbourliness, kindness and compassion. We should try to establish a basis for dialogue among different groups that oppose each other. This would offer a space for dialogue between NGOs and multinationals, which in other conditions would be highly improbable. We have a chance to break this cordon. This is a creative response to the challenge. I think we should also make use of information technology to inform and learn from each other.

SULAK: We should, I think, be a small group, but try to influence in a big way. Countries in our region, such as Thailand, Malaysia, Indonesia, Philippines, Korea, and so on, should come together and conduct a dialogue with the IMF and the World Bank. International financial organisations cannot control our alternatives. At the same time, the governments should be more compassionate towards their people. It should consult and discuss with the people the ways in which they can become self-reliant. I think the government needs not so much to help the people, but to become more compassionate towards them. It can create conditions and opportunities for the people to help themselves and protect themselves from exploitation. I have learned this experience from the Thai situation with the Assembly of the Poor. The government did not help them but rather harmed them. I asked the Prime Minister, Mr Thaksin Shinawatra, not to help them and at the same time not to harm them, but to learn from them. This is more important than trying to help them without understanding them. The government so far has been trying to help them without learning from them. If we learned to learn from the people, they would be very happy.

Many NGOs used to be very critical of the government. Some were even anti-government. They see that the government has to become strong to resist the TNCs. I think the government also needs the people to become strong. It is important to recognise the fact that without the people's support governments are susceptible to greater manipulation by the TNCs. This is where my King does not see the point. He is in the pocket of CP, a Thai multinational corporation. He gives them money and they offer their expertise. The King believes their expertise to be right. He knows that he has no idea of the poor and has a very low opinion of the NGOs. I hope we can change his opinion also.

JEFFREY SUNG: I think the ideas of Sidney Webb, the British socialist, are more relevant in this context. Lee Kuan Yew was studying in England during Sidney Webb's time and was greatly influenced by Webb's ideas. The idea that we must have a big government to counterbalance the MNCs may have begun here. The Singapore model that Lee Kuan Yew gave rise to was clearly based on this approach. This is why we have a huge public sector. We also find that the private sector is very weak in Singapore. The government deals in all the strategic industries and the rationale is to neutralise the role and influence of the MNCs.

SULAK: We have to change now. If the government wants to be strong then NGOs should also be made strong. The government cannot do everything. Let the NGOs also participate. Let us encourage the people to do it themselves. The Thai government issued a decree on education with an emphasis on a dominant role of the government. This is wrong because everyone is brainwashed by the government.

People – the monks, the mosque, the church and so forth – should run education. The government could, of course, have a minimal role. The government can insist that children learn about national identity and our common history, but should let the people do the rest. Let them give rise to good Christians, Buddhists and Muslims. The government need not interfere.

PRACHA: How do you see the present crisis of leadership in Asia and in the world at large?

WAHID: Of course, we do not have giants like Abraham Lincoln or Churchill or Roosevelt. The most important thing is that the system should be established and developed in the right way, to ensure that so-called ordinary people may emerge as leaders of the country in ways that will benefit the country as a whole. They need not become great leaders. Let us take, for example, Tony Blair from Britain or Gerhard Schroeder from Germany. They are good examples in this context. I would consider Jiang Zemin from China as good, despite his attitudes on democracy and human rights within China. This so-called ordinary leader actually faces several challenges in China that are not ordinary at all. Anybody who can lead China in tackling her difficulties is a great leader because of the many problems facing the country. This is also true of India and Japan. Do not forget about Japan. I do not rely on the greatness of a leader.

SULAK: What you said sounds very good but can I contradict or disagree? We now have to realise that capitalism is the dominant force. Someone like Tony Blair may be very nice; people liked him before he became the Prime Minister of the UK. People believed that he would change the Labour Party and also help restore his country's traditional values. But Blair has proved that he is part of the global capitalist system and can be controlled by the USA. Bill Clinton is also a very nice man, but to become President of the USA you have to be more or less controlled by the big capitalists, particularly the arms and tobacco merchants. That is why they have to keep on waging wars. The Gulf wars, for instance, are good indications of their oil interests. This is despite the fact that the United States was defeated in Vietnam. I feel that unless these leaders are free from the control of capitalists, they cannot work for the people. The people in the UK no longer believe that Mr Blair is with them. That is why we think that you should remain with the people. I do believe that the IMF, the World Bank and the transnational corporations will move away from you if you are closer to the people. I also notice that the international press has been attacking you from all sides. They initially thought that you were 'God'. Since you have not changed things in their way or as drastically as they wanted, they have started criticising you. The only problem is that the more the international press attacks you, the more some people in your own country will, unfortunately, begin to believe them.

WAHID: We should move step by step, gradually. We cannot do everything at once. This is very important. We can hear some hopeful voices, even among the capitalists. For example, during the 1830s, US President Andrew Jackson formed the American Federal Resource System, against the selfishness of the industrialists. This was to be organised for the benefit of all the people, not only for the industrialists. We can see now that the American Federal Resource System is attending toward the needs not only of the industrialists but also of the common people. I do think that if we undertake this kind of initiative we can eventually 'tame the industrialists'. We will, of course, be out of power if we fail. This is what I said to you. This is also very important to remember. Of course, the press would campaign against me, but as long as the people are with me I am not afraid. You can see that today I go everywhere in Indonesia. People feel that I am one of them and support me in elections. In Indonesia now, so many people, including the intellectuals, say that I am wrong about this or that, but I do not care. I do whatever I think is right. I am not responsible to my critics but to the people. You can see that yourself. That is my stance, and parliament referred recently to my 'guilt' for adopting it. I do believe that the parliament itself will be changed by the people in the long run.

As I mentioned earlier, the key here is gradualism. We cannot force things too quickly. But we have to be determined. We have to be persistent. That is the key word. Take, for instance, when people like Mary Robinson say that they would like to rip the army. The question, for me, is: where is the army? We will need them to protect us. It is, of course, necessary to resist those who work against the wishes of the government and civilian rule. The cardinal rule for the army is always to remain loyal to the government. This is very important for us to understand.

SULAK: I feel that both in Indonesia and my own country, Thailand, the army has become less of a threat now. The real threat, in my view, is likely to come from the IMF and the transnational corporations. As you can see in your own case – you have been the President of Indonesia for nearly a year now – the rupiah has gone down steadily throughout this period. This is of course due to the international agencies that control the money. They want you to fail. In my opinion, it is not the army or the people who pose the threat. Big business and the capitalists are the real threat. I do think that your becoming successful also means that people's power will grow. I do not think that the major capitalists would allow that. I may be wrong. But how can you compete with this situation when the rupiah is going down all the time?

WAHID: People have to choose between two things. The first choice is democracy, my approach to life. The second is the so-called nepotism of the past. I think people will not sacrifice democracy because without that they cannot compete. We have to use this opportunity to strengthen ourselves. This is not because we are against the International Monetary Fund; anyway, the IMF is only an instrument. The President of Egypt said that it should be disbanded, that there should be no IMF at all. He renamed it the International Misery Fund. But for me it is an instrument that can be changed. We can change it to suit our own needs, to serve the people and to emphasise the people's welfare. The principle is also very important. If the principle of achieving economic development is to concentrate power in the government's hands and not let the market place decide, then the IMF and other monetary agencies will be against us. But that is not our plan. Even if we are able to pay the IMF (and the World Bank) and decide that we will not take loans from them any more, we will yet continue to apply the same principles on which the IMF is based. They are competition, open management and democratic values. We may have a different meaning for 'democracy' and 'democratic values'. We define 'open management' and 'rule of law' in a different way.

SULAK: I find this a skilful strategy. The United States at one time used to call its client states democracies, whether they were dictatorships or any other kind of rule. Until recently, Indonesia used to be called a client state of the USA. This is also true of Thailand. I think your argument is very sound. They cannot use the same approach any more. I think they must uphold democratic principles and democratic practices. You are doing that. But I am also interested in knowing which way you would develop democratic practice in order to be more Asian or, say, more Indonesian? How would you use Islamic spiritual traditions and other traditions ecumenically to shape this country beyond 'the usual Western democracy'? As you know, Buddhism and Hinduism influenced early developments within your country. And, of course, you also have Christian minorities now.

WAHID: Remember also the pre-religious traditions of the so-called indigenous system. This is important as well. We have to learn from our history. We have to know whether our country is the place where they try to mix things or the place where they develop original theories. I think it is the first one. You know that we do not have an original cuisine, the cuisine of Indonesia. We took it from the Indians and the Chinese. We developed an exquisite Indonesian cuisine by blending Indian and Chinese foods. Our genuineness lies in making things work for us by changing them. If you ask about our original cuisine I can only point to the aborigines' food. We can either boil it or fry it over the fire.

SULAK: Indonesian cuisine is wonderful. If I had a choice between the aborigines' boil-and-burn and the fast food of Kentucky Fried Chicken or McDonald's, I would go for the indigenous food. For me KFC and McDonald's represent a greater danger. This is not because of the food alone but also because of the monoculture that they impose on our societies and nation states.

WAHID: I think we have to be careful. In the long run we have to inform and educate the people about fast food. We need to tell them about other implications as well.

SULAK: Have you been educating them?

WAHID: Oh yes! But little by little. The younger people easily accept the fashion of eating fast food in the Western way. We have to introduce our 'own blend' and have them served more and more in the restaurants. But the most important thing is to remember that it will take time. It is a matter of social and cultural education.

SULAK: The media campaign and the advertisements are really powerful. Unless we are very skilful with our social education we cannot succeed in our struggle against the multinational companies. Your country reminds me of the Bandung Conference, which was a great success and achievement for the Third World. Unfortunately the major figures that played a prominent role in Bandung had their own shortcomings. Mr Sukarno played an active role in the formulation in 1945 of Pancasila, Indonesia's guiding ideology, but unfortunately he failed because the people around him were so corrupt and dictatorial. Then Mr Nehru, a great man himself: he was also the political heir of Mahatma Gandhi, but he was quite different from Gandhi. Mr Nehru admired Western science and technology. He wanted India to remain part of the British Commonwealth. He himself claimed that he was the last Englishman ruling the country. Of course, the majority of Indian people did not understand the science and technology that he advocated, but they all believed in it.

I am quite certain that you see these two historical personalities clearly and understand their relevance for the future. We are exploring to find the middle path with regard to our attitude, understanding and application of science and technology. Gandhi was entirely against science and technology because he felt that they were meant to help only the rich and not the poor. He, of course, had several important arguments against modern science and the concept of modernity. You know about Mr Sukarno as well.

WAHID: Of course, I do not entirely oppose science and technology. They are only tools. As tools, science and technology may be fashioned to our needs and not only to the needs of the capitalists. I think we should lay more stress on co-operation and solidarity among developing nations. When I was in Cairo for the G15 meeting, it was quite clear that people divide into two camps. One group wants to use the so-called structural and political analysis of the situation. This group feels that the whole exercise profits only international capital-holders, and would therefore like to see the IMF dismantled. The other group consists of Latin Americans who are heavily indebted to the IMF and other international economic institutions. They refuse to accept this kind of structural analysis and instead stress 'the ordinary business' of credit and so forth. Hence they want to talk to each other in order to use the instrument effectively to overcome their situation and ultimately develop another perspective. This is what I did in Cairo.

SULAK: Wonderful!

WAHID: At the moment the role of people like myself is to try to make South–South dialogue more intense and meaningful than in the past. This important task should be done before we begin our dialogue with the North. People like Mahathir Mohamad and Fidel Castro are so bitter about the IMF, and we have to give full recognition to these and other opponents of free trade. People like Mahathir Mohamad and Fidel Castro should play a more active role in South–South dialogue. This is why I asked Fidel Castro to lead the people of the South, but he said, 'No, I am too old for that. It will be better if Mahathir Mohamad leads.' I agreed with him.

I would like to divide the work into three parts. There should be an institution in each region of the South – Africa, Asia and Latin America – to collect information and undertake policy analysis. Leaders will be chosen from each region to direct each institution on a rotational basis. These three institutions will share and co-ordinate their efforts with the South Centre in Geneva. In this way we will be able to 'make ourselves ready'.

SULAK: Struggles for freedom and democracy also exist in Asia. Incidents of human and democratic rights abuse are not uncommon. We are concerned about the developments regarding Anwar Ibrahim in Malaysia. I am quite certain that he will become the President of Malaysia. There is no marked change in the attitude of the Burmese military junta towards Aung San Suu Kyi or in the Chinese response to the Tibetan situation. Developments inside China also indicate an attitude of preparedness on the part of the rulers to suppress dissent.

WAHID: There is one important thing for us to remember about China. The leadership has been trying to develop things gradually into a democracy, at least a more open system. The problem is that the Western-educated people would like to have that too soon. Therefore the Chinese leadership is left with no option but to remain stern against the protesters. Let us take the example of the events in Tiananmen Square in 1989. The Chinese government had no alternative means to handle such a situation. The students were not only fighting for their rights, but were also opposed to the Chinese government. If they had been allowed to have their way the government would have crumbled. There was no choice left for the Chinese leadership and the government. This extraordinary situation was not always seen in the right perspective.

SULAK: I am raising this concern with you, since you are meeting the Chinese Vice-President and you have a good relationship with the Chinese. The Chinese have been severed from their cultural roots. They have a long cultural history and represent an ancient civilisation. But Maoism has uprooted them and now from Maoism they embrace capitalism and consumerism. My friend Tui Wei Ming, who teaches at Harvard and is the best Chinese scholar on Confucianism, thinks that the Chinese need to go back to Buddhism, Taoism, Confucianism. He has also been talking to a number of scholars and thinkers in China. They agree with him. China could perhaps be a really great country with such moral leadership. Otherwise they will be in turmoil. I hope your dialogue with them may be very meaningful. You can perhaps urge them gently.

WAHID: The most important thing to remember is that the Chinese should detach themselves from communism as an ideology. Ideology is not a way of life. Another important thing is that the ideology has its origins in the West. The best thing to do is to remind them always that they are Eastern people. They have to follow Eastern ways.

PRACHA: Is there any concept of state in Islam?

WAHID: It is an interesting question to answer. What is Islam's concept of the state? How far have Islamic intellectuals themselves dealt with it? And what consequences flow from this concept, if it exists? What is the consequence of the concept itself? The answer to this series of questions could be simplified, in my view, with one word: none. I think Islam, as a way of life, has no clear concept of state. The basis of the answer is the absence of any standard opinion in the Islamic world about two cases: first, Islam does not recognise any clear point of view about leader succession.

The prophet was succeeded by Sayyidina Abu Bakar three days after his death. During that time, Muslim society, at least in Medina, waited patiently to see how the case was resolved. After the three days, all agreed that it was Sayyidina Abu Bakar who replaced the prophet through allegiance or homage to religion. The leaders of tribes or their representatives uttered their commitment, and thereby disaster was avoided for Muslims. Before his death, Sayyidina Abu Bakar stated to the Muslim community that Umar bin Khattab was to become his successor, which meant that the succession had been settled before the succeeded passed away. This is, of course, the same as the appointment of vice presidents in the modern era. When Umar was trusted by Abdurrahman bin Muljam, and at the end of his life, he asked that an electoral college be designated, which would consist of seven people, including his son, Abdullah, who was not permitted to be his successor. Afterwards, they agreed to take Ustman bin Affan as head of state/government. Next, Ustman was replaced by Ali bin Abi Thalib. At that time, Abu Sufyan was preparing his descendant to take charge of the above position, as successor to Ali bin Abi Thalib.

Then the Kingdom system was born, where, on the death of a king, the elite put up candidates for the next king/sultan. There was, in fact, no clear concept of nation in Islam. The prophet left Medina with no clear form of government for the Muslims. In the era of Umar bin Khattab, Islam was an imperial world from the eastern Atlantic seaboard to South-east Asia. There were some views about government form, but no precise explanation of what the Islamic state should be like; whether it should be a nation state, city state or another form was debatable.

It becomes very important, because expressing ideas about an Islamic state without a clear conceptual basis, means letting the idea fragment according to the difference of views of Islamic leaders themselves. For instance, take the conflict in Iran between the 'moderate' leaders like President Khatami and the 'conservative' mullahs such as Rafsanjani right now. The only matter they agree upon is the 'Islamic' name itself. They might disagree about the 'kind' of Islam that should be applied in the country: should it be Shi'a or something more 'universal'? If we must follow the Shi'ite sect, would not the idea of an Islamic state then belong only to a minority group? Is Shi'ism not the view of only one in eight Muslims in the world? Clearly, then, there is no one idea of an Islamic state followed by the majority of Muslims. It was thought of by a number of leaders, who always consider Islam only from its institutional aspect. Furthermore, should they or their state still properly be called Muslim? Are they the majority of the religion's adherents?

PRACHA: What is the relationship between the state and Islam in Indonesia?

WAHID: In the last few years, many have wished to make Islam the state ideology, in place of Pancasila [five principles]. In my opinion, this follows from the narrowness of their idea of Pancasila. There is only one way to comprehend Pancasila, and that is with a veiw to maintaining power. Other ways of expressing Pancasila should be understood more widely. Let me put it another way. Indonesia has only one state ideology: Pancasila. To try to usurp this is wrong. However, the assumption is widespread that the growth of Islam in this state will be as an alternative to Pancasila. Therefore, we should maintain the plural character of Islam, and in this way it cannot become the state ideology. Then Islam would have the same function as nationalism, socialism or any other world-view. It is the difference between Pancasila as the state ideology, which has a pluralistic character, and several others developing in this country, such as nationalism, socialism, and so on. As a nation, we certainly only have one state ideology, but with different social interpretations.

PRACHA: Is there any specific approach to the economy or economic orientation in Islam?

WAHID: According to the Islamic perspective, the goal of human life is to reach happiness in heaven and earth by positioning that life in a structure of devotion to Allah. This is known by one of His commandments, which says: 'I create human and genie for no reason but to worship Me'. In this context, the human being will always feel the need for God, and will not just do as he pleases; there will be a control over his behaviour throughout his life. The nature of this conduct is to seek righteousness and to prevent sinfulness. Thus the most appropriate Muslim prayer is: 'God, please provide us with righteousness in this life and after life'. What I am describing is the microstructure of a Muslim life. It is a fundamental of human life, and directly related to the Muslim belief that there is no God but Allah and that the Prophet Mohammed is His messenger. Without faith in these two basic principles, technically a man cannot be considered a Muslim.

In the macro structure, man is a social being who cannot live alone, because he is part of a community. A famous saying on this matter is: religion cannot take any form without a community, and there will be no community without a leadership, and there will be no leadership without a leader. Therefore, according to Islam, the roles and responsibility of a leader are very hard. A leader should create a strong, obedient and loyal community. To accomplish these goals, he has to follow a comprehensive strategy to strengthen his community, meaning that he should be able to apply two important things to do so: he has to establish it as just and prosperous. It is stated in the preamble to the 1945 Constitution.

The appropriate orientation in leadership includes a distinct economic orientation. Government policy, the action taken and the regulation applied in the economy since independence, almost all tend to facilitate large and giant enterprise. It indicates an economic orientation that ignores the interests of small and medium enterprises. Now it's time for us to change our economic orientation from the tendency to protect large enterprises, to supporting small and medium enterprises, especially providing low-interest loans as a capital basis.

This change of orientation means that we change from our focus on exports, which gives little benefit to government in the form of taxes, which in turn provides a lot of leeway for exporters. We should focus on expanding our domestic market. This requires three things: an increase in capital income to improve purchasing power, the promotion of industrialisation to supply the domestic market, and the promotion of overall economic independence from international market trade. This means that we have to maintain honest competition and efficiency, and establish a functioning network for small and medium enterprises, either to promote domestic production or to establish a domestic market. So we have to maintain clean and competitive international trade, and extend our tax base from 2 million people at present to 20 million people in the future. Then we could increase the income of civil service and military officers tenfold, eliminate leakage, and abolish the current levies.

That kind of economic order will enable us to obtain better prosperity, referred to in the 1945 Constitution preamble as the establishment of a just and prosperous community. Islamic legal theory says that 'a leader's wisdom and action on the community led should be closely related to the prosperity of that community'. This also applies in the economic sector. An economy oriented to the ability to be independent will establish a system that is in accordance with Islam. Whether this kind of economy should be referred to as an Islamic economy or simply a national economy is not relevant. The important thing is that the economic structure developed, both the order and the orientation, should be consonant with Islam. I believe that this kind of economy is also consonant with other religions.

Therefore the term 'Islamic economy' is not required, because what is important is the application of the system and not the usage of the term. In this structure, the importance of the micro economy in obtaining contentment on earth and in heaven is at the same level as the development of the macro economy, which focuses on justice and prosperity for all. We can do it when there is the political will to do it. The national economy is much too important to be resolved by economists without the involvement of the whole citizenry. Because it is related to the prosperity of all nations, then all nations should resolve it together. Before taking such a decision, we should engage in intense debate.

SULAK: How do you apply this to the situation in Indonesia?

WAHID: The situation in our country now is different. We are safe and we can continue this way. We have progressed economically. Foreign investment, of course, does not come that easily. Two months after becoming President, I realised that we would have no more foreign investment. This, of course, implies the need for stability, security and more improvements in the bureaucracy. But I cannot hope to deliver. We have therefore changed the strategy towards a promotion of exports. Our earlier estimate for the year 2000 was US$38 billion, but we exported US$50 billion and maybe more. You can see that clearly. I went to Nigeria, Yemen and the United Arab Emirates to sell aircraft. We have been able to sell eleven planes and a few fighters. The Malaysian Prime Minister has agreed to buy seven helicopters. We have an agreement with China for production and sales. Our major problem is that the infrastructure does not exist for this kind of expansion. We are therefore trying to build the complete infrastructure soon.

We are more likely to witness better economic progress. The first policy initiative of the government was to undertake a reforestation programme. It is important for us to plant new trees and plants in all parts of the country. We want to reforest Indonesia so that arid places will rapidly change into forest and we may re-establish our country as the lung of the world. Besides that, we have deliberately changed our whole strategy towards economic growth. We need not emphasise industrialisation and exports. We will have to concentrate on building the 'people's economy'. This will cater to the domestic market rather than foreign investment. If we cannot survive then we will invite foreign investment. We would like to see the growth of the people's economy. Hence we have to be careful about our entry into the world market and trade. This also means that out of greediness we may have to import many things from the West. I do not think our nation is ready for that yet.

RABIA ROBERTS: How does a country like Indonesia deal with such a situation where you begin to manoeuvre economically? Every country, through excessive consumption, is rapidly over-using the natural resources that belong to all the generations to come. Our environment is another form of God's revelation. As we destroy it, quite frankly, we are only destroying the opportunities for the human spirit to know itself. Could you comment on the political, economic and environmental challenges facing us in the future, and on your responses to meet those challenges?

WAHID: As I have already explained to you, direct trade among so-called developing countries should complement the good-neighbour policy. First, this will put the trade question on to a new basis, that of mutual sharing of resources, and so on. This is important because, as you know, the resources of the world are limited. If we cannot regulate their usage we will be deprived of them very soon. We need to discipline ourselves. Population growth will soon make it necessary for us to ration our resources. I would like to see the emergence soon of a more balanced relationship among countries. We should establish more 'humane' communication and a system of sharing. I do not know how you see it. My vision of information technology [IT] is that it should serve our efforts to establish an identity. For instance, the process of autonomy is slowly eroding the national identity of Indonesia. I do not know whether this phenomenon exists in the US or not. Our purpose with IT, I think, is to explore whether it can strengthen our national identity, and help to reverse the trend.

RABIA: You have to prevent American IT from entering your country.

WAHID: No! We would like to welcome them. First, they should be able to help us develop our national identity. This is what I mean. Second, I believe the use of national language is very important. I speak the national language besides my mother tongue, Javanese. The use of the national language is so widespread in Indonesia. Almost everyone can use and understand it, except a few, who may constitute only 5 per cent of the population, mostly immigrants. The language we use in IT is going to be the national language of our country. It is not going to be English or any other foreign language. We have to create new stations and terminals so that we can translate English and other foreign languages into Indonesian and vice versa. We are planning to set up 20 such centres. This would help to strengthen national identity, which has been under stress due to demand for devolution and decentralisation. The third element, which is very important, is the so-called complementary elements of national development in the economic field. For instance the Javanese always needed the products of Javan and Sumatran forests. The gas from Iriaya would be used for the vehicles here, and within ten years we will switch from gasoline to methanol gas, which is cleaner and available in abundance here. The use of IT will contribute to this process of mutual assistance and interdependence between different provinces in Indonesia. These three things will be reinforced by the use of IT. More importantly, the adoption of our national language as the language of IT is crucial to this transition.

RABIA: The long-term effect will be that everyone in Indonesia will be bilingual. They will be able to speak their mother tongue and the national language.

WAHID: There are still many people who do not speak the national language, Indonesian. The change will surely come and it is being taught in schools now.

RABIA: Is there any resistance to these kinds of initiatives?

WAHID: Yes! There are different dialects in our country and we often have jokes about that.

RABIA: Oh yes! We have a similar situation in the US. We often do not understand each other. I think this is a strong move with IT. How can you balance the pressures for increased trade and foreign investment with the environmental concerns of your country?

WAHID: First, we have to protect the environment, especially the forests. We have already enacted laws. The NGOs, for instance, demanded that the government should ban the export of logs for 40 years. This is a far-fetched proposal. It would mean the loss of livelihood for millions of people. We can then specify certain areas for forestry, industrialisation, infrastructure and so forth. We have to change our policy of internal migration: people should move by themselves and we need not ask them. In this we follow the American concept of the Homestead Act of 1862.

RABIA: Where will the people come from? Is it from the cities, an out-migration? Or is it from the villages to other places?

WAHID: Village people from Java to other islands. In Java, 60 per cent of the Indonesian people live on 7 per cent of the Indonesian land. It is really lopsided. The environmentalists have warned that in the next fifty years, if we are not careful, half of Java will become a desert. We have to stop this cutting down of trees and deforestation in the country.

According to literature some parts of our country used to be rich with forests. I asked a university faculty of forestry to conduct a study. There is a lady, truly a wonderful person, who went about forty years ago into a dry area about 30 km south of Jogjakarta city. Since then she has changed the entire place. This place never had many plantations and she has reforested the whole area.

RABIA: I am interested in this Homestead Act; it needs to be accompanied by some education programme.

WAHID: Oh yes! We need education. There is an indigenous group of very able people. They work hard and can withstand hardship. They are a bit arrogant, and there is too much of an in-group feeling. But we have to keep their endurance and so on. But I am afraid that with the growing population, the pressure on land and resources will become more intense.

RABIA: The natural resources are, in fact, your major draw for foreign investment.

WAHID: I think so. It is also the most important market base for us. We are earning US$210 million, and it will grow to US$245 million in ten years. Each year it will grow by 3–4 per cent. I learnt from Ajarn Sulak that Thailand has become a market for Western products. It is a terrible situation. It has also caused a great deal of ugliness and the loss of the cultural beauty that was Thailand.

Do not forget about AIDS. It is terrible both here and in Thailand. The newspapers are not telling the truth. I know that millions of people are affected by it now. We do not like to talk about it because we call ourselves Muslims. That is why we hide. There is no worse nation at hiding the truth than Indonesia.

RABIA: What do we mean by justice now, at the beginning of the twenty-first century? Is it equal opportunities for everyone? Or is it equal distribution of wealth for everyone? Is it land reform? What are the major concerns for you in ensuring that Indonesia is a just society?

WAHID: First, we have to create jobs for everyone. Second, we have to treat everybody fairly on an equal basis. This is what our constitution advocates. It speaks of treating everyone equally. That is the fight we have now.

RABIA: It has been hard for us to determine what equality is. It is something that causes constant debate and discussion among women and men in our country.

WAHID: In that sense, we have to denote the importance of fairness and equal opportunity. This is very important. I try to stress that everybody must have an equal chance and opportunity for education. This is why I consider education an important instrument of liberation. I am proud of the fact that so many in Indonesia, from very poor backgrounds, have become professors, doctors, scientists and doctorate holders. We are lucky in the fact that the Dutch in the past provided us with the so-called objective chance for everybody in education. We certainly have to improve on that. What I mean is that everybody should have an equal chance to develop.

RABIA: Do you think that it is possible to continue maintaining small villages and individual farms in Indonesia?

WAHID: Oh yes! The problem with us in Java is that the farm holding is becoming smaller and smaller. We can stop this by having migration from Java to other islands. A second thing is that we have the Reform Law of 1961, according to which a family can have only five hectares of land. If we enforce this law directly, which I intend to do in the next three years, then we will be able to achieve our purpose. The present problem is the concentration of land in the hands of only a few.

We have not been able to implement this, but the law is there. We hope to implement it now, the law of limited land-holding. A family can have only 15 acres. A company may have around 100 acres, but it can work together with the farmers. The company will not engage in production, but limit itself to processing. Only the farmers themselves will be engaged in production. Then the produce will be processed by the companies and sold abroad.

RABIA: Can foreign investors own land in Indonesia?

WAHID: No. We have to evaluate the proposals submitted to the government to extend the period of hiring land. Currently it is only for 35 years. It should be extended to 100 years. But I will have to examine that first.

JEFFREY SUNG: In Singapore you can lease for up to 99 years and in Thailand for 33 years.

PRACHA: Could you summarise your view on globalisation from an Islamic perspective?

WAHID: Globalisation, at present, is often interpreted as open competition, total submission to competition and total recognition of international trading represented by the World Trade Organisation (WTO). In the other words, economic globalisation aims to justify the giant enterprise domination of the economy of developing countries, which surely hampers those countries. Therefore, protests against the WTO and globalisation in that sense came from non-governmental organisations domiciled in the developed countries. Open objection to the WTO by international NGOs in Seattle influenced developing countries, and it became a subject at the WTO conference in Qatar. However, the dispute against economic globalisation was not followed up by a mass campaign for new perspectives on globalisation itself. What happens is the negative approach, in which resistance against one idea is not followed up by mass campaign for a positive approach to globalisation. This failure to present a positive strategy will perpetuate the negative perspective on globalisation.

In understanding globalisation from a different perspective, we could take into account the religious idea of national development. The idea, from what Islam refers to as the function of the economy in a community, is based on two main factors. The meaning of goods and services for human beings, and how the society uses the goods and services. According to this idea, capital is something that is needed to produce goods or services for human beings. By considering capital from this perspective, profit will be a secondary result, which is not only to improve the life of the capital owner but will also bring benefit to the buyer/user of the goods. In other words, profit functions not only as a benefit for the capital owner but also to create justice among producers and consumers. In short, profit should not be manipulative in nature, a production factor should not be used to manipulate the other party. According to this idea, goods and services should provide benefit to both sides. This will eliminate the exploitative nature of an economic transaction. What is prevented by Islam is not the attempt to obtain profit in an economic transaction but the exploitative nature of the attempt. Here lies the important role of government, to make sure that no citizen is being done down by an economic transaction.

Globalisation in the old perspective, which focuses on the interests of one party, should be changed to a new perspective, which will focus on the balance between the user/buyer of a product and the producer. Then, obtaining benefit/ profits in globalisation should not be considered as total freedom to liquidate the opponent. Instead it should aim to reach a balance between the interests of consumer and producer. An adjustment between the interests of these two parties will become a point of adjustment among nations in economy and trade. From this perspective, the Islamic idea states the need to balance the interests of goods- and service-producer countries and those of the countries that utilise the goods and services. This will result in an international economic and financial balance. Justice does not allow globalisation to be used in or against the interests of a certain country or nation.

Index

Index